LISTEN, AMERICA!

Jerry Falwell

LISTEN, AMERICA!

A DOUBLEDAY-GALILEE ORIGINAL

DOUBLEDAY & COMPANY, INC.
GARDEN CITY, NEW YORK, 1980

Permission to quote material from the following sources is gratefully acknowledged:

The Eleventh Hour, by General Lewis Walt, copyright © 1979 by Caroline House Publishers, Inc., Post Office Box 738, Ottawa, Illinois 61350, used by permission; *Campus Shock: A Firsthand Report on College Life Today*, by Lansing Lamont, copyright © 1979 by Lansing Lamont, reprinted by permission of E. P. Dutton, a Division of Elsevier-Dutton Publishing Co., Inc.; *Whatever Happened to the Human Race?*, by Francis A. Schaeffer and C. Everett Koop, M.D., copyright © 1979 by Franky Schaeffer V Productions, Inc. Used by permission; *Free to Choose*, by Milton and Rose Friedman, reprinted by permission of Harcourt Brace Jovanovich, Inc., copyright © 1980, 1979, by Milton Friedman and Rose D. Friedman; *The Death of a Nation*, by John Stormer, copyright © 1968 by John A. Stormer. Reprinted by permission of Liberty Bell Press; *None Dare Call It Treason*, by John A. Stormer, copyright © 1964 by John A. Stormer. Reprinted by permission of Liberty Bell Press; *What Is a Family?*, by Edith Schaeffer, copyright © 1975 by Edith Schaeffer, published by Fleming H. Revell Company, used by permission; *A Time of Truth*, by William E. Simon, copyright © 1978 by William E. Simon, reprinted by permission of McGraw-Hill Book Company; *The Exploring Spirit: America and the World Then and Now*, by Daniel J. Boorstin, copyright © 1976 by Daniel J. Boorstin, used by permission of Random House, Inc.; *When Free Men Shall Stand*, by Senator Jesse Helms, copyright © 1976 by Jesse Helms, published by Zondervan, used by permission; "Frightening Facts About Children and Drugs," by Peggy Mann, *Family Weekly*, November 25, 1979, copyright © 1979 by *Family Weekly*. Used by permission of *Family Weekly*, 641 Lexington Avenue, New York, N.Y. 10022; "America Shrugged," *New Times*, January 8, 1979, copyright © 1979 *New Times*, used by permission; excerpts from "A Cry for Leadership," "Was Robin Just a Hood?," "The Stampede to Tragedy," "Rock's Outer Limits," reprinted by permission from *Time*, The Weekly Magazine, copyright © 1979 Time Inc.; excerpts from "Are the Marines Obsolete?," September 10, 1979, and "The Great American Bureaucratic 'Perks' Machine," December 17, 1979, copyright © 1979 *U.S. News & World Report*; "Critique of Western Society," by A. Solzhenitsyn, reprinted by permission of *Evangelical Newsletter*, copyright © 1978, Evangelical Ministries, Inc., 1716 Spruce Street, Philadelphia, Pa. 19103; "Half-Educated Generation," by Fred Reed, from the Washington *Post*, December 29, 1979, copyright © 1979 the Washington *Post*; "Jesus Is Still the Answer," copyright © 1974 by Lanny Wolfe Music Company, a division of The Benson Company, Nashville, all rights reserved, international copyright secured, printed by permission; "Lesbian Homes for Child Homosexuals," the New York *Times*, December 2, 1979, copyright © 1979 by the New York Times Company, reprinted by permission; "American Dream Found Alive and Well," the Washington *Post*, December 16, 1979, copyright © 1979 the Washington *Post*.

Library of Congress Catalog Card Number 79–6279
ISBN: 0-385-15897-1
Copyright © 1980 by Jerry Falwell

To my godly and faithful wife, Macel, and to our children
Jerry, Jr.
Jeannie
Jonathan
and to their generation—from whom our future leaders must
come.

ACKNOWLEDGMENTS

I am deeply indebted to Ruth Tomczak McClellan for her editorial assistance in developing the material for this book; Kathy Vandegriff for assistance in co-ordinating and typing; and Della Jane Brooks for her research assistance.

CONTENTS

PART III.   PRIORITY—REVIVAL IN AMERICA

According to recent polls, including a George Gallup poll, there are in America today more than sixty million people who profess to be born-again Christians, sixty million others who consider themselves religious promoralists, and fifty million others who are idealistic moralists, who want their children to grow up in a moral society. More than eight out of every ten—84 per cent of the American people—believe that the Ten Commandments are still valid for today. And yet, as we look at these statistics, we must admit the sad fact that we, the American people, have allowed a vocal minority of ungodly men and women to bring America to the brink of death.

As I address issues that are corrupting America today when speaking to people all across America, I am met with a plaintive cry and a despairing question: "We have never heard these things before! Why have we not been informed long ago?" It is now well past time that moral Americans band together to save our beloved nation. Moral people of character and integrity from all walks of life and from every religious persuasion must arise out of their apathy. We must withdraw our lot from that of the silent majority in order to defend and maintain the freedoms that allow us to live and believe as we so choose.

There is hope for America, but we must act quickly.

LISTEN, AMERICA!

Part I

LIBERTY—
WILL WE KEEP IT?

I MUST LISTEN

Recently I was returning to Lynchburg, Virginia, at midnight after having preached at a church missions conference in Tulsa, Oklahoma. It was one of those rare times when I was not accompanied by members of my staff who travel with me to conduct business during flight time. That night my thirteen-year-old son, Jonathan, and I were alone. We had had an extremely exhausting day, but fatigued as I was, I could not rest. As we flew over the heartland of these United States of America, I reminisced about my trip the previous week in the country of Thailand.

My thoughts centered on the atrocities I had witnessed in Southeast Asia. I thought of the land that we had traversed near the Cambodian border, where more than 300,000 refugees are living in holding centers in refugee camps. I had spent much time in two of those camps. There I witnessed unparalleled suffering. I had seen innocent Cambodians dying. I did not know it was possible to survive in such terrible conditions. As we flew through the air, the faces of those thousands of little children who had walked with me through the pathways of those refugee camps haunted me. I thought of the children who are suffering permanent brain damage because of malnutrition. I thought of the little girl I had taken in my arms, being careful not to hurt her thin, fragile body and her brittle, reedlike arms and legs. I had looked down at her swollen belly and was overwhelmed with the fact that thousands like her were dying. No one could visit the camps I had visited and seen the things I had seen without having his heart moved.

I remembered that on the day I left Thailand to come back to Lynchburg, Virginia—January 11, 1980—the headlines of the Bangkok paper read, "Border Alert for Refugee Avalanche." The newspaper warned Thailand border officials to brace themselves to meet an avalanche of almost 740,000 refugees, who were reported to have gathered in pockets along the Cambodian border. They were expected to cross over to seek temporary asylum in Thailand within 30 days.

These people are victims of a war between the Vietnamese Communists supported by Russia and the Khmer Rouge led by Pol Pot, supported by Red China. Millions of Cambodians have been murdered. The nation, which in 1970 had a population of 8 million people, now has a population of 3½ million.

In that same Bangkok newspaper, I had read the headline, "Pirates Plunder VN Boat People." I had read what others had already told me: "Thai authorities and relief workers are cooperating in an attempt to track down at least some of the Thai pirates who raped, looted, and killed more than 70 Vietnamese refugees in a New Year's Eve orgy of violence on Koh Kra off southern Thailand.

"A relief officer said the pirates killed 70 male refugees, then towed the survivors to the deserted island 'to rape and hunt at will.' One 8-year-old girl reportedly was raped by 100 men during the week. She and 120 other survivors were held on Kra." The article went on to describe many other gruesome attacks upon the boat people.

I had talked personally with many children and adults in those terrifying refugee camps. Stories of bravery coupled with catastrophe abounded. Some of the saddest stories I have ever heard were told to me by refugees who have suffered great family tragedies. I will never forget Vang Kong, a 12-year-old boy who made a daring escape from communism. Vang's family had come from a small village of about 300 people in Laos. The entire village claimed themselves Christians. When the Communists took over Laos, they announced that only 30 per cent of the village's people could profess Christianity. They slaughtered the adjoining village in the valley so that the Christians would know that their threat was not an empty one. While at the border, seeking a way of escape, Vang's father was shot to death. Knowing what was coming, Vang's mother took him and his brother to the Mekong River, which separates Communist Laos from free Thailand. (The Mekong River is approximately a quarter-mile wide and is treacherous even for a skilled swimmer.) Vang's baby brother, only a few months old, was tied to Vang's back. His mother then pushed them into the water. She tried to swim herself but, unable to maneuver the swift current, she was retrieved and arrested on the bank by the Communists. Vang does not know what happened to her. He and his baby brother now live in the refugee camp in northern Thailand that I visited. My heart went out to these brave children.

After Pol Pot took control of Cambodia in 1975, he and his Khmer Rouge soldiers began to eliminate all professional people. Doctors, lawyers, educators—any skilled person was immediately killed. I thought of the young 16-year-old girl I had met in one of the refugee camps. Her father had been a doctor. She was a brilliant girl who spoke English, French, Cambodian, and Thai, but she had been spared because she had pretended to be deaf and dumb. She had thrown away her glasses so the Communists would not know that she was educated. She had watched the Communists kill her mother, her father, her brothers, and all of the other members of her immediate family. She watched the Communists chop off her parents' heads and then carry them around by the hair.

As my plane continued across the heartland of the United States my thoughts would not be silenced. Millions of people across the globe are running away from communism. They long for freedom and they long for life. One hundred forty-seven million people have been murdered by the Communists since the Bolshevik Revolution in 1917.

After four years of mass terror and murder under the Khmer Rouge, the Vietnamese invaded Cambodia last December and installed a puppet regime headed by President Heng Samrin. Vietnamese soldiers backed by Soviet Russia now control Cambodia. Pol Pot was deposed and is now living in the mountains. His Khmer Rouge soldiers are protecting him and are fighting against the Vietnamese, who have 200,000 soldiers in Cambodia. The Cambodian people are the victims in the middle.

Cambodia is truly a country devastated by war. It is a country that is soaked in blood, and literally millions are starving to death. It is a tragic and terrible thing to watch people starve or be ravaged by diseases such as dysentery, malaria, and tuberculosis. It is a fearful thing to look into the faces of starving mothers who cradle hollow-eyed children. I doubt that any nation on earth has experienced more agony and suffering than have the people of Cambodia. And still the horror goes on.

Every American should read a report, "Murder of a Gentle Land," in the February 1977 issue of the *Reader's Digest*. It is a graphic account of the horror that swept over Cambodia after the Communists took over in 1975. The gruesome atrocities described therein could not even be imagined by the average American.

It is no wonder that I could not sleep on that plane as I thought of the suffering going on at that very moment in another part of the world, suffering so deep and pervasive that few could describe it. There, in the darkness of the cabin of that plane, I looked intently at my son, who was asleep. I could not help but thank God that he has never gone hungry a day in his life. He knows little but what he has read about communism. As I looked at him while he slept, I prayed that God would turn America around so that he would know the America I have known. I vowed that I would never turn my back on the firm decision and sacred commitment I had made to myself and to God that I would preach and work and pray to stop the moral decay in America that is destroying our freedoms.

I fear that the people of the United States have taken the blessings of God for granted. I was born free. Every American living today who was born in these United States can make that statement. For forty-seven years I have enjoyed the privileges of being an American. The Declaration of Independence, our Constitution, the Bill of Rights, and other great documents have guaranteed to me rights that few but Americans enjoy. But that night in that airplane, although I knew that I lived in the greatest country in the world, I knew that I had to face the grim truth that America, our beloved country, is indeed sick. Our people must be made aware of that fact and be called together to turn this country around before it is too late.

It is time that we come together and rise up against the tide of permissiveness and moral decay that is crushing in on our society from every side. America is at a crossroads as a nation; she is facing a fateful "Decade of Destiny"—the 1980s. I am speaking about survival and am calling upon those Americans who believe in decency and integrity to stand for what is good and what is right. It is time to face the truth that America is in trouble.

I have read the recent best sellers on the stands of America's bookstores. I have read the books of men of courage who are not afraid to stand and tell the American public the dangers they see. Nobel Laureate economist Milton Friedman, who has written the best seller *Free to Choose*, speaks of the suicidal course along which our beloved nation is proceeding. In his best seller *A Time for Truth*, William E. Simon, Secretary of the Treasury from 1974 to 1977, a period of the worst inflation and recession to rock our country in forty years, speaks of leaving Washington "a very frightened man." He states in his book that he declared time and time again to hundreds of subcommittees on Capitol Hill that "all the rhetoric about deficits and balanced budgets obscures the real danger that confronts us: the gradual disintegration of our free society." William Simon says, "Our country today sits at the very crossroads between freedom and totalitarian rule. If a majority of Americans do not soon understand this reality and help to turn the tide toward freedom, they ultimately will have no choice but to understand it at a time when it will be too late to do anything about it."

General Lewis W. Walt, who was assistant commandant of the Marine Corps from 1968 to 1971 and who served in combat during World War II, the Korean War, and in Vietnam, winning two Navy Crosses, two Distinguished Service Medals, the Silver Star Medal, two Purple Hearts, and numerous other decorations, pleads with the American people in the Preface to his book *The Eleventh Hour*, "to fight a battle now to prevent a war tomorrow. Unless you respond—both veteran and youth—the sacrifices of the past and the promises of the future will vanish down the drain of history." In his best seller *Restoring the American Dream*, Robert J. Ringer says to Americans, "For you and me, the picture is pretty clear; we either restore the American dream right here and now or we most certainly will never live to experience it again." I could list many other excellent books that warn of our collapse.

At one time these men would have been called alarmists, but the truth is that many American people are coming to the realization that something must be done. They are ready to listen. Americans are looking at the 1980s with uncertainty.

I respect the writers of the books I have mentioned. They are intelligent men who are knowledgeable and who have concrete answers to the problems they pose in their area of expertise. But I do not believe that America will be turned around solely by working in the areas of politics, economics, and defense, as important as these may be. These are crucial issues that face us in the 1980s, but America can only be turned around as her people make godly, moral choices. When history records these ten years, I think it will be fair to project that this will have probably been, since the days of the American Revolution, the most important decade this nation has known. This is a grave statement because I believe that the outcome of how we stand as a free people at the end of this decade will depend upon the moral decisions we as a people make in the very near future.

Before we discuss America's moral dilemma let me summarize our military, economic, and political malaise. Even in these areas, a return to our founding principles is our sure and only hope.

The United States is for the first time, in my lifetime, and probably in the lifetime of my parents and grandparents, no longer the military might of the world.

I have read about the War Between the States; indeed that was a perilous time. No one questioned the fact, however, that our nation would survive that time. The First World War, that war that was to end all wars, was a very difficult time. Thousands perished, but no one ever doubted the survival of our republic. I was born in 1933 and do not recall the Great Depression. But I know that the Great Depression was a horrible time for many families and for our nation as a whole; but again, our existence was not at stake. I remember the Second World War. I remember well listening to the radio the day the Japanese bombed Pearl Harbor. The worst war in history occurred during a 4½-year period that none of us can forget. There were 50 million deaths in that war. Hitler was certainly a formidable opponent, but yet, as an elementary-school student eight years of age when we entered the war, I cannot remember anything but an optimistic outlook on the part of America's citizens. My schoolteachers, the news commentators, and everyone who spoke of the war spoke with a note tempered with encouragement and hope, even though everything was dark in those first months of the war. We believed that we were fully capable of rising to the occasion, and we did. I could go on and on. There was Korea, then Vietnam, but again the existence of our republic was never in question. The survival of this nation has been secure from long before I was born.

This is not true today. Recently I watched a film entitled *The SALT Syndrome*. This film was produced by the American Security Council and is a numerical and dramatic comparison of the military strength, both conventional and nuclear, of the United States and the Soviet Union. Much could be said about this film, but the bottom line reveals that in offensive nuclear weaponry, the United States is behind the Soviet Union two to one. That separation is widening daily as the United States spends less proportionately than the Soviet Union and as the Soviet Union continues to accelerate its expenditures. The

United States is behind forty-seven to one in defensive weap-onry. That breach is also widening due to a policy adopted in the United States in the 1960s. It is called Mutual Assured De-struction. The American people and the Soviet population have been placed in positions of hostages of one another, both reasonably concluding that the other would not attack.

Our legislators and governmental officials have not taken into consideration that the Soviets think nothing of lying and cheat-ing. It is a fact that of the past twenty-seven treaties America has made with the Soviet Union, twenty-seven of them have been broken by the Soviet Union. Top governmental officials in our nation once said that if we would treat the Russians humanely, if we would show our sincerity by unilaterally dis-arming, by pulling back, by making concessions, that the Soviets would reciprocate because they too are decent people. Two nights after the Afghanistan invasion, the report came from Washington, D.C., that it was finally concluded that the inten-tions of the Soviets "are not good."

It is sad that it has taken a crisis like the invasion of Afghani-stan to make our leaders realize the terrible threats of commu-nism. The Soviet Union has watched the United States re-spond, not from what was once a point of strength, but from what is now a point of weakness. I believe that the Soviets had no doubt of what the reaction of the United States would be before they moved into Afghanistan.

It is only common sense that disarmament is suicide. The leaders of our country are responsible for taking care of the families of this nation. For the first time in two hundred years, we face a decade when it is doubtful if Americans will survive as a free people.

We as Americans can, as the old cliché goes, "put our heads in the sand." We can laugh and assume that things will always be as they are, when we really know that this is not being realis-tic. The fact is that we have a "will crisis" in this country today. We are not committed to victory. We are not committed to greatness. We have lost the will to stay strong and therefore have not won any wars we have fought since 1945.

The Soviets have always had only one goal, and that is to destroy capitalistic society. They are a nation committed to communism and to destroying the American way of life. Because of the overwhelming conventional and nuclear strength of the Soviet Union, it is now possible that the Soviet Government could demand our capitulation. Our unwillingness to pay the price of a nuclear conflict could well force our leadership into lowering our flag and surrendering the American people to the will of the Communist Party in Moscow. There has never been a time in our history when such a condition existed.

In the September 2, 1979, issue of the Detroit *News* we find this quote released by UPI: "Former U. S. Secretary of State Henry Kissinger assailed Western military policies Saturday and warned the time is fast approaching when the Soviet Union will be able to determine the world's destiny.

" 'If present trends continue, the 1980s will be a period of massive crisis for all of us,' Kissinger told a symposium on the future of NATO. 'The dominant fact of the current military situation is that the NATO countries are falling behind in every significant military category. Never in history has it happened that a nation achieved superiority in all significant weapons categories without seeking to translate this at some point into some foreign-policy benefit.'

"He added: 'The Soviets have been building forces for traditional military missions capable of destroying the forces of the U.S., so that in the 1980s we will be in a position where many of our strategic forces and all land-based forces will be vulnerable.' "

I believe that John Gorton summed it up well when he said at the time he was Prime Minister of Australia: "I wonder if anybody has thought what the situation of comparatively small nations would be if there were not in existence a United States of America with a heritage and a willingness to see that small nations who might otherwise not be able to protect themselves, are given some shield. Imagine what the situation would be if they were not a great and giant country prepared to make such sacrifices!"

America is in desperate trouble economically. A strong national defense requires the monies to maintain that defense. Common sense tells us that you cannot spend more than you are taking in for a long period of time without eventual bankruptcy. When government begins to print more and more money without backing, it soon becomes worthless, and financial collapse then becomes inevitable. Economists are quick to point out that freedom is directly related to our free-enterprise system and that our Congress is responsible for the economic and energy crises that America is now experiencing.

Economist Milton Friedman points out that currently more than 40 per cent of our income is disposed of on our behalf by government at the federal, state, and local levels. He points out in his book *Free to Choose* that as late as 1928 federal government spending amounted to only 3 per cent of the national income.

Today government has become all-powerful as we have exchanged freedom for security. For all too many years, Americans have been educated to dependence rather than to liberty. A whole generation of Americans has grown up brainwashed by television and textbooks to believe that it is the responsibility of government to take resources from some and bestow them upon others. This idea certainly was alien to the Founding Fathers of our country.

Welfarism has grown because Americans have forgotten how to tithe and give offerings. Until the early days of this century, it was widely recognized that churches and other private institutions carried the primary responsibility, not merely for education, but also for health care and charity. The way to defeat welfarism in America is for those who wish to see God's law restored to our country to tithe fully to organizations that will remove from government those tasks that are more properly addressed by religious and private organizations.

Our nation's growing welfare system alone threatens our country with bankruptcy. It is time that we realized the working population of America cannot indefinitely carry on the burden of governmental spending.

Currently, our government is running annual deficits of more than fifty billion dollars. Our government's accumulated long-term debt is more than five trillion dollars. The inflation rate in the United States is nearly 19 per cent. Our government is now printing money at a rate that is more than twice as fast as our economy is growing. Our currency does not have substantial gold backing, and consequently has shockingly little value.

Milton Friedman points out, "The economic controls that have proliferated in the United States in recent decades have not only restricted our freedom to use our economic resources, they have also affected our freedom of speech, of press, and of religion." (p. 39)

The free-enterprise system is clearly outlined in the Book of Proverbs in the Bible. Jesus Christ made it clear that the work ethic was a part of His plan for man. Ownership of property is biblical. Competition in business is biblical. Ambitious and successful business management is clearly outlined as a part of God's plan for His people. Our Founding Fathers warned against centralized government power, concluding that the concentration of government corrupts and sooner or later leads to abuse and tyranny. Robert Ringer sums up the economic situation in America, "If the devastating cycle of politically expedient promises/government-function, spending/direct taxation and inflation is not halted and drastically reduced, attempts to use free enterprise as a scapegoat will accelerate. And as taxation and regulation of business increase, motivation to produce will die, leading inevitably to a nationalization of industry. This is the step which will take America from the decaying stage to the death stage. It happened in Greece; it happened in Rome; it happened in every civilization that tried to provide the free lunch for its citizens and then blamed businessmen for its financial collapse." (p. 299)

The third crisis facing our nation today is a vacuum of leadership. One of the greatest needs in our nation today is for effective leadership. A special section of an August 6, 1979, *Time* magazine issues "A Cry for Leadership" and quotes Ortega y Gasset: "Before long there will be heard throughout the planet a formidable cry, rising like the howling of innumerable dogs to the stars, asking for someone or something to take command. . . ." In this special section, historian Eugene Genovese is quoted as saying, "It would be very difficult to point out a set of values about which you could say that most Americans could agree. I think our society has become largely purposeless." The special section continues, "The task of the nation's leaders in the eighties will be to rediscover new themes of purpose in American life." *Time* quotes former U. S. Commissioner of Education Ernest Boyer as saying, "Conditions are building that will revitalize leadership. People are not willing to live endlessly with ambiguity. There is something within us that is violated by feeling that we are adrift."

The all-too-prevalent feelings of many Americans about leadership in America today is summed up by Douglas Fraser, UAW president. When asked by *Time* correspondents, "What living American leaders have been most effective in changing things for the better?" Mr. Fraser made this comment: "I can't think of any leaders. Isn't this sad? That's what's wrong with this country! That's exactly what's wrong." An April 16, 1979, *U. S. News & World Report* states the findings of its sixth nationwide leadership survey, "Who Runs America," and reports that more than ever top Americans are doubting the quality of the nation's direction and that influential citizens are hungry for decisive White House leadership. Florida Attorney General Jim Smith says in this article, "Americans are crying out for persons in responsible elected positions to provide leadership. Unfortunately, most elected public officials spend too much time analyzing the political angles rather than making the tough decisions. The American people will accept some hardships." This survey indicates that sixteen of the twenty most influential citizens in the United States have positions in government. "Although finding fault with leadership in the White House and on Capitol Hill, America's policymakers have little disa-

greement on who runs the United States: the federal government and its officials."

The sad fact today is that many of our top governmental
officials care more about getting a vote than doing and standing
for what is right and good for America. Edmund Burke once
said, "Men are qualified for civil liberties in exact proportion to
their disposition to put moral chains upon their own appetites."

It is indeed true that "In recent years there has been a rising
tide of criticism of 'the system.' The criticism, for the most part,
has been neither fair nor valid. The system is excellent; the primary fault lies with politicians and legislators and bureaucrats
and judges in high places who have manhandled, not only the
system, but the very meaning of freedom itself. As a consequence, the future of the country, as long as they are in charge
of it, is depressingly bleak." (Helms, p. 77)

In the thirteenth chapter of the Book of Romans in the Bible
we find these verses: "Let every soul be subject unto the higher
powers. For there is no power but of God: The powers that be
are ordained of God. For rulers are not a terror to good works,
but to the evil. Wilt thou then not be afraid of the power? Do
that which is good, and thou shalt have praise of the same: For
he is the minister of God to thee for good. But if thou do that
which is evil, be afraid; for he beareth not the sword in vain:
For he is the minister of God, a revenger to execute wrath upon
him that doeth evil. Wherefore ye must needs be subject, not
only for wrath, but also for conscience sake. For this cause pay
ye tribute also: For they are God's ministers, attending continually upon this very thing."

Obvious facts can be concluded from these verses. The authority, "the higher powers"—the President, the Congress, the
judiciary—are ordained of God. This does not imply that all persons in places of authority are godly people. It does, however,
mean that they are in their position, whether they are aware of
the fact or not, by divine ordination. The Bible states that rulers
are not a terror to good works, but to evil works. Law-abiding
citizens need not be afraid of leaders. The leader is the minister
of God to the people for good. Because they are to respect and

obey the leaders in authority, Americans have a grave responsibility to vote in those leaders who will rule America justly, under divine guidance. Good citizens are concerned, informed, active, and law-abiding. The only grounds for citizens refusing to obey the law would be when human law violates divine law.

Why do we have so few good leaders? Why is it that political and judicial decisions are made that horrify America? You will find that when society begins to fall apart spiritually, what we find missing is the mighty man, that man who is willing, with courage and confidence, to stand up for that which is right. We are hard-pressed to find today that man in a governmental position, that man of war, that judge, that prophet, that preacher who is willing to call sin by its right name. Vanishing from the scene is the prudent, the wise person, the ancient, the old, the honorable people, the grandparents who will stand up for righteousness year after year, generation after generation, and be an example to us. For the first time in history, we have few elderly honorable people on the national scene. We have few we can look to and say, "Here is an example of godliness in leadership." Instead we find confusion and selfishness, which is destroying the very basis of our society.

We must review our government and see where our leadership has taken us today and where our future leaders must take us tomorrow if we are to remain a free America. It is a sad fact today that Americans have made a god of government. They are looking to government rather than to God, who ordained government. The United States is a republic where laws rule. Although the people of the United States have a vote, America is not a democracy in the sense that the majority rules. Her citizens elect representatives who represent them and govern them by laws. I believe that God promoted America to a greatness no other nation has ever enjoyed because her heritage is one of a republic governed by laws predicated on the Bible.

America is facing a vacuum of leadership not only in regard to her elected officials, but also among her citizens who are not standing for what is right and decent. We need in America today powerful, dynamic, and godly leadership. Male leadership in our families is affecting male leadership in our churches, and it is affecting male leadership in our society. As we look across our nation today we find a tremendous vacuum of godly men who are willing to be the kind of spiritual leaders who are necessary not only to change a nation, but also to change the churches within our nation and the basic units of our entire society, our families.

If a man is not a student of the Word of God and does not know what the Bible says, I question his ability to be an effective leader. Whatever he leads, whether it be his family, his church, or his nation, will not be properly led without this priority. God alone has the wisdom to tell men and women where this world is going, where it needs to go, and how it can be redirected. Only by godly leadership can America be put back on a divine course. God will give national healing if men and women will pray and meet God's conditions, but we must have leadership in America to deliver God's message.

We must reverse the trend America finds herself in today. Young people between the ages of twenty-five and forty have been born and reared in a different world than Americans of years past. The television set has been their primary baby-sitter. From the television set they have learned situation ethics and immorality—they have learned a loss of respect for human life. They have learned to disrespect the family as God has established it. They have been educated in a public-school system that is permeated with secular humanism. They have been taught that the Bible is just another book of literature. They have been taught that there are no absolutes in our world today. They have been introduced to the drug culture. They have been reared by the family and by the public school in a society that is greatly void of discipline and character-building. These same young people have been reared under the influence of a government that has taught them socialism and welfarism. They have been taught to believe that the world owes them a living whether they work or not.

I believe that America was built on integrity, on faith in God, and on hard work. I do not believe that anyone has ever been

successful in life without being willing to add that last ingredient—diligence or hard work. We now have second- and third-
generation welfare recipients. Welfare is not always wrong.
There are those who do need welfare, but we have reared a generation that understands neither the dignity nor the importance
of work.

Every American who looks at the facts must share a deep concern and burden for our country. We are not unduly concerned
when we say that there are some very dark clouds on America's
horizon. I am not a pessimist, but it is indeed a time for truth.
If Americans will face the truth, our nation can be turned
around and can be saved from the evils and the destruction that
have fallen upon every other nation that has turned its back on
God.

There is no excuse for what is happening in our country. We
must, from the highest office in the land right down to the shoe-
shine boy in the airport, have a return to biblical basics. If the
Congress of our United States will take its stand on that which
is right and wrong, and if our President, our judiciary system,
and our state and local leaders will take their stand on holy living, we can turn this country around.

I personally feel that the home and the family are still held in
reverence by the vast majority of the American public. I believe
there is still a vast number of Americans who love their country,
are patriotic, and are willing to sacrifice for her. I remember the
time when it was positive to be patriotic, and as far as I am concerned, it still is. I remember as a boy, when the flag was raised,
everyone stood proudly and put his hand upon his heart and
pledged allegiance with gratitude. I remember when the band
struck up "The Stars and Stripes Forever," we stood and goose
pimples would run all over me. I remember when I was in elementary school during World War II, when every report from
the other shores meant something to us. We were not out demonstrating against our boys who were dying in Europe and Asia.
We were praying for them and thanking God for them and
buying war bonds to help pay for the materials and artillery
they needed to fight and win and come back.

I believe that Americans want to see this country come back to basics, back to values, back to biblical morality, back to sensibility, and back to patriotism. Americans are looking for leadership and guidance. It is fair to ask the question, "If 84 per cent of the American people still believe in morality, why is America having such internal problems?" We must look for the answer to the highest places in every level of government. We have a lack of leadership in America. But Americans have been lax in voting in and out of office the right and the wrong people.

My responsibility as a preacher of the Gospel is one of influence, not of control, and that is the responsibility of each individual citizen. Through the ballot box Americans must provide for strong moral leadership at every level. If our country will get back on the track in sensibility and moral sanity, the crises that I have herein mentioned will work out in the course of time and with God's blessings.

It is now time to take a stand on certain moral issues, and we can only stand if we have leaders. We must stand against the Equal Rights Amendment, the feminist revolution, and the homosexual revolution. We must have a revival in this country. It can come if we will realize the danger and heed the admonition of God found in 2 Chronicles 7:14, "If my people, which are called by my name, shall humble themselves, and pray, and seek my face, and turn from their wicked ways; then will I hear from heaven, and will forgive their sin, and will heal their land."

As a preacher of the Gospel, I not only believe in prayer and preaching, I also believe in good citizenship. If a labor union in America has the right to organize and improve its working conditions, then I believe that the churches and the pastors, the priests, and the rabbis of America have a responsibility, not just the right, to see to it that the moral climate and conscience of Americans is such that this nation can be healed inwardly. If it is healed inwardly, then it will heal itself outwardly.

It is not easy to go against the tide and do what is right. This nation can be brought back to God, but there must first be an awareness of sin. The Bible declares, "Righteousness exalteth a nation: But sin is a reproach to any people." (Pr. 14:34) It is right living that has made America the greatest nation on earth, and with all of her shortcomings and failures, America is without question the greatest nation on the face of God's earth. We as Americans must recommit ourselves to keeping her that way. Our prayers must certainly be behind our President and our Congress. We are commissioned by Scripture (1. Tm. 2:1–3) to pray for those who are in authority, but we would also remind our leaders that the future of this great nation is in their hands. One day they will stand before God accountable with what they have done to ensure our future. God has charged us as Americans with great privileges, but to whom much is given "much is required." We are faced with great responsibilities. Today, more than at any time in history, America needs men and women of God who have an understanding of the times and are not afraid to stand up for what is right.

Americans have been silent much too long. We have stood by and watched as American power and influence have been systematically weakened in every sphere of the world.

We are not a perfect nation, but we are still a free nation because we have the blessing of God upon us. We must continue to follow in a path that will ensure that blessing. We must not forget the words of our national anthem, "Oh! thus be it ever, when free men shall stand/Between their loved homes and the war's desolation!/Blest with victory and peace, may the heav'n rescued land/Praise the Power that hath made and preserved us a nation./Then conquer we must, when our cause it is just,/And this be our motto: 'In God is our trust.'" We must not forget that it is God Almighty who has made and preserved us a nation.

Let us never forget that as our Constitution declares, we are endowed by our Creator with certain inalienable rights. It is only as we abide by those laws established by our Creator that He will continue to bless us with these rights. We are endowed our rights to freedom and liberty and the pursuit of happiness by the God who created man to be free and equal.

The hope of reversing the trends of decay in our republic now lies with the Christian public in America. We cannot expect help from the liberals. They certainly are not going to call our nation back to righteousness and neither are the pornographers, the smut peddlers, and those who are corrupting our youth. Moral Americans must be willing to put their reputations, their fortunes, and their very lives on the line for this great nation of ours. Would that we had the courage of our forefathers who knew the great responsibility that freedom carries with it. Patrick Henry said, "It is natural to man to indulge in the illusions of hope. We are apt to shut our eyes against a painful truth. . . . Is this the part of wise men, engaged in a great and arduous struggle for liberty? Are we disposed to be a number of those who, having eyes, see not, and having ears, hear not, the things which so nearly concern their temporal salvation? For my part, whatever anguish of spirit it may cost, I am willing to know the whole truth; to know the worst and to provide for it. . . . Is life so dear or peace so sweet, as to be purchased at the price of chains or slavery? Forbid it, Almighty God! I know not what course others may take, but as for me, give me liberty or give me death!"

More than ever before in the history of humanity, we must have heroes, those men and women who will stand for what is right and stand against what is wrong, no matter what it costs. Today we need men and women of character and integrity who will commit themselves to letting their posterity know the freedom that our Founding Fathers established for this nation. Let us stand by that statement in the Declaration of Independence that cost our forefathers so much: ". . . with a firm Reliance on the Protection of divine Providence, we mutually pledge to each other our lives, our Fortunes, and our sacred Honor."

Our Founding Fathers separated church and state in function, but never intended to establish a government void of God. As is evidenced by our Constitution, good people in America must exert an influence and provide a conscience and climate of morality in which it is difficult to go wrong, not difficult for people to go right in America.

I am positive in my belief regarding the Constitution that God led in the development of that document, and as a result, we here in America have enjoyed 204 years of unparalleled freedom. The most positive people in the world are people who believe the Bible to be the Word of God. The Bible contains a positive message. It is a message written by 40 men over a period of approximately 1,500 years under divine inspiration. It is God's message of love, redemption, and deliverance for a fallen race. What could be more positive than the message of redemption in the Bible? But God will force Himself upon no man. Each individual American must make His choice.

Peter Marshall knew that the choices of individuals determine the destiny of a nation. He immigrated to the United States as a young man and worked his way through seminary by digging ditches and doing newspaper work. His years in the ministry culminated with the pastorate of the historic New York Avenue Presbyterian Church in Washington, D.C. (Abraham Lincoln's church), located two blocks from the White House. Dr. Marshall became chaplain of the Senate in January 1947. He died suddenly in January 1949 while still holding office. He was a dynamic Christian and was called by many a reporter the "conscience of the Senate."

Peter Marshall summed it up well when in a sermon to the New York Presbyterian Church he challenged its members with these words: "Today, we are living in a time when enough individuals, choosing to go to hell, will pull the nation down to hell with them. The choices you make in moral and religious questions determine the way America will go. The choice before us is plain, Christ or chaos, conviction or compromise, discipline or disintegration. I am rather tired about hearing about our rights and privileges as American citizens. The time has come, it now is, when we ought to hear about the duties and responsibilities of our citizenship. America's future depends upon her accepting and demonstrating God's government. It is just as plain and clear as that."

Americans must no longer linger in ignorance and apathy. We cannot be silent about the sins that are destroying this nation. The choice is ours. We must turn America around or prepare for inevitable destruction. I am listening to the sounds that threaten to take away our liberties in America. And I have listened to God's admonitions and His direction—the only hopes of saving America. Are you listening too?

THE RISE AND FALL OF EMPIRES

We the American people have to make a choice today. Will it be revival or ruin? There can be no other way. One has only to turn to history to find that this is a proven fact. But the words of a familiar cliché hold ironic significance for our nation: "Men have learned only one thing from history, that being that men do not learn from history." History provides us with valuable lessons that Americans must carefully examine and heed in our present crisis. Abraham Lincoln declared, "If destruction be our lot, we ourselves will be its author and its finisher."

The rise and fall of nations confirm the Scripture that says, "Be not deceived; God is not mocked: Whatsoever a man soweth, that shall he also reap." (Ga. 6:7) Psalm 9:17 admonishes, "The wicked shall be turned into hell, and all the nations that forget God." America will be no exception. If she forgets God, she too will face His wrath and judgment like every other nation in the history of humanity. But we have the promise in Psalm 33:12, which declares, "Blessed is the nation whose God is the LORD." When a nation's ways please the Lord, that nation is blessed with supernatural help.

General Douglas MacArthur indeed spoke the truth when he said these profound words: "History fails to record a single precedent in which nations subject to moral decay have not passed into political and economic decline. There has been either a spiritual awakening to overcome the moral lapse or a progressive deterioration leading to ultimate national disaster."

The Book of Judges in the Old Testament records a chaotic period of history. The age-long story of the Jews is described in Judges, Chapters 17 and 21. During this time Israel had no King, and Scripture declares, "every man did that which was right in his own sight." Because there was no King, there were no rules or regulations, and therefore, with no code of ethics, every man did whatever pleased himself. During this period the Jewish people went through a time of bloodshed, horror, disorder, and lawlessness. They were repeatedly in and out of captivity because of God's judgment upon them. God would have destroyed them had it not been for His promise to Abraham.

History books are replete with illustrations of how, down through six thousand years of human history, empires, governments, kingdoms, and nations have ceased to exist when they have fallen into sin. The Roman Empire is probably the prime illustration of a society that went from nothing to the highest pinnacle of greatness ever known, only to lose it all by ceasing to make the effort to be and to do those things that had elevated her to her greatness.

Rome was invaded and destroyed in A.D. 410. There are distinct reasons why the greatest nation the world had ever seen fell. As pleasure and hedonism became the rule of the day in Rome, morality disappeared, and with it diligence, commitment, and sacrifice.

Politically Rome allowed power to gather in the hands of a few. Economically under Caesar Augustus, the people began greatly to depend on the government to provide for their needs. A welfare system came into being. Taxation reached such a high point that producers lost the incentive to work; hard work disappeared. There was false prosperity in Rome. As the government began to decay, more and more pressure was placed on its citizens to allow a totalitarian state.

Economists agree that economic freedom is directly related to political freedom. It is true that high taxation and centralization of government contributed to the fall of Rome, but the ultimate collapse was a direct result of Rome's spiritual condition. Had her spiritual vitality not eroded, she would have had the strength and wisdom to have maintained herself politically, economically, and militarily.

The Romans tried to build their society upon gods who were finite and limited. These gods were amplified humanity. Caesar Augustus was worshiped as a genius; it was obligatory for the people to worship him.

Morality prevailed in the early days of the Roman Empire, but with prosperity came change. Near the end of its glory Rome was noted for its loose sexual morals, for its corruption, and for its violence. Rome fell because of its own internal rottenness. A culture without high moral standards is not a stable culture. When man feels no moral responsibility to God or to those around him, he loses regard for all men. In Rome, a breakdown of morals preceded a dictatorship that led to oppression and downfall.

Ironically enough, Rome had conquered Greece, and yet Rome allowed Greek teachers to corrupt her society with humanism. In the ruins and in the history of Greece we see what happens to a civilization that worships and idolizes the human mind and body. In spite of her unending knowledge and great contributions to the world, Greece fell.

It is shocking to study history and to find that it was fashionable for Romans to hire teachers who taught their children humanistic philosophies. In order to accommodate the women who clamored for more rights, new marriage contracts were designed, including "open marriages." The progression of big government is amazing. A father's authority was lost first to the village, then to the city, next to the state, and finally to the empire. Unemployment became a problem, and civil-service jobs were created. People complained of the high cost of living, of crime in the streets, etc.

The days of the Roman Empire were numbered when she brought great and terrible persecution upon Christians who had established a flourishing New Testament Church.

In the nineteenth century, Great Britain was in her glory. She seemed to be in a golden age, both economically and politically. Her slogan proclaimed, "The sun never sets on the British Empire." But today we know the sad truth that the sun has indeed set on her glory. Today Great Britain has a socialist government.

Prime Minister Margaret Thatcher is making bold moves to restore Great Britain. She has stated that socialism increases the power of the state and that this increase of power produces neither greater wealth nor greater liberty, but the reverse. Socialism in Britain has led to a feel of oppressiveness among her people, with resultant loss of incentive. Says Margaret Thatcher regarding the future of Britain: "Unless we change our ways and our direction, our greatness as a nation will soon be a footnote in the history books, a distant memory of an offshore island lost in the mist of time like Camelot."

Britain once produced some of the greatest preachers the world has ever known, men like John Wesley and George Whitefield. These men were labeled fanatics and extremists, and they were barred from many churches in England. They taught that a new birth experience is necessary for each and every citizen. Whitefield proclaimed the "good news" to the multitudes of England. Men and women were regenerated by the thousands. Many readily admit that England was changed during Wesley's fifty-year ministry. In 1922, the British Prime Minister, David Lloyd George, stated that Great Britain ". . . owed more to the movement of which Wesley was the inspirer and leader than to any other movement in the whole of its history . . . there was a complete revolution effected in the whole country." During his time as Prime Minister, Lord Baldwin said that historians ". . . who filled their pages with Napoleon and had nothing to say of John Wesley, now realize that they cannot explain nineteenth-century England until they can explain Wesley."

But England's Industrial Revolution brought man-centered self-sufficiency back to the foreground. Britons forgot the God-centered message of the Wesleys.

A decisive question now in the headlines of the news of

America asks, "Is the United States going the way of a once-great Britain?" This question worries a great number of Americans. They remember the Britain of the past that was a world power, a wealthy country, and an industrial leader. Prime Minister Thatcher has dedicated herself to reversing Britain's low wages, low productivity, and low expectations. Quoted in the February 5, 1979, *U. S. News & World Report,* Milton Friedman warned fellow Americans that if they follow the path that Britain has taken, they will have even higher inflation than they do now, they will see government take a larger part of their freedom, and their vaunted productivity will decrease. U. S. Senator Jesse Helms summed it up well in *When Free Men Shall Stand*: "The devil is still at work today promising the whole panoply of material wealth to those nations that disavow their Christian heritage and accept him as prince of this world. Nation after nation has accepted the devil's bargain, only to find themselves deceived, betrayed, and then destroyed." (p. 118)

FREEDOM'S HERITAGE

I believe America has reached the pinnacle of greatness unlike any nation in human history because our Founding Fathers established America's laws and precepts on the principles recorded in the laws of God, including the Ten Commandments. God has blessed this nation because in its early days she sought to honor God and the Bible, the inerrant Word of the living God. Any diligent student of American history finds that our great nation was founded by godly men upon godly principles to be a Christian nation. Our Founding Fathers were not all Christians, but they were guided by biblical principles. They developed a nation predicated on Holy Writ. The religious foundations of America find their roots in the Bible.

Our Founding Fathers firmly believed that America had a special destiny in the world. They were confident that God would bless their endeavors because they did not forget to acknowledge Him in all their doings. America must not forget her motto, one that was founded and established in the early days of her history. America's coins as well as her postage stamps bear that motto: "In God We Trust." America's currency bears the inscription, "Annuit Coeptis" (He has favored our undertakings). We must remember, as our coins depict, that "In God We Trust" stands for "Liberty." Our religious heritage and our liberty can never be separated. America is in trouble today because her people are forgetting the origin of their liberty, and questioning the authority and the inerrancy of the Bible.

At one time Benjamin Franklin uttered these profound words: "God surely was no idle spectator when this great nation was born in his name and with his grace." Our Declaration of Independence declares: "We hold these Truths to be self-evident, that all Men are created equal, that they are endowed by their Creator with certain unalienable Rights, that among these are Life, Liberty, and the pursuit of Happiness." It is our Creator who has endowed us with "certain unalienable Rights." These rights were given to us with the condition and the responsibility of acknowledging and obeying Him. Freedom *is* conditional upon precisely that—the acknowledgment of and obedience to the laws of our Creator. When the majority of our population forgets that this is indeed "one nation under God," we do not deserve to survive. The choice is ours; God is waiting for Americans to return to Him so He can give America a spiritual rebirth. "Ultimately, the author of human liberty is almighty God, who endows each human being with free will. Every human being since Adam has been free to obey the laws of God or to disobey them; to enjoy, in the words of Scripture, the glorious liberty of the sons of God, or to submit to his own slavery in sin. God Himself does not constrain our wills; in His infinite majesty, He respects the choices made by man." (Helms, p. 19)

The heritage of the United States of America is one of courageous men and women who came to these shores desirous of religious freedom. The heritage of the Puritan Pilgrims is one not of a church, but of a nation; these were men and women who were not only the progenitors of a state, but also the ancestors of a nation. We can thank these courageous people who laid the religious foundation of our nation for the freedom and liberty we so liberally enjoy today.

In 1607 Puritans established the first settlement in this country at Jamestown. They had come in search of a place where they could freely worship God and live in total commitment to His laws. Before coming to America, many Puritans had chosen to leave England for Holland because of religious persecution involving the Church of England, which was then a state church. "The Pilgrim Fathers, then, did not see the New World as an opportunity to new-fashion society. Rather to old-fashion it to the perfect biblical model," says 1975 Pulitzer Prize winner Daniel J. Boorstin in his book *The Exploring Spirit*. (pp. 21–22)

Many of the Puritan Pilgrims lived successfully in Holland for a time, but found it necessary to seek a new land when they found that their children were being corrupted by "the great licentiousness of youth in that countrie, and the manifold temptations of the place (Boorstin)." Governor Bradford gave this as the final reason for the Pilgrims' leaving Holland for America: ". . . a great hope & inward zeall they had of laying some good foundation, or at least to make some way therunto, for ye propagating & advancing ye gospell of ye kingdom of Christ in these remote parts of ye world; yea, though they should be but even as stepping stones unto others for ye performing of so great a work. . . ."

No matter what persecution the Puritan Pilgrims suffered before coming to America, they remained completely dedicated to following God and obeying His laws. Governor Bradford wrote, "The one side laboured to have ye right worship of God & discipline of Christ established in ye church, according to ye simplicitie of ye gospell, without the mixture of men's inventions, & to have and to be ruled by ye laws of God's word, dispensed in those offices, & by those officers are of Pastors, Teachers, & Elders, &c. according to ye Scripturs." This is what was important to the Puritan Pilgrims, and they paid a price to live and to die for these beliefs.

The official document providing for the settlement of Jamestown was the First Charter of Virginia. This Charter was written before the Puritan Pilgrims arrived in America. It is here that we find America's beginnings. The Charter is dated April 10, 1606, and in it we find these sentiments: "We, greatly commending, and graciously accepting of, their Desires for the Furtherance of so noble a Work, which may, by the Providence of Almighty God, hereafter tend to the Glory of His Divine Majesty, in propagating of *Christian* Religion to such People, as yet live in Darkness and miserable Ignorance of the true Knowledge and Worship of God, and may in time bring the Infidels and Savages, living in those Parts, to human Civility, and to a settled and quiet Government."

When the settlers who founded the Jamestown colony landed at Cape Henry in April of 1607, they erected a large wooden cross and held a prayer meeting. It was their first act in the new land that they had come to settle. On November 11, 1620, the Pilgrims arrived on the *Mayflower* at Cape Cod Harbor. It was on that day that the men of their company signed the immortal *Mayflower* Compact. The *Mayflower* Compact begins with these words: "In The Name of God, Amen. We, whose names are underwritten . . . Having undertaken for the Glory of God, and Advancement of the Christian Faith and the Honor of our King and Country, a Voyage to plant the first colony in the northern Parts of Virginia: Due by these Present solemnly and mutually in the Presence of God and one another covenant and combine ourselves together into a civil Body Politic, for our better Ordering and Preservation, and Furtherance of the Ends of Aforesaid; And by Virtue hereof do enact, constitute, and frame, such just and equal Laws, Ordinances, Acts, Constitutions, and Offices. From time to time, as shall be thought most meet and convenient for the General good of the Colony; unto which we promise all ado, Submission, and Obedience."

The weather was very bad during November, and the Pilgrims, under the leadership of Captain Standish, made an exploration of the cape. After days and nights of stormy weather, they arrived at a small island. William Bradford, who was historian and governor of the Plymouth Colony, wrote, "God gave them a morning of comforte & refreshing (as usually He doth to his children) . . . and they found them sellvs to be on an iland secure from ye Indeans . . . and gave God thanks for his mercies, in their manifould deliverances. And this being the last day of the weeke, they prepared ther to keepe ye Sabath." It was not until December 16 that the *Mayflower* actually reached Plymouth Harbor. When the party finally embarked on the shore, Governor Bradford wrote of their first act, "Being thus arrived in a good harbor and brought safe to land, they fell upon their knees and blessed the God of heaven. . . ."

These Puritan Pilgrims merit the description of Macaulay in his "Essay on Milton," of which one line reads: "The Puritans brought to civil and military affairs a coolness of judgment and an immutability of purpose which some writers have thought inconsistent with their religious zeal, but which were, in fact, the necessary effects of it." The Puritan Pilgrims paid a price for their religious beliefs.

The first Constitution written in America was the Fundamental Orders of Connecticut, written in 1639. This written Constitution created a government, and it included words stating that it pleased the Almighty God by the wise disposition of His divine providence to order and dispose of things. It declared that where our people were gathered together, the Word of God required that to maintain peace and union of such a people, there had to be an orderly and a decent government established according to God. The Constitution went on to speak of the maintenance and preservation of liberty, and of the purity of the Gospel of Jesus Christ which they professed and which was the discipline of their churches.

The Pilgrim Puritan movement was actually a crusade for righteousness. These people wanted to be left alone to worship God in their own way. "Their desires were sett on the ways of God and to enjoye His ordinances." They were consecrated men and women of God whose lives were dominated not by temporal gain but by spiritual truths.

One has only to research all the early documents of American history to find that, time and again, our Puritan Pilgrim heritage was centered around advancing the Kingdom of God. Liberty was directly related to this end. On May 19, 1643, the early settlers of our country formed the New England Confederation. It begins with these words: "Whereas we all came into these parts of America with one and the same end and aim,

namely, to advance the Kingdom of our Lord Jesus Christ and
to enjoy the liberties of the Gospel in purity with peace . . ."

It is interesting to observe that many of the first colonial institutions required that a person make a public profession in
Jesus Christ before he could hold a public office. The first
schools in America were conducted in churches, and the first
teachers in the American school system were pastors. The first
textbook in American education was the Bible. Before they
came to America, the Pilgrims decided to incorporate into the
Mayflower Compact that they would, upon reaching the new
land, establish schools in order to teach their children to read
the Scriptures.

The first three American universities established upon this
continent—Harvard, Yale, and Princeton—were originally built
in order to train pastors for the ministry. There were many
university men in the first ships that came into Boston. By
1639, there were about seventy university graduates known to
have been in New England. Strong personalities in the Puritan
colonies included great preachers like John Cotton, Roger Williams, John Davenport, Thomas Hooker, and John Eliot. They
were ministers of commanding ability, magnetism, and intelligence.

By the 1700s affluence, peace, and prosperity in America
began to cause people to forget their heritage. At those times of
backsliding in America, great preachers revived the nation. John
Wesley and George Whitefield came to America preaching the
Gospel of Jesus Christ and spreading revival throughout the
land. Benjamin Franklin reports that he listened to George
Whitefield preach blocks away and could hear his voice echoing
across the countryside calling America to repentance. Some believe that his influence laid the foundation for the Great Awakening that gave us the character to fight for independence.

If you will go back to the early days of the history of this nation, you will find that local churches played a tremendous role
in the establishment and in the nurture and growth of this
republic. The local churches and the preachers provided the
conscience, the strength, and the spiritual and moral fiber with

which this great nation was put together. The first Jamestown settlement centered around a church. Early Puritan Pilgrims built their church before they even built their homes. The church was a place to worship, love, and serve God. It was a rallying place where everything important was discussed. It was the focal point of the total lives of those first settlers who came and established America.

The church is important to the history of this land. Calvin Coolidge, the thirtieth President of the United States, said, "America was born in a revival of religion. Back of that revival were John Wesley, George Whitefield, and Francis Asbury."

Thousands of men and women were brought to their knees after hearing Jonathan Edwards' powerful sermon, "Sinners in the Hands of an Angry God." Edwards propounded the message that all men are created equal according to the Word of God, and that no man should be under tyranny. In 1758, Jonathan Edwards became the president of Princeton University, and a generation later, his grandson, Timothy White, was twice the President of Yale.

Universities such as Princeton, the University of Pennsylvania, Rutgers, Brown, and Dartmouth were begun as Christian universities. Daniel Boorstin has written, "In England, the higher learning as well as religion had been a monopoly of the Established Church. Nonconformists had difficulty securing admission to Oxford or Cambridge (the only English universities till the early nineteenth century), while Catholics and Jews were absolutely excluded. The dissenting academies, which set high scholarly standards, had no power to grant degrees. In America, by contrast, at the time of the Revolution, nearly every major Christian sect had a degree-granting institution of its own. By the early eighteenth century, New England Puritans and their secessionists had set up Harvard and Yale, while Virginia conformists of the Church of England had their College of William and Mary. The flourishing variety of sects nourished a variety of institutions. New-Side Presbyterians founded Princeton University; revivalist Baptists founded Brown University in Rhode Island; Dutch Reformed revivalists founded Queen's

College (later Rutgers University) in New Jersey; a Congregational minister transformed an Indian missionary school into Dartmouth College in New Hampshire; Anglicans and Presbyterians joined in founding King's College (later Columbia University) in New York City and the College of Philadelphia (later the University of Pennsylvania)." (p. 46)

The establishment of these colleges and universities was a direct result of the Great Awakening. A potential student had to demonstrate that he had been "born again" before he was accepted into these institutions when they were first established.

History tells us of the great revivals that took place at these institutions in their founding years. After George Whitefield preached at Harvard, a revival broke out on the campus. Before Whitefield went to Boston, President Willard of Harvard University wrote to a friend complaining of the moral decay in the college. He wrote: "Whence is there such a prevalency of so many immoralities amongst the professors? Why so little success of the gospel?" President Willard later wrote describing the revival that had come because of George Whitefield's preaching: "That which forbodes the most lasting advantage is the new state of the college. Gentlemen's sons that were sent here only for a mere polite education, are now so full of zeal for the cause of Christ and the love of souls as to devote themselves absolutely to the study of divinity. The college has entirely changed; the students are full of God—and will I hope come out blessings to this and succeeding generations."

The story is often told about the French political philosopher who visited America when she was just a young nation. Alexis de Tocqueville said he came to the United States to find what magic quality enabled a handful of people to defeat the mighty British Empire twice in thirty-five years. He looked for the greatness of America in our harbors and rivers, in her fertile fields and in her boundless forests, mines, and other natural resources. This man studied America's schools and her Congress and her matchless Constitution. It is said that it was not until he went into the churches of America and heard pulpits that were aflame with righteousness did he understand the secret of

America's genius and strength. De Tocqueville returned to France and wrote the sagacious sentiment, "America is great because America is good, and if America ever ceases to be good, America will cease to be great."

With the passage of time, and with what the colonists felt was undue control and domination by the mother country, England, America began her travels on the long road of revolution. Let us examine a few instances that exemplify our Founding Fathers' dependence upon God.

On September 4, 1774, the Reverend Jacob Duché opened the First Continental Congress with prayer. He read Psalm 35, which includes these verses: "Plead my cause, O LORD, with them that strive with me: Fight against them that fight against me. And my soul shall be joyful in the LORD: It shall rejoice in his salvation. And my tongue shall speak of thy righteousness and of thy praise all the day long."

We find in the journals of the Continental Congress a declaration of the causes and necessity of taking up arms, dated July 6, 1775. In this document we find these words: "But a reverence for our great Creator, principles of humanity, and the dictates of common sense, must convince all those who reflect upon the subject, that government was instituted to promote the welfare of mankind, and ought to be administered for the attainment of that end. . . . We esteem ourselves bound by obligations of respect to the rest of the world, to make known the justice of our cause. Our forefathers, inhabitants of the island of Great-Britain, left their native land, to seek on these shores a residence for civil and religious freedom. At the expense of their blood, at the hazard of their fortunes, without the least charge to the country from which they removed, by unceasing labour, and an unconquerable spirit, they effected settlements in the distant and inhospitable wilds of America. . . . We most solemnly, before God and the world, declare, that, exerting the utmost energy of those powers, which our beneficent Creator hath graciously bestowed upon us, the arms we have been compelled by our enemies to assume, we will, in defiance of every hazard, with unabating firmness and perseverance, employ for the preservations of our liberties; being with one mind resolved to die freemen rather than to live slaves."

Next we find the Continental Congress going in a body from the State House to attend the service of fasting and prayer set apart by themselves on July 20, 1775, in Christ Church in Philadelphia. On this occasion, we again find the Reverend Jacob Duché participating. He had been asked by the Congress to preach a sermon from Psalm 80, which he did.

Christ Church of Philadelphia, which is still standing, was President George Washington's home church for six years during his term of office. Three distinguished signers of the Declaration of Independence were pewholders there; Benjamin Franklin served several years as vestryman; Francis Hopkinson was the rector's warden and an organist there for some time. Robert Morris, one of the great financers of the Revolution, attended services there regularly.

The road to revolution was becoming a very busy thoroughfare. On the night of April 18, 1775, Samuel Adams and John Hancock were at Lexington preparing to leave for a meeting of the Second Continental Congress in Philadelphia. They were awakened about midnight by Paul Revere, who had ridden from Boston with word that British soldiers were on their way to arrest them both. Adams, knowing that the British would be met soon by the fire of American minutemen, is said to have remarked, "This is a glorious day for America." It was at this second session of the Continental Congress that John Adams nominated George Washington as commander-in-chief of an army for all the colonies, and it was approved unanimously.

At the Third Continental Congress, in 1776, John Adams spoke these profound words: "Before God I believe the hour has come. My judgement approves this measure, and my whole heart is in it. All I have, and all that I am, and all that I hope in this life, I am now ready here to stake upon it. And I leave off as I began, that live or die, survive or perish, I am for the Declaration. It is my living sentiment, and by the blessing of God it shall be my dying sentiment, Independence now, and Independence forever!" The Revolutionary War was one that involved much bloodshed, as seen in the Battles of Concord, Lexington, Cambridge, New York, Charleston, and Valley Forge. It was a war in which citizens were proud to sacrifice their utmost.

Patrick Henry was not only a great orator and an ardent pursuer of liberty, but he was also a great colonel as well. He organized the 1st Independent Company of Volunteers in Virginia and was a valuable contributor to the Continental Congresses and the Virginia Revolutionary Conventions. It was at the second Virginia Revolutionary Convention, which met in St. John's Church on March 23, 1775, when Patrick Henry, moved to arm the colony, gave his great "Liberty or Death" speech that I have previously quoted.

After the Third Virginia Revolutionary Convention, Patrick Henry was appointed commander-in-chief of all the Virginia forces. At the fifth and final Virginia Revolutionary Convention, held May 6, 1776, Patrick Henry called upon Congress to make a Declaration of Independence. It was here that he was elected the first governor of an independent state.

From reliable documented history, it is evident that Patrick Henry was a great Christian. He is reported to have said, "I would only wish that I could leave my family my faith in Jesus Christ; for without that nothing else is worthwhile." Hearing that some people had questioned whether he was a Christian, Patrick Henry had said, "I hear it said . . . that some good people think I am no Christian. This thought gives me much more pain than the appellation of Tory; because I think religion is of infinitely higher importance than politics; and I find much cause to reproach myself, that I have lived so long, and have given no decided and public proofs of my being a Christian."

So it was that on June 11, 1776, a committee gathered to draw up a Declaration of Independence. Thomas Jefferson drafted the document in seventeen days, and Congress adopted it on July 4, 1776. For six months, several signatures on the Declaration of Independence were kept secret. These men knew the full significance of the last paragraph, in which they pledged their lives, their fortunes, and their sacred honor. Fifty-six men placed their signature beneath that pledge. The Old Dominion had taken the road to revolution and her leaders were soon to avow their purposes before the world and "take their chances, very narrow chances, of becoming founders of the greatest nation in the world, or of adorning with their fine, powdered heads the gallows on Tower Hill, London." (Campbell, *Patrick Henry*, p. 186)

The men who laid the foundation for our liberties were men of integrity. They were successful men of means who were extremely prosperous and who were wealthy landowners. They were men of character. They were willing to pay a great price for the liberties that we enjoy today. Of the fifty-six men who signed the Declaration of Independence, fourteen lost their lives as captive soldiers or casualties in the war for independence. Many lost their sons and saw their lands and properties devastated. Knowledge of the lives of the men who signed the Declaration of Independence should cause each and every citizen of the United States to appreciate their costly heritage. These men of high principles and deep moral values willingly endured tremendous personal sacrifice to create a nation with the highest ideals of freedom, justice, and morality in the world. The fifty-six brave men who placed their signatures on the Declaration of Independence were all denounced as rebels and traitors to be hanged if caught. These men knew they were signing their own death warrants. Here is the story of just a few of these brave men:

Carter Braxton of Virginia, a wealthy planter and trader, saw his ships swept from the seas. To pay his debts, he lost his home and all his property and died in rags.

Thomas Lynch, Jr., owned a large plantation. After he signed the Declaration, his health began to fail. With his wife he left for France to regain his health, but their ship never arrived in France and he was never heard from again.

Thomas Nelson, Jr., of Virginia raised two million dollars to provision our allies, the French fleet. After the war, he personally paid back the loans, wiping out his entire estate. In the final battle at Yorktown, he urged General Washington to fire on his home, which was occupied by Cornwallis. Nelson's home was destroyed; he died bankrupt and was buried in an unmarked grave.

Francis Lewis had his home and everything he owned destroyed. His wife was imprisoned and died shortly thereafter. Lewis Morris saw his land destroyed and his family scattered. Philip Livingston died from the hardships of the war.

John Hart was driven from his wife's deathbed. Their thirteen children fled for their lives in all directions. For more than a year he lived in forests and caves and returned home after the war to find his wife dead and his children and property gone. He died a few weeks later of exhaustion and a broken heart.

Of the fifty-six signers, few were long to survive. Five were captured by the British and tortured before they died. Twelve had their homes searched and looted or burned. Two lost their sons in the army. Nine died in the war from its hardships or from enemy bullets.

These fifty-six were mostly men of means who enjoyed much ease and luxury in their personal lives. They knew, however, that liberty and freedom were more important than security, so they pledged their lives, their fortunes, and their sacred honor. They paid the price. Little did John Adams know how significant his words would be when he spoke to his wife, Abigail, on the passing of the Declaration of Independence and said, "I am well aware of the toil, and blood, and treasure, that it will cost to maintain this declaration, and support and defend these states; yet, through all the gloom, I can see the rays of light and glory. I can see that the end is worth more than all the means."

Many other men suffered greatly, as did their families. Among the seventy-odd minutemen who stood on the Lexington green and returned shots, thus beginning the Revolutionary War on April 19, 1775, was Jonathan Harrington. From an upstairs window of their home his young wife watched as he was shot in the chest and stumbled toward their house. She ran down the steps, caught her husband, and watched him die at her feet. Janet Livingstone Montgomery's husband, Richard, who was one of eight brigadier generals of the Continental Congress, was killed in battle. Mrs. Montgomery was widowed almost before her honeymoon was ended. She made these comments regarding her husband's death: "As a wife I must ever mourn the loss of a husband, friend, and lover; of a thousand virtues, of all domestic bliss; the idol of my warmest affections, and in one word my every dream of happiness. But, with America, I weep the still greater loss of the firm soldier and the friend to freedom."

When General Anthony Wayne joined George Washington at Valley Forge in 1777, Wayne had not been home in sixteen months. In explaining why he could not come at the time, he wrote to his wife: "I can't be spared from camp. I have the confidence of the General and the hearts of the soldiers who will support me in the day of action. . . . The Times require great Sacrifices to be made. The Blessings of Liberty cannot be purchased at too high a price. The Blood and treasure of the Choicest and Best Spirits of the land is but a trifling consideration for the Rich Inheritance."

Many great women, wives, and mothers deserve credit for their great part in the fight for liberty. In researching the lives of many of the wives of the generals and other men who fought with Washington in the Revolution, we find that in hundreds of letters to their husbands there is not one word of regret at their husband's course, not one word of pity for themselves or for their children who were left alone. These women did not complain. They were united with their husbands in the fight for freedom, and they suffered much for the cause. They counted the cost and willingly paid it. In 1776, Thomas Payne wrote: "What we obtain too cheaply, we esteem too lightly; it is dearness only that gives everything its value. Heaven knows how to put a price upon its goods, and it would be strange indeed if so celestial an article as freedom should not be highly rated."

When speaking of sacrifice, we cannot overlook Nathan Hale. This schoolteacher and graduate of Yale was a good example of a courageous man who gave his all for the cause of liberty when things looked very bleak for the American cause. General Washington, short of both men and materiel, was in desperate need of information as to the enemy's strength and plans. A core of rangers was organized, and Captain Hale eagerly accepted the opportunity to join the special unit. At a meeting of its officers, it was reported that Washington suggested sending someone behind the enemy's lines to gather intelligence on British preparations and movements. Nathan Hale immediately stepped forward as a volunteer. He slipped through enemy lines and was apparently caught while returning from his mission. He was carrying notes and plans in his shoe. General William Howe ordered that he be hanged. Captain John Montresor, an aide to General Howe, witnessed the hanging. Later that day, under a flag of truce, he reported to American Captains Alexander Hamilton and William Hall that the spy had demonstrated unusual bravery at the gallows. As the noose was about to be placed around his neck, Nathan Hale said: "I only regret that I have but one life to lose for my country."

To those who sacrificed for our freedom, the end was worth the painful means. No one, however, forgot the sacrifices and the help God had afforded the struggling nation. When, after the representatives who had met in 1787 to write the Constitution of the United States struggled for several weeks making little or no progress, eighty-one-year-old Benjamin Franklin rose and addressed the troubled and disagreeing convention that was about to adjourn in confusion. It seemed that their attempt to form a lasting union had apparently failed. Benjamin Franklin said, "In the beginning of the contest with Britain, when we were sensible of danger, we had daily prayers in this room for Divine protection. Our prayers, Sir, were heard and they were graciously answered. All of us who were engaged in the struggle must have observed frequent instances of a superintending Providence in our favor. . . . And have we now forgotten this powerful Friend? Or do we imagine we no longer need His assistance?

"I have lived, Sir, a long time, and the longer I live, the more convincing proofs I see of this truth: 'that God governs in the affairs of man.' And if a sparrow cannot fall to the ground without His notice, is it probable that an empire can rise without His aid? We have been assured, Sir, in the Sacred Writings that except the Lord build the house, they labor in vain that build it. I firmly believe this. I also believe that, without His concurring aid, we shall succeed in this political building no better than the builders of Babel; we shall be divided by our little partial local interest; our projects will be confounded; and we ourselves shall become a reproach and a byword down to future ages. And what is worse, mankind may hereafter, from this unfortunate instance, despair of establishing government by human wisdom and leave it to chance, war, or conquest.

"I therefore beg leave to move that, henceforth, prayers imploring the assistance of Heaven and its blessing on our deliberation be held in this assembly every morning before we proceed to business." Benjamin Franklin then proposed that the Congress adjourn for two days to seek divine guidance. When they returned they began each of their sessions with prayer. The stirring speech of Benjamin Franklin marked a turning point in the writing of the Constitution, complete with a Bill of Rights.

The Constitution of our United States begins with these words: "WE THE PEOPLE of the United States, in Order to form a more perfect Union, establish Justice, insure domestic Tranquility, provide for the common defence, promote the general Welfare, and secure the Blessings of Liberty to ourselves and our Posterity, do ordain and establish this CONSTITUTION for the United States of America." It is indeed a grand statement, "the Blessings of Liberty."

George Washington proudly proclaimed his dependence, as well as our nation's dependence, upon God. Washington said, "No people can be bound to acknowledge and adore the Invisible Hand which conducts the affairs of men more than those of the United States. Every step by which they have advanced to the character of an independent nation seems to have been distinguished by some token of providential agency." In 1782, the first English-language Bible was printed in the United States and was approved and recommended by the United States Congress. George Washington is reported to have said, "It is impossible to rightly govern the world without God and the Bible."

In his first inaugural address, on April 30, 1789, before the Senate and the House of Representatives, George Washington spoke of the reverence and great privilege he felt to be summoned by his country, "whose voice," he said, "I can never hear but with veneration and love." He acknowledged the great responsibility of the job ahead of him, "the magnitude and the difficulty of the trust to which the voice of my country called me." The second paragraph of his address begins, "Such being the impressions under which I have, in obedience to the public summons, repair to the present station, it would be peculiarly improper to omit in this first official act my fervent supplications to that Almighty Being who rules over the universe, who presides in the counsels of nations, and whose providential aids can supply every human defect, that His benediction may consecrate to the liberties and happiness of the people of the United States a Government instituted by themselves for these essential purposes, and may enable every instrument employed in its administration to execute with success the functions allotted to his charge. In tendering this homage to the Great Author of every public and private good, I assure myself that it expresses your sentiments not less than my own, nor those of my fellow-citizens at large less than either. No people can be bound to acknowledge and adore the Invisible Hand which conducts the affairs of men more than those of the United States. Every step by which they have advanced to the character of an independent nation seems to have been distinguished by some token of providential agency; and in the important revolution just accomplished in the system of their united government the tranquil deliberations and voluntary consent of so many distinct communities from which the event has resulted cannot be compared with the means by which most governments have been established without some return of pious gratitude, along with an humble anticipation of the future blessings which the past seem to presage. These reflections, arising out of the present crisis, have forced themselves too strongly on my mind to be suppressed. You will join with me, I trust, in thinking that there are none under the influence of which the proceedings of a new and free government can more auspiciously commence . . . the foundation of our national policy will be laid in the pure and immutable principles of private morality, and the preeminence of free government be exemplified by all the attributes which can win the affections of its citizens and command the respect of the world . . . there is no truth more thoroughly established than that there exists in the economy and course of nature an indissoluble union between virtue and happiness . . . we ought to be no less persuaded that the propitious smiles of Heaven can never be expected on a nation that disregards the eternal rules of order and right which Heaven itself has ordained and since the preservation of the sacred fire of liberty and the destiny of the republican model of government are justly considered, perhaps, as deeply, as finally, staked on the experiment intrusted to the hands of the American people."

It can be found when reading the inaugural addresses of all of our Presidents that there is reference to the Almighty God as Author of our liberty or to His Providence, without which we would not be blessed. In every one of the constitutions of our fifty states, there is an appeal or a prayer to the Almighty God.

It is indeed proper that we as Americans set aside a day in which to give thanks to God for the blessings of our liberty. It is commendable that as early as 1677, the first regular Thanksgiving proclamation was printed in Massachusetts. It was soon an annual custom to set aside a day of thanksgiving in all the colonies. During the Revolutionary War, the people in the Continental Army observed an annual Thanksgiving Day by the proclamation of the Continental Congress. It was discontinued until 1789, and Washington's proclamation was only occasionally followed by other Presidents. Washington's first Thanksgiving proclamation in an official act reads, "Whereas it is the duty of all nations to acknowledge the Providence of Almighty God, to obey His will, to be grateful for His benefits, and humbly implore His protection and favor . . ." It goes on to call the nation to thankfulness to God. In 1864, President Abraham Lincoln issued a proclamation appointing the fourth

Thursday of November, with a view of having the day kept, thereafter, annually without interruption.

It has, without question, been established that our forefathers paid a great price so that their posterity could live in freedom. Dare we be willing to pay any less a price for the same ends? Scripture declares, "Unto whomsoever much is given, of him shall be much required." (Luke 12:48) God is the Author of our liberty, and we will remain free only as long as we remember this and seek to live by God's laws. By looking at the statements and the documents made by the generation who laid the foundation of our government, it is evident that they were deeply religious men. They made it clear that they were guided in their thinking, their decisions, and their writings by scriptural teachings.

America's great lawmaker Daniel Webster spoke profoundly when he said, "I believe Jesus Christ to be the Son of God; I believe that there is no other way of salvation than through the merits of His atonement; I believe that the Bible is to be understood and read." Andrew Jackson too knew the importance of the Bible when he remarked to a friend, "That Book, Sir, is the Rock on which our Republic rests." I believe that God is the Author of our liberty and that freedom's light is indeed "Holy." I sing with pride, "Our fathers' God, to Thee, Author of liberty, To Thee we sing: Long may our land be bright With freedom's holy light; Protect us by Thy might, Great God, our King!"

It is clear that America is a land that has had a great heritage, one that evidences mighty blessings of God. I am glad that our country was born in the tradition of respect for God and the love of Jesus Christ and that the national buildings and monuments in our capital are ripe with religious symbolism. Next time you travel to Washington, D.C., remember to look for these:

The cornerstone of our magnificent Capitol building was laid by George Washington. Later a box was inserted in the cornerstone that contained a number of documents including a manuscript written by Daniel Webster, who was then Secretary of State. His manuscript concludes with these words: ". . . And all here assembled, whether belonging to public life or, to private life, with hearts devotedly thankful to Almighty God for the preservation of the liberty and happiness of the country, unite in sincere and fervent prayers that this deposit, and the walls and arches, the domes and towers, the columns and the entabletures, now to be erected over it, may endure forever. God save The United States of America."

Inside the Capitol building you will see in the rotunda a picture of the Pilgrims about to embark from Holland on the sister ship of the *Mayflower*, the *Speedwell*. The great chaplain, Brewster, who later joined the *Mayflower*, has open, on his lap, the Bible, and there very clearly are the words, "the New Testament according to our Lord and Savior, Jesus Christ." On the sail is the motto of the Pilgrims, "In God We Trust, God With Us."

Engraved on the metal cap on the top of the Washington Monument are these words: "Praise be to God." Lining the walls of the Washington Monument are many phrases, including these: "In God We Trust; May heaven to this union continue its beneficence; God in Our Native Land; Search the Scriptures; Holiness to the Lord; Train up a child in the way he should go, and when he is old he will not depart from it; Suffer the children to come unto me and forbid them not for of such in the Kingdom of God."

Every session of the House, the Senate, and the Supreme Court begins with prayer. If you were to go to listen to the proceedings of the Supreme Court, you would find they begin with a crier quoting these official words: "Oyez, Oyez, Oyez! All persons having business before the Honorable, the Supreme Court of the United States, are admonished to draw near and give their attention, for the Court is now sitting. God save the United States and the Honorable Court." In that courtroom is a great winged angel of God defending the forces of justice on one side, and on the other side holding back the forces of evil. Above the head of the Chief Justice of the Supreme Court are the Ten Commandments, with the great American eagle protecting them.

In the Senate, across from the eyes of the President of the Senate, who is the Vice President of the United States, are the words, "In God We Trust." Above the American flag that is behind the Speaker of the House of Representatives you will find in large words inscribed in the marble, "In God We Trust." In the Senate there are busts of some of the greatest senators in history. In that chamber there are twenty-three large medallions of the great lawgivers in history. On the western wall are a row of saints. There is only one medallion that is not in profile. It is a medallion in full-front face, and it sits right over the main entrance of the House of Representatives. It is the face of Moses.

On the walls of the various rooms of the Library of Congress you will find statements such as these: "What doth the Lord require of thee, but to do justly and to love mercy and to walk humbly with thy God," and "That this nation under God, shall have a new birth of freedom; that government of the people, by the people, for the people, shall not perish from the earth." "The Heavens declare the glory of God; and the firmament showeth his handiwork." "Wisdom is the principal thing; therefore get wisdom and with all thy getting get understanding."

John Adams, the first President to live in the White House, had these words inscribed over the fireplace: "I pray Heaven to bestow the best of Blessings on this White House and on all that shall here after inhabit it. . . ."

America must not forget where she came from. Let us not forget the warning God gave to the Israelites, which is the same warning that applies to America today. Deuteronomy, Chapter 8, verses 10, 11, 18, and 19 says: "When thou hast eaten and art full, then thou shalt bless the LORD thy God for the good land which he hath given thee. Beware that thou forget not the LORD thy God, in not keeping his commandments, and his judgments, and his statutes. But thou shalt remember the LORD thy God: For it is he that giveth thee power to get wealth, And it shall be, if thou do at all forget the LORD thy God, and walk after other gods, and serve them, and worship them, I testify against you this day that ye shall surely perish."

America must not turn away from the God who established her and who blessed her. It is time for Americans to come back to the faith of our fathers, to the Bible of our fathers, and to the biblical principles that our fathers used as a premise for this nation's establishment. We must come back lovingly but firmly, and establish as our priorities once again those priorities that are God's priorities. Only then will we become important to God, and only then will we once again know the great blessings of the Power that has made and preserved us a nation!

OUR REPUBLIC

After representatives at the Constitutional Convention had completed their work, this question was put to old Ben Franklin: "Well, Dr. Franklin, what have you given us?" Dr. Franklin replied to the lady who had asked the question, "You have a republic, madame, if you can keep it." James Russell Lowell, an American poet and statesman of the late nineteenth century, was asked, "How long do you think the American republic will endure?" Lowell replied, "So long as the ideas of its Founding Fathers continue to be dominant."

The framers of our Constitution knew the great sacrifices that bought our liberty. They had worked diligently to produce a Constitution that would guarantee to their posterity that their liberty would never again be usurped, abused, misused, or denied. One of the framers of the Constitution, James Madison, explained the nature of the American republic: "We have staked the whole future of American civilization, not upon the power of government, far from it. We have staked the future of all of our political institutions upon the capacity of mankind for self-government; upon the capacity of each and all of us to govern ourselves, to control ourselves, to sustain ourselves according to the Ten Commandments of God."

Today we find that America is more of a democracy than a republic. Sometimes there is mob rule. In some instances a vocal minority prevails. Our Founding Fathers would not accept the tyranny of a democracy because they recognized that the only sovereign over men and nations was Almighty God. A republic is a government of law. In a republic there are checks and balances, and the majority represents the individual.

More than forty years ago, Dr. Nicholas Murray Butler, who was then the president of Columbia University, wrote in his book *Why Should We Change Our Form of Government?* ". . . there is under way in the United States at the present time a definite and determined movement to change our representative republic into a socialistic democracy . . . if it is successful, it will bring an end to the form of government that was founded when our Constitution was made. . . ." Our Founding Fathers intended that individuals be the master, and the state the servant. Thomas Jefferson said, "Man is not made for the State, but the State for man."

In his first inaugural address, George Washington spoke of the "Republican model of government." Article 4, Section 4 of the Constitution of these United States states, "The United States shall guarantee to every State in this Union a Republican Form of Government." It was important to the framers of the Constitution that the rights of all Americans be protected and that the authority of every branch of government be limited. It was important to protect the rights of individuals. The goal of the republic, as our Founding Fathers established it, was to prevent the consolidation of political power.

When M. Frederic Auguste Bartholdi, designer of the Statue of Liberty, sailed into New York Harbor, he said, "We will rear here, before the eyes of the millions of strangers seeking a home in the New World, a colossal Statue of Liberty; in her upstretched hand the torch enlightening the world; in her other hand the Book of Laws, to remind them that true liberty is only found in obedience to law. . . ." Our Founding Fathers had profound respect for the law and knew that true liberty is found only in obedience to law because they recognized the fallen nature of man as recorded in the Bible. They understood that they needed law as a guide.

Let us remember as we pledge allegiance to the flag of the United States of America that it is "to the republic" that we make this pledge. And let us do more than remember; let us live by the laws recorded in God's Word.

The Issue of Church and State

We have seen that the goal of the framers of our Constitution was to govern the United States of America under God's laws, as evidenced by the fact that the guidelines for, as Hamilton later called it, "Our Experiment in Liberty" are directly based on the Ten Commandments. Most of the Ten Commandments are still written into the statute laws in the various states.

Our Founding Fathers based our system of government on the First Commandment. Man was created to serve God, not the state. Since man was created in God's image, government could be used to help secure man's God-endowed rights. The goal of institutionalized government since the founding of our nation has been to be a servant of mankind, never the master of man. Our Founding Fathers sought to do this by advocating that people govern themselves under God's laws. Thomas Jefferson said, "God grant that we should never have a government that we can feel."

Of major concern in the United States today is a problem regarding the issue of "church and state." There are presently before the Congress of the United States several bills dealing with this issue. The First Amendment to our Constitution states, "Congress shall make no law respecting an establishment of religion, or forbidding the free exercise thereof . . ." This was included in the Bill of Rights because in England the state church had been determined by the religion of the monarchy; the intention of our Founding Fathers was to protect the American people from an established government church, a church that would be controlled by the government and paid for by the taxpayers. Our Founding Fathers sought to avoid this favoritism by separating church and state in function. This does not mean they intended a government devoid of God or of the guidance found in Scripture.

U. S. Senator Jesse Helms has pointed out that the same day that the First Amendment was adopted by Congress, that same Congress said that Washington could proclaim a national day of prayer. To separate personal religious preference from a forced establishment of religion is far different from separating godliness from government. The establishment of a state religion such as that which was established in England, the Church of England, and severing the relationship between God and government are two entirely different matters. Our Founding Fathers most certainly did not intend the separation of God and government.

Cicero once said, "It is impossible to know the truth and not be held responsible." We find in America today millions of apathetic people who realize that something has gone wrong in our country, but who have not taken the initiative or the interest to find out what is at the root of our problems and what steps must be taken to solve those problems. We must now begin to face the duties and responsibilities of our citizenry, or soon we will be unwillingly experiencing the disciplines of tyranny.

Resounding throughout the West in recent years has come the voice of Alexandr Solzhenitsyn. Alexandr Solzhenitsyn, recipient of a Nobel Prize for literature, is an intellectual, a teacher, a writer, a decorated war hero, and a man who once wrote a letter in which he made some "unflattering comments" about Stalin. Because of this letter, he spent eleven years in Siberian prison camps. One of the most famous books of our time, *The Gulag Archipelago*, came out of his experience. Alexandr Solzhenitsyn is a man who knows from firsthand experience the situation in Soviet Russia. After he was expelled from the Soviet Union in February 1974, Mr. Solzhenitsyn visited America and horrified his listeners with his denunciation of communism. He spoke of the catastrophic world situation and of "the West's fantastic greed for profit and gain." He asked of America, "Is it possible or impossible to warn someone of danger?" And he quoted a Russian proverb, "When it happens to you, you'll know it's true." His words fell on an all-too-apathetic public.

Too many Americans blame our corrupt politicians for "the sad state we find America in today." We cannot place the full blame upon our national leaders. It is we, the American people, who voted them into office. Now it is time for us to face the truth responsibly and do something to turn America around. We can warn, as do some key figures in America, about the accelerating evolution of our society into a collectivist state, wherein government officials become rulers rather than servants. We agree with the top economists of our country who are trying to warn Americans that there is a bond among personal freedom, political freedom, and economic freedom that is an indissoluble one. We can talk about inflation, about big government, about crime in the streets, about America's lack of defense, and about a host of other critical subjects—and we will discuss these and other topics throughout the course of this book. But the fact remains that at the root of America's problems today is the decay of our individual and national morals. This has resulted in the subsequent decadent state and instability of everything else in America—including economics, politics, defense, etc. The choices we as Americans have made in moral and religious questions have determined the way America is going today.

In the first twelve days of November 1979, the Washington *Post* conducted a nationwide poll entitled, "Americans' Hopes and Fears About the Future." In the poll results, printed in the December 16, 1979, issue of the Washington *Post*, we read, "Clearly expressed in the survey answers is the survival of living religious faith—once considered threatened by the secular prosperity of the post-World War II generation. God is very much alive for most Americans of all persuasions—73 per cent consider themselves 'very religious' or 'somewhat religious.' And 31 per cent of the people feel that religion is more important to them than it was to their parents, while 28 per cent feel it is less important."

This survey points out that citizens felt most threatened by national and international events beyond their personal control, by war, depression, shortages, nuclear war, oil crises, economic disaster, too much dependence on foreign nations, no leadership, etc. Washington *Post* writers explain the American temperament using words such as "narcissism," "alienation," and "malaise."

Some of the soundings of the decade of the seventies were ominous. There was turmoil and unrest. Let us examine the decade of the seventies and determine what was the climate then and what is the actual climate of the vast majority of the American people today.

On May 4, 1970, a volley of fire was directed into a crowd on the campus of Kent State University. Before students knew what had happened, thirteen students had been shot—two in the front, seven in the side, four in the back. Four lay dead. Angry students ushered in the decade of the seventies. They were violent students, many who thought nothing of burning the American flag, throwing rocks, shouting obscenities, and violently protesting the Vietnam War.

Within days after the Kent State shootings, nearly a thousand U.S. universities and colleges were either shut down or came close to being shut down. Demonstrations swept throughout our country. "Kent was the United States in a kind of microcosm, with all its good and its potential and all its bad at the same time," related Gordon W. Keller, associate vice president of academic and student affairs at Kent State. The tumultuous seventies began with student revolutions and carried through with Vietnam demonstrations, Watergate, oil embargoes, gasoline shortages, inflation, big government, and the dwindling dollar.

What was the general consensus of life in America in the seventies? Several magazine articles provide insights. In his editorial entitled, "What Kind of People Are We?" in the February 5, 1979, *U. S. News & World Report*, Marvin Stone asked, "What has happened to the America we knew?

"That plaintive cry is sounded time and again in letters from our readers, by people we meet on our trips, by those close to home.

"What kind of people have we become?" Mr. Stone quotes the farewell issue of *New Times* magazine, "Come July it will be ten years since Neil Armstrong stepped on the moon—and ten years since Teddy Kennedy and Mary Jo Kopechne rode off Dike Bridge. Of the two events, Chappaquiddick far better presaged the decade ahead. It was so callous, so sloppy.

"We shrug off almost everything now, moving on—with a lot of help from the omnivorous media—to the next fleeting titillation.

"It's as if we're beyond making distinctions, beyond caring. . . . Third-graders are selling dope, White House aides are buying it. Our appetite for violence is insatiable.

"Exhausted from our exertions of the sixties, all we ask for now is relief. Six hours of TV help to get us through the day —life once removed is close enough, thanks. The impetus to rethink-reform-transform has long since slid into the ennui.

"After two centuries, we have reached a consensus of indifference."

Mr. Stone continues, "So we ask: If we have really come to that, is there any turning back?

"The answer has to come from intangibles not readily calibrated. But the answer is crucial, because our future will surely be endangered if we continue aimlessly to drift." Mr. Stone went on in his editorial to discuss America's retreat from dominance, her economic disorder, big government and its misfeasance, loss of respect for government, lack of voter participation, degeneration in education, and other issues. He ended his editorial with these comments: "Certainly we have the intelligence to understand that we are going through one more social revolution in this country and the challenge is to preserve the best of the past and embrace the good and the new. But it will take leadership to define and inspire a common purpose, and desire by the rest of us to pursue it."

A February 26, 1979, *U. S. News & World Report* article entitled, "The Doubting American—a Growing Breed," reports "pessimism, distrust of leaders, laxity in standards—all raise a basic question about the U.S.: Whatever happened to belief?" The article begins with these statements: "Belief, the energizer of progress and the cement of civilization since the dawn of history, is running into trouble—in America, of all places.

"In speeches, surveys, sermons and editorials, Americans are being told of a 'credibility gap' and the decline of old certitudes, whether secular or religious, that once bred faith in leaders, institutions and the U.S. future.

"The growth of disbelief—whether thoughtful skepticism or casual cynicism—is all the more striking in a nation long viewed as an exemplar of idealism and faith in the future."

In the November 12, 1979, issue of the Washington *Post*, staff writer Kathy Sawyer reports in an article entitled, "A Sleeping Lion: The 'Me Generation' of Nonvoters" responses from people who do not vote, including these: "It seems like a vote doesn't have very much power. Promises aren't kept. . . . It just seems sort of pointless." "Regardless of what I do, see, it's not going to have any effect. . . . After you take so much water in a boat, you're not going to save the ship." Kathy Sawyer includes Republican pollster Robert N. Titter's report that of the seventy-five million Americans who reached voting age since 1960, about fifty million have not even registered to vote. She points out that "among blue-collar workers in the twenty-seven-to-thirty-five age group, nearly half never even have registered."

"Recent interviews with nonvoters around the country revealed a mosaic of bitterness, cynicism or merely indifference—a feeling that voting is unconnected to the concerns of their lives. Among all age groups, voting has declined and cynicism toward politics has risen." A young man sums up the attitude of many: "There is only one word I can use to describe myself—and I'm speaking for a lot of people: cynicism. It's very hard to believe in anything anymore."

Dennis Carey was one of those students who stood on that hill at Kent State ten years ago and saw the shots and heard the screams of that awful tragedy. The agony of Kent State led to the formation of a new program for the university that attracted

Carey's attention. At the time of the shooting, he was finishing his graduate work in psychology. Since that time, Carey has been involved in a peace studies program at Kent State and is acting director of the Kent Center for Peaceful Change. In a December 16, 1979, Washington *Post* article by Haynes Johnson, Carey is reported to have made these comments: " 'Kids who come into our program are still very much influenced by the belief you can do something, that you can make a difference,' he says. 'But other kids that we get in our classes will say, "Yes, I see your point, but there isn't a lot we can do about that. It's too big, it's gone too far down the road. And at this point I measure the boundaries of my personal application of energy to what it is I need to carve out a life for me, to make money and stay out of trouble."

" 'Many of them simply believe they may not survive their lifetime. They honest-to-God believe that, deep down. And perhaps the main reason they carve so small a place for themselves is there's no point in trying something else: They think they have this time to enjoy this much. I think the arms race is real to them, and that spells a kind of imminent disaster. Not being able to get a job like they've been told they're going to be able to get, and the economic collapse of the country are real enough. And, unlike years ago, they don't see profound political problems causing that. They simply think it's the system running out. And what do you do in these circumstances? You say, "Look, you've convinced me. I believe it. Okay. Leave me alone and let me enjoy what I've got."

" 'It's frightening, really frightening, because the motivations have become so narrow.' " Sadly enough, this has been the all-too-prevalent condition in our country for about thirty years. People are discouraged and defeated. Americans have a no-win policy in their hearts because they have lost respect for their government and for their leaders. People in America are realizing that the world is losing respect for America.

We could go on and on. The headlines ring out, "Is the malaise real? Nation's mood in Autumn. Americans today are dismayed by the sick economy, worried about social decline, concerned over lack of leadership in Washington." (*U. S. News & World Report*, November 12, 1979)

"To friend and enemy alike, America seems to be slipping," reports a November 26, 1979, *Newsweek* article entitled, "Has the U.S. Lost Its Clout?"

"Americans were living in an age of innocence prior to the Johnson presidency, and people assumed that our government was honest and that we were the most moral people around. All those generalities have now been questioned, and once confidence is shaken on a national basis, it is going to be very difficult to re-establish," says Angus Campbell, professor of psychology and sociology at the University of Michigan, in an interview in the December 24, 1979, *U. S. News & World Report*.

The January 7, 1980, issue of *Time* magazine, in an article entitled "Epitaph for a Decade," discusses the "Me Decade." Lance Morrow says, "In a sense, life styles (a very seventies preoccupation) were the distinguishing characteristic of the decade. Social critic Tom Wolfe, in a 1976 essay, called it the Me Decade, a term that caught the epoch's dreamily obsessive self-regard. The seventies were given over to building private, not public morale."

Lance Morrow is optimistic about the 1980s, hoping that "the U.S. is emerging from the privatism and divisions of the Me Decade."

Is there reason for optimism in the 1980s? Can we truly write an epitaph for the Me Decade?

The 1970s were characterized by an obsession with consciousness expansion, self-awareness, and a type of narcissism. The supposed new narcissism of the seventies expounded the ideas that within each individual there is a glorious talented personality, that each individual is possessed with an inner divinity that he alone can bring out in himself; each individual must think only of himself and do exactly what he or she feels like doing. The seventies proposed exactly what the Bible speaks of when it says, "Every man did that which was right in his own eyes." (Jg. 17:6)

Until sin is eliminated, it will never be possible to write epitaphs for the "Me Decade." People have not changed. The only difference with the decade of the seventies was that it produced new terminology for human sin. The basic questions asked in the seventies were the same questions man has always asked: "Who am I? Why am I here? Where am I going?" These questions spring from a dissatisfaction with life that results with alienation from God.

We are living in a society today that is quite sophisticated and very educated. Ours is indeed a clever generation, but one that is suffering because men are doing what is right in their own eyes and disregarding God's immutable laws. If a person is not a Christian, he is inherently a failure because he has rejected that one third of his being that must be satisfied—the human spirit. While he is working to please the body and soul, he is ignoring the part of man that yearns for God. He needs a new birth, and this is a second birth—one in which an individual invites Jesus Christ, the Lord, in the person of His Holy Spirit, to come and indwell him.

In the third chapter of the first book of the Bible we have the story of the fall of man. Adam and Eve were placed in the Garden of Eden. They were completely innocent, never having committed sin even though they were capable of sinning. There were other creatures in the garden, including Lucifer, the son of the morning. This was Satan, who revealed himself as a serpent. God had told Adam and Eve that they could partake of all the fruit, and the vegetables, and the offerings of the garden, but they were warned not to partake of the tree of the knowledge of good and evil. Satan first tempted Eve, and then Eve tempted Adam. Both Adam and Eve disobeyed God and sinned. Because they sinned, they died. Because of them every human being who has ever and who will ever live, is doomed to one day die.

In the first verse of Chapter 3 of Genesis, Satan approached Eve and asked her a question, "Yea, hath God said?" The official satanic campaign to discredit the Bible, the Word of God, began with that question mark regarding Holy Scripture.

Adam and Eve knew well that God had said, "Thou shalt not eat of it: for in the day that thou eatest thou shalt surely die." God was speaking of spiritual and physical death. Because Adam and Eve partook of that forbidden fruit, they were doomed to spiritual and physical death.

The satanic campaign to discredit the Bible continues to this day. It has continued down through every generation to this present hour. Why is it wrong to refuse to accept the Genesis account of creation? If man is not basically bad; if he is not inherently evil, having received from the fall the very nature of sin and having had death passed upon him and all men; if the depravity of man is not a fact from the very fall in the garden, then the death, the burial, and the resurrection of Jesus Christ were needless and worthless.

Man was created in the image of God, with a body, a soul, and a spirit. Man was created a free moral agent with the choice of either obeying God or sinning and disobeying God. If man did not sin and fall from his original state, there is no need to accept the Gospel message. This is the concept of modern-day humanism and naturalism that has permeated our country and led men and women to believe foolishly that they are good and can pick themselves up by their own bootstraps. I here propose that man by nature is not good. One has only to look at the chaotic condition of our nation and our world to confirm the fact that men without Christ have no lasting peace and security. Each and every man and woman alive today needs a new birth experience. Man must be born again; he must be regenerated and believe in the death, the burial, and the resurrection of Jesus Christ and accept the shed blood of the Savior as the atonement for his sin in order to be complete.

A thorough study of the Bible will show that it is indeed the inerrant Word of the living God. The Bible is absolutely infallible, without error in all matters pertaining to faith and practice, as well as in areas such as geography, science, history, etc.

The disintegration of our social order can be easily explained. Men and women are disobeying the clear instructions God gave in His Word. Because of this, we live in a world of people with confused priorities who are giving maximum time to that which is of minor importance. It is no wonder that we see materialism on every hand today. People are living and dying for money. We see drug addiction and alcoholism and people worshiping the idol of and the god of sex. These people are spending their time, their talent, and their energies lusting after things that only lead to a dead end. We live in a world of confused and depressed people because, having violated divine laws, they have dissipated and ruined their lives. They have found that the pleasures of sin are but for a season.

The law of sowing and reaping is as immutable as the law of gravity: ". . . whatsoever a man soweth, that shall he also reap." In the Old Testament it is also stated this way: "Be sure your sin will find you out." Today we are living in an amoral society where millions of people are discounting the reality of sin as taught in the Bible.

Sin is a transgression of God's law, and God's law is unalterable. To sin is to voluntarily disobey God and His divine laws. When man does what is right in his own eyes, he is really saying that it does not matter to him what God thinks about it. He is endorsing what God has condemned, whether God likes it or not. The Bible clearly points out in Proverbs 14:34, "Righteousness exalteth a nation: But sin is a reproach to any people." Righteousness uplifts a nation. Sin brings reproach upon a people. This is the reason we are in a nosedive as a nation.

Psychiatrist Karl Menninger, in his book *Whatever Became of Sin?* asks: "The very word 'sin,' which seems to have disappeared . . . was once a strong word, an ominous and serious word. It described a central point in every civilized human being's life plan and life style. But the word went away. It has almost disappeared—the word, along with the notion. Why? Doesn't anyone sin anymore?" Dr. Menninger believes, "To revive the half-submerged idea of personal responsibility and to seek appropriate reparation might turn the tide of our aggressions and of the moral struggle in which much of the world's population is engaged. A conscious sense of guilt, and implicit or explicit repentance, would be consequences of the revival of an acknowledgment of error, transgression, offense, and responsibility—in short, of sin." (pp. 16, 218)

Men and women today try to rationalize their sins by calling them shortcomings or errors. Many modern theologians evade the word "sin." It is time that we began calling sin by its right name and calling for what is America's only hope—a biblical and spiritual awakening in the lives of her people. The Bible declares, "For the wages of sin is death; but the gift of God is eternal life through Jesus Christ our Lord."

We live in a world under God's judgment. Until man realizes that his greatest problem is sin and that this is what has alienated him from God, his Creator, there can be little hope of curing the chaotic conditions in our nation and world. Countless people are searching desperately for something that will bring inner peace and stability to their lives. People are lonely and filled with fear about the future, about failure, about death.

Men and women cannot ignore God, live as they please, and expect to be happy and blessed. This is, however, precisely what has happened. Men and women have placed their priorities on acquiring tangible possessions and achieving tangible goals. Man, rather than God, has been placed at the center of all things. Humanism in some form has taken the place of the Bible. Secular humanism has become the religion of America. Through education and the media, man is constantly being told that he is nothing more than a machine.

According to Webster's New Collegiate Dictionary, humanism is "a doctrine, attitude, or way of life centered on human interests or values; a philosophy that asserts the dignity and worth of man and his capacity for self-realization through reason and that often rejects supernaturalism." Humanism is man's attempt to create a heaven on earth, exempting God and His Law. Humanists propose that man is in charge of his own destiny. Humanism exalts man's reason and intelligence. It advocates situation ethics, freedom from any restraint, and defines sin as man's maladjustment to man. It even advocates the right to commit suicide and recognizes evolution as a source of man's existence. Humanism promotes the socialization of all humanity into a world commune.

Christianity is ruled out of humanism and is said to be an obstacle to human progress and a threat to its existence. Mao Tsetung once said, "Our God is none other than the masses of the people. Ye shall be as Gods." The first version of the *Humanist Manifesto* appeared in 1933. The second version appeared in 1973 and was printed in its entirety in the New York *Times*. *Humanist Manifesto I* and *Humanist Manifesto II* openly deny the existence of a Creator, urge abolition of national sovereignty in favor of world government, and embrace complete sexual freedom, abortion, homosexuality, and euthanasia.

Naturalism also has gained a stronghold. Naturalism looks on man as a kind of biological machine. To those who believe this philosophy of life, sexual immorality is just another bodily function, as is eating or drinking. The birth of a child is no different than the birth of an animal. Man lives a sort of meaningless existence in life, and it really doesn't matter what significance he thinks he has or what goals he is headed for. The only thing that really is important for man is to try to make himself happy in the immediate now. "If something feels good, do it." It is this philosophy that is destroying the basis and foundation of our nation today.

America's decadent state is evident. A highly respected "key figure" in society today is Harvard psychologist B. F. Skinner. Skinner's hypothesis is that every man and woman is merely a bundle of behaviors determined by an environment and nothing more. He believes that through evolution the environment selected the behaviors that survive in man's genes and that environmental conditioning shapes the lives of each and every individual. He does not believe that men and women possess "inalienable rights." In more than forty years of psychological research, Skinner has developed techniques for the modification of behavior by operant conditioning. Behaviorists all across America are completely committed to Skinner's view. They accept man as a machine and treat him that way. Many of these men are now controlling the educational process in America.

When mankind absolves his Christian base, he loses respect for human life. This is clearly shown in America's recent change of attitude toward abortion. As men and women fall under the satanic effects of humanism and naturalism, they begin to lose value for the most important thing in God's universe—human beings. Humanists do not value humankind; they value themselves.

A biology professor at Rutgers University, Dr. David Erhenfeld, makes these comments in his book *The Arrogance of Humanism:* "Evidence is piled all around us that the religion of humanity is self-destructive and foolish, yet the more it fails, the more arrogant and preposterous are the claims of its priests." (p. 58)

In his commencement address at Harvard University in 1978, Alexandr Solzhenitsyn made these comments: "Society appears to have little defense against the abyss of human decadence, such as, for example, misuse of liberty for moral violence against young people, motion pictures full of pornography, crime, and horror.

"Such a tilt of freedom in the direction of evil has come about gradually but it was evidently born primarily out of a humanistic and benevolent concept according to which there is no evil inherent to human nature; . . . Strangely enough, though the best social conditions have been achieved in the West, there still is criminality. . . . How has this unfavorable relation of forces come about? How did the West decline from its triumphal march to its present sickness? . . . The West kept advancing socially in accordance with its proclaimed intentions, with the help of brilliant technological progress. And all of a sudden it found itself in its present state of weakness.

"This means that the mistake must be at the root, at the very basis of human thinking in the past centuries. I refer to the prevailing Western view of the world which was first born during the Renaissance and found its political expression from the period of the Enlightenment. It became the basis for government and social science and could be defined as rationalistic humanism or humanistic autonomy: the proclaimed and enforced autonomy of man from any higher force above him. It could also be called anthropocentricity, with man seen as the center of everything that exists . . . we turned our backs upon the Spirit and embraced all that is material with excessive and unwarranted zeal. This new way of thinking, which had imposed on us its guidance, did not admit the existence of intrinsic evil in man nor did it see any higher task than the attainment of happiness on earth. It based modern Western civilization on the dangerous trend to worship man and his material needs. Everything beyond physical well-being, an accumulation of material goods, all other human requirements and characteristics of a subtler and higher nature were left outside the area of attention of state and social systems, as if human life did not have any superior sense. That provided access for evil, of which in our days there is a free and constant flow. Merely freedom does not in the least solve all the problems of human life and it even adds a number of new ones."

The Bible declares that men and women who do not acknowledge God, although professing themselves to be wise, become fools. God desires to give America revival. But before there can be revival, there must first be a conviction of sin, and there cannot be a conviction of sin until there is awareness of sin. The hope for America is for her people to believe the Bible to be the Word of God and to begin to live by the laws of God.

A LOOK AT OUR GOVERNMENT TODAY

When America was founded, the legitimate purpose of government was to protect the lives, the liberties, and the property of the citizens. It was not the purpose of government to redistribute resources or to enforce any particular results in the relationships and dealings of the citizenry among themselves. Simply stated, government was to protect the God-given rights of the people.

The framers of our Constitution instituted a system of representative government, with clear limits upon what government could and could not do. This was done to ensure individual freedom. A system of checks and balances was instituted to make sure that government would not have the power to deprive individual men and women of rights that the Constitution stated were "endowed by their Creator." Our Founding Fathers recognized that the individual was God's precious earthly creation, and therefore men and women were born equal before God.

Individuals should be free to build their own lives without interference from government. Our Declaration of Independence states that governments derive "their just Powers from the Consent of the Governed," and that "whenever any Form of Government becomes destructive of these Ends, it is the Right of the People to alter or to abolish it . . ." The premise that our Founding Fathers established that those who govern do so only with the consent of the governed is being severely attacked. We find today that government is threatening our basic freedoms because it is becoming, in the words of many of our modern freedom fighters, a "monster."

In his book *The Sum of Good Government*, Philip Crane quotes Dr. Roger Freeman: "By its massive entry over the past two decades into the field of domestic public services, the national government has decisively altered the nature of the American federal system. In establishing a federal structure with an intricate system of checks and balances, the Founding Fathers had aimed to disperse authority so widely that no one branch or level of government—and no one man—could prevail over the others. They concluded from history that concentration of power corrupts and sooner or later leads to abuse and tyranny. Whenever the wisdom of the age-old lesson is disregarded, its truth is brought home to the nation sooner or later with a brutal shock. . . . American society has strayed far from its beginnings. Instead of desiring freedom from governmental interference; instead of looking to the government primarily as a source of protection from foreign or domestic enemies and not as the provider of services and benefits, Americans have embraced the very centralized government the Founding Fathers urged them to fear and hold in check." (pp. 22, 23)

Our government now takes more than 40 per cent of the nation's personal income. Our government must print money to finance annual deficits of more than fifty billion dollars. Our government's total accumulated long-term debt and obligations (more than five trillion dollars) are more than the total worth of our economy. A vast number of government bureaucrats in Washington and across the nation are running our government and destroying the freedom that our Founding Fathers established at the birth of our nation. Our system of government is in a precarious state because men and women of America have their priorities mixed up. U. S. Senator Jesse Helms has summed it up well when he says, "when you have men who no longer believe that God is in charge of human affairs, you have men attempting to take the place of God by means of the

Superstate. The Divine Providence on which our forefathers relied has been supplanted by the Providence of the All-Powerful State. I believe that this is the source of deep weakness in America, because it is a transgression of the first and greatest of the Ten Commandments. Atheism and socialism—or liberalism, which tends in the same direction—are inseparable entities."

A majority of Americans are unaware of how their representatives run our government. It is the responsibility of each and every citizen to be informed about what is going on in his government. Woodrow Wilson was a keen student of history. He made this statement: "The history of liberty is a history of limitations of governmental power, not the increase of it. When we resist, therefore, the concentration of power, we are resisting the powers of death, because concentration of power is what always precedes the destruction of human liberties." (Crane, p. 118) Let us look at how the concentration of power in our government today is seeking to strangle the freedoms and liberty each one of us Americans enjoys.

The United States of America was experiencing a deep time of trouble in the election year of 1932. The terrible Depression had left millions of people out of work, and breadlines were common sights. People were desperate; they had lost trust in the prevailing economic system. Franklin Delano Roosevelt offered hope to the American people. He promised the American people many things, which gradually grew into his "New Deal." It is important to review this time because our top economists agree that it was this period that marked the beginning of a changing role of government.

Economist Milton Friedman points out: "One simple set of statistics suggests the magnitude of the change. From the founding of the republic to 1929, spending by governments at all levels, federal, state, and local, never exceeded 12 per cent of the national income except in time of major war, and two thirds of that was state and local spending. Federal spending typically amounted to 3 per cent or less of the national income. Since 1933 government spending has never been less than 20 per cent of national income and is now over 40 per cent, and two thirds of that is spending by the federal government. True, much of the period since the end of World War II has been a period of cold and hot war. However, since 1946 nondefense spending alone has never been less than 16 per cent of the national income and is now roughly one third of the national income. Federal government spending alone is more than one quarter of the national income in total, and more than a fifth for nondefense purposes alone. By this measure the role of the federal government in the economy has multiplied roughly tenfold in the past half century." (*Free to Choose*, p. 92)

Belief in individual responsibility, laissez-faire, and a decentralized and limited government changed to belief in social responsibility and a centralized and powerful government. Those men who advised Roosevelt felt that there had to be a change in the economy, which involved an increase in government ownership and operation of the means of production. Friedman points out that Roosevelt's advisers were ready to view the Depression as a failure of capitalism. They saw as the remedy the intervention of central government. Friedman points out, "World War II interrupted the New Deal, while at the same time strengthening greatly its foundations. . . . The war's effect on public attitudes was the mere image of the Depression's. The Depression convinced the public that capitalism was defective; the war, that centralized government was efficient. Both conclusions were false. The Depression was produced by a failure of government, not of private enterprise." (*Free to Choose*, p. 94)

In this viewing of history, we can see that government began to expand greatly. It was at this time that governmental intervention in business mushroomed. Today we see bigger and bigger government in the form of our welfare programs and regulatory activities. We have in our country today hundreds of governmental welfare and income-transfer programs. Friedman points out, "The Department of Health, Education, and Welfare, established in 1953 to consolidate the scattered welfare programs, began with the budget of $2 billion, less than 5 per cent of expenditures on national defense. Twenty-five years later, in 1978, its budget was $160 billion, 1½ times as much as total spending on the Army, the Navy, and the Air Force. It had the third largest budget in the world, exceeded only by the entire budget of the U. S. Government and of the Soviet Union." (*Free to Choose*, p. 96)

We know that HEW was subdivided and a separate Department of Education was established in late 1979, but the fact is that our economy is in deep financial trouble today. We find much fraud and corruption in governmental intervention in our economy. Governmental intrusion, rather than helping the American people, has actually reduced the sense of responsibility and initiative in her citizens. It is the way of socialism and communism to reduce a man's incentive by taking away from him the fruits of his labors. The sad fact is that government is the major source of our economic instability in this country.

Our Founding Fathers knew that free enterprise was the best economic organization to maintain the free society they had created. Milton Friedman points out in his book *Capitalism and Freedom*, "The kind of economic organization that provides economic freedom directly, namely, competitive capitalism, also promotes political freedom because it separates economic power from political power and in this way enables the one to offset the other." (p. 9) Free enterprise in a capitalistic society, where free men trade with other free men without the interference of other people, works. Men want to reap the rewards of their own labors.

Free enterprise is consistent with freedom. It naturally rises from a country that has liberty. America has enjoyed the highest standard of living in the world, since the founding of our nation, as a direct result of the free marketplace. We have only to look at history to find that no nation has survived long when its citizens were denied the free market and individual initiative. Government was never meant to dominate the economic affairs of its citizens; this is not the way of freedom. As we continue to move toward collectivism, individual freedoms are eroded.

Protection of each and every individual's right to acquire property is a necessity of freedom. To destroy or to control a man's right to own and use property is to diminish him as an individual, for property rights are human rights. Freedom to own property is a basic tenet of this society.

More and more today, we are seeing our government run by thousands of bureaucracies that destroy the productive institutions they supervise. It is all too obvious that Congress is becoming more and more antibusiness. The attack on business is ultimately an attack upon the principles of free enterprise. In his book former Secretary of the Treasury William Simon points out: "Government control of production results in artificial shortages which produce crises, and if not corrected, it will culminate in a drive to economic dictatorship. The principle is inviolate. Our capacity for innovation must decay, our standard of living must drop, and our wealth and freedom—and the wealth and freedom of those nations which depend on us—must deteriorate until the principle is finally understood." (Simon, p. 85) Immigrants by the millions have come to the United States. They knew that in this country they could make a way for themselves and their families if they worked hard enough, and most were not afraid of hard work.

The pattern is fitting together that when men take their eyes off the principles in the Word of God, there is trouble in every area. God said in the first book in the Bible, Genesis, that we are to earn our bread by the sweat of our brow. He was giving us the principles of reward for work. The principles established by Almighty God work in every area of our lives.

It is clear that our freedoms are being eroded today because of economic trouble in our country. Americans have violated Scripture, and with it their freedoms. Dwight D. Eisenhower said: "When shallow critics denounce the profit motive inherent in our system of private enterprise, they ignore the fact that this is the economic support of every right we possess and that without it, all rights will soon disappear. Their conclusions emphasize the results: more and more bureaus, more and more taxes, fewer and fewer producers, and finally, financial collapse and the end of freedom."

Let us now look at government spending and see where our

tax dollars go. I have heard it said that it is unbelievable but true that taxpayers are paying for their own destruction. With the government taking more than one third of every dollar of income generated in the United States, it follows that the erosion of freedom results as people have less and less choice as to what they are doing with their money. No power has been more abused by Congress than that of the free spending of each and every citizen's tax money. The taxation of the American people is today an overwhelming burden.

According to the Tax Foundation, the typical taxpayer works from January 1 to April 30 for money he never sees. It is only right that citizens share in the responsibility of the functions of their government, but when government is not responsible, its citizens become overburdened. Our forefathers did much to emphasize the idea of a limited and frugal government. When he left office on September 19, 1796, President Washington said in his farewell address, "Avoid likewise the accumulation of debt, not only by shunning occasions of expense, but by vigorous exertion in time of peace to discharge the debts which unavoidable wars may have occasioned, not ungenerously throwing upon posterity the burden which we ourselves ought to bear."

In the first 124 years of our national existence, the federal government of the United States spent $16.5 billion; in the next 40 years (1901–40), the government spent $149.5 billion. From 1941 to 1950, the federal government spent $535 billion. From 1951 to 1960, it spent $744 billion. From 1961 to 1970, it spent $1.4 trillion. And from 1971 to 1977, the federal government spent $2.1 trillion. The total expenditures of our federal government (actual and estimated) were $450.8 billion in 1978, $493.4 billion in 1979, and $531.6 billion in 1980. That represents an increase of federal spending of 117.9 per cent in the last two years.

Government spending is out of control. Government spending is rising far faster than the economy can support it. There are today more than one thousand federal programs for the transferral of a producer's income to a non-producer's pocket. Our government is the nation's largest employer. Defense spending is the only category of federal spending that has been reduced drastically in the last several years.

We find a growing internal encroachment of government bureaucrats who distribute rules and regulations, many times called "guidelines." Programs initiated by the bureaucrats have been an economic burden and an inflationary pressure on the people of our nation. A special report in a December 17, 1979, *U. S. News & World Report* entitled "The Great American Bureaucratic 'Perks' Machine," states, "Working for Uncle Sam pays off in a lot more than money. Elected officials, judges, military personnel and bureaucrats receive fringe benefits that seem endless—and cost U.S. taxpayers millions." One must read this article to find the horrifying and extravagant expenses that are paid for by American tax dollars. I will here quote a very small portion of the article: "Rising salaries, expanding staffs, generous pension benefits and a growing list of office 'perks' have driven up the cost of operating Congress to more than a billion dollars a year—triple the expense of ten years ago.

"Every lawmaking body needs a staff, critics concede. But aides to members of Congress now cost taxpayers about $301 million a year, representing one of the most valued perquisites on Capitol Hill, especially at re-election time.

"The Senate, which first authorized the hiring of personal aides in 1885 at the rate of $6.00 per day, now has 7,148 staff members—double the number of a decade ago. Each of the hundred senators gets up to $1 million for staff payroll, depending on his state's population. The House has 11,738 aides, with each of the 435 representatives receiving $288,156 to pay up to 18 employees.

"To accommodate the expanding staffs that lawmakers insist are needed to meet public demands for service, Congress is building a sixth office building. The nine-story structure, to be named after the late Senator Phillip A. Hart, first was proposed in 1972 at a cost of $48 million. It now is expected to cost $137.7 million.

"The price tag would have been even higher had not the House balked at inclusion of a rooftop restaurant, a gymnasium, saunas, and $2.3 million in walnut paneling for a building to serve only senators. Even so, the structure, which is only one third office space, will have marble facing, leading Senator William Roth to call it a new 'marble and bronze-gilded castle.' "

Let us look at our welfare system. Our whole welfare system is built on a basic premise that is detrimental to our society. We cannot survive economically when the working population of America is faced with an ever-increasing burden of governmental spending to support a tremendously large nonworking segment of our society.

In the Bible, in the third chapter of 2 Thessalonians, we find the Apostle Paul writing to a congregation in the city of Thessalonica regarding the subject of work. This is not a labor or management discussion. It is a spiritual discussion. Paul says, "Now we command you, brethren, in the name of our Lord Jesus Christ, that ye withdraw yourselves from every brother that walketh disorderly, and not after the tradition which he received of us. For yourselves know how ye ought to follow us: For we behaved not ourselves disorderly among you. Neither did we eat any man's bread for naught, but wrought with labor and travail night and day, that we might not be chargeable to any of you: Not because we have not power, but to make ourselves an example unto you to follow us. For even when we were with you, this we commanded you, that if any would not work, neither should he eat. For we hear that there are some which walk among you disorderly, working not at all, but are busybodies. Now them that are such we command and exhort by our Lord Jesus Christ, that with quietness they work and eat their own bread. But ye, brethren, be not weary in well-doing."

The work ethic is a biblical principle. I am not totally anti-welfare; those who need help, those who cannot care for themselves, the sick and the aged should be taken care of. God will bless our country for doing so. There have been times in our country's history when there were not enough jobs to go around, or when the jobs did not provide enough money to buy the food necessary to keep the family alive. There are times when we should help those people who are able to work, but who because of extenuating circumstances simply cannot. But I believe that, generally, there are now enough jobs to go around. Too many people who could work, do not. Have they forgotten what the word "work" means? Will they live off giveaway programs, supported by those people who work hard for a living, forever? We must not forget that our government does not give away anything that it does not take from someone else.

During the past decade the number of citizens living on welfare has increased 500 per cent. A January 1979 issue of *U. S. News & World Report* says that without government help, some forty-three million Americans—that is, 20 per cent of the population—would be classified as being poor. Many experts are puzzled that this figure has remained stagnant for the past twelve years despite rising wages and millions of new jobs being available.

Food stamps are only one of a random number of food-assistance programs, and some nineteen million Americans receive them once a month. The food-stamp program alone is a multibillion-dollar program. When the government cares for its people, why should its people care for themselves? Welfare programs tend to destroy one's initiative, skill, work habits, and productivity.

It is time for our welfare program to be examined and much of it done away with. People will not starve to death, although their standard of living may not be sustained. We have two dogs at our home. They are big, beautiful Irish setters. The fellow who gave them to us is a dear friend who owns a supermarket. When he gave me the dogs, he told me what kind of meat they had to have and where I could buy it. The more he talked the more I realized that I could not afford to keep the dogs, but when he left, I went up to the store and bought a big bag of brown nuggets, dumped them into two pans, and put them outside for the dogs. Sure enough, at first they would not eat them, but four days later they did. They did not eat luxuriously, but they did eat.

Another alarming expenditure of our federal government is

the use of tax funds that support public-relations efforts that can best be described as purely political in nature. Recently our President issued a memorandum to federal department heads urging them to use their tax-supported offices to persuade people to support the passage of the Equal Rights Amendment. Another massive tax-supported public-relations campaign was that of trying to persuade the people to give away the Panama Canal. More than one million dollars of tax money was used to persuade citizens to support the second Strategic Arms Limitation Treaty with the Soviet Union. We could go on and on with such examples.

In order to pay for its budget items, as well as those items that are not included in the budget, government has been printing more and more money every year. Inflation destroys free enterprise, and is a form of theft. In his book *Restoring the American Dream*, Robert Ringer makes this statement: "When a person finds that his higher income of today buys less than did his income of five years ago, he is living in a country that is being deluded (and destroyed) by false prosperity. He is living in a nation where the combined income of the population exceeds the total production of goods and services. He is living in a nation that is courting economic collapse." (p. 54) It is the deficit borrowing of our Congress that sets off the deadly inflationary spiral. Before 1917 the federal budget only exceeded $1 billion. The $100 billion mark was not reached until 1962. From there it skyrocketed until at the rate it is now going, federal spending could reach $1 trillion by the mid-1980s. Deficit spending is the primary cause of inflation. Financial experts now tell us that the national debt has hit $892.8 billion. Interest on the national debt is roughly $85 billion, or 85 per cent of our current budget for national defense. It is no wonder that millions of Americans are finding that their standard of living is going down with each passing year. When Calvin Coolidge was President he made this comment: "Inflation is a repudiation of the just possessions of all. Its chief cause is government spending beyond its income."

Another form of welfare and a great expenditure of American

tax dollars is foreign aid. In the past 35 years, foreign aid has cost the taxpayers of this country almost $200 billion. No wonder our federal debt has increased tremendously; foreign aid has been responsible for a large percentage of our national debt. The sad fact is that we often give freely to those countries that repudiate everything freedom stands for.

In this day of great energy crisis William Simon provides valuable insights: "Government planning and regulation of the economy will ultimately lead to shortages, crises, and if not reversed in time, some form of economic dictatorship. That is precisely what happened in the realm of energy production in the United States. Years of incoherent government intervention strangled energy production, domestic supplies diminished, artificial shortages emerged, a foreign embargo on oil precipitated a crisis. There was a violent, public outcry for an instant solution, an energy 'dictatorship' was established to allocate the rare commodity. . . . Most existing regulation is so irrational that it should be worked out by law, along with the bureaucracies that have spawned it. This is a disease of government; it is not government." (Simon, pp. 45, 46, 186)

It is very evident from this cursory overview of our government that it is time that the size of government decreased. We could list page after page of answers and solutions that our economists present. The fact is that we must return to the concept of government proposed and enacted by our Founding Fathers, one in which individual liberty was foremost and a limited constitution of government made our nation the envy of the world.

Milton Friedman is optimistic; he concludes his book *Free to Choose* with these words: "Fortunately, we are waking up. We are again recognizing the dangers of an overgoverned society, coming to understand that good objectives can be perverted by bad means, that reliance on the freedom of people to control their own lives in accordance with their own values is the surest way to achieve the full potential of a great society.

"Fortunately, also, we are as a people still free to choose which way we should go—whether to continue along the road we have been following to ever bigger government, or to call a halt and change direction." (pp. 309–10)

Robert Ringer's solution to restoring the American Dream is in educating the young. He admonishes, "The redistribution-of-the-wealth functions of government should be phased out, which means cutting government spending to the bone. . . . Within a matter of a few years, this cutback would begin to turn our whole economy around." (p. 292)

Thomas Jefferson, the third President of the United States, spoke these words in his first inaugural address on March 4, 1801: ". . . acknowledging and adoring an overruling Providence, which by all its dispensations proves that it delights in the happiness of man here and his greater happiness hereafter—with all these blessings, what more is necessary to make us a happy and a prosperous people? Still one thing more, fellow-citizens—a wise and frugal Government, which shall restrain men from injuring one another, shall leave them otherwise free to regulate their own pursuits of industry and improvement, and shall not take from the mouth of labor the bread it has earned. This is the sum of good government, and this is necessary to close the circle of our felicities."

I want to quote General Douglas MacArthur once again as saying, "History fails to record a single precedent in which nations subject to moral decay have not passed into political and economic decline. There has been either a spiritual awakening to overcome the moral lapse or a progressive deterioration leading to ultimate national disaster." The answer to every one of our nation's dilemmas is a spiritual one. When we as a country again acknowledge God as our Creator and Jesus Christ as the Savior of mankind, we will be able to turn this nation around economically as well as in every other way.

If you were to read *The Selected Works of Lenin*, you would find these words on page 298 of Volume 7: "As long as capitalism and socialism exist, we cannot live in peace; in the end, one or the other will triumph. A funeral dirge will be sung over either the Soviet Republics or over world capitalism."

Karl Marx, known as the nineteenth-century "father of communism," was a university-trained intellectual who had a doctorate in philosophy. Marx's theory of dialectical materialism was a blending of Feuerbach's atheistic materialism with Hegel's theory that everything in nature is in a state of constant conflict. As a self-proclaimed scientist, Marx developed certain "scientific theories." These included: "There is no God. When Communists deny God, they simultaneously deny every virtue and every value that originates with God. There are no moral absolutes, no right and wrong. The Ten Commandments and the Sermon on the Mount are invalid." Lenin said, "We do not believe in eternal morality—our morality is entirely subordinated to the interests of the class struggle."

The next "scientific law of communism" says: "Man is simply matter in motion. As such, he is without soul, spirit, or free will and is not responsible for his own acts." Marx taught that man was an evolutionary animal and as such had no eternal life. His third law states: "Man is an economically determined animal. Qualities of human intelligence, personality, emotional and religious life merely reflect man's economic environment. The evil a man does is just a reflection of his environment." Marx taught that capitalism must be destroyed and replaced with socialism. Then, under socialism, the Communist Party should work toward the establishment of communism. Socialism is actually a transitional stage in a society between capitalism and communism.

Nicolai Lenin was a Russian revolutionary and an ardent student of Marx. Lenin developed a plan for organizing the Communist Party. His plan called for a highly disciplined and dedicated core of professional revolutionaries. Joseph Stalin spelled out Lenin's theory in detail in his book *Stalin on China*. He wrote: "The most powerful enemy can be conquered only by exerting the utmost effort, and by necessarily, thoroughly, carefully, attentively, and skillfully taking advantage of every, even the smallest 'rift' among enemies, of every antagonism of interest of the bourgeoisie of the various countries and among the various groups or types of bourgeoisie within the various countries, and also by taking advantage of every, even the smallest opportunity of gaining a mass ally, even though this ally be temporary, vacillating, unstable, unreliable, and conditional. Those who do not understand this do not understand even a particle of Marxism, or of scientific modern socialism."

Before Lenin died in 1924, he formulated a plan for world domination. Lenin's plan included: "First, we will take Eastern Europe, then the masses of Asia, then we will encircle the United States, which will be the last bastion of capitalism. We will not have to attack. It will fall like an overripe fruit into our hands."

In July 1959, President Eisenhower invited Khrushchev to America. Khrushchev was one of Stalin's most trusted killers. Before he arrived in the United States, the House Committee on Un-American Activities documented Khrushchev's bloody record. In seven volumes they showed that Khrushchev personally conceived and executed the mass starvation and liquidation of six to eight million Ukrainians in the early 1930s. Khrushchev was the chief executioner for the bloody Moscow Purge Trials in 1936. He supervised the killing of thousands. Khrushchev, during a second two-year reign of terror in the Ukraine in 1937–1938, slaughtered another 400,000 people. Khrushchev's postwar Ukrainian Purge liquidated or exiled hundreds of thousands to slave labor camps.

If we will look at history, we will find that every time the Soviets were in peril, at the point of collapse, the United States came to their aid in the form of food, relief, and medical and other supplies. We find that it was men of expertise from the United States who opened up Russia's oil fields and assisted her in building many of her plants. When the U.S.S.R. was faltering again in 1933 it was the United States who recognized her. With U.S. diplomatic recognition came access to the credit and money markets of the world. For this act upon the part of the United States, the Communists promised in writing that the Soviet Union would not interfere in our internal affairs. Before the agreements were even signed, the Soviets were busy setting up spy networks in agencies in the United States. The Communists have never been trustworthy.

In *Restoring the American Dream,* Robert Ringer quotes Alexandr Solzhenitsyn, "It is American trade that allows the Soviet economy to concentrate its resources on armaments and preparations for war. Remove that trade, and the Soviet economy would be obliged to feed and clothe and house the Russian people, something it has never been able to do. Let the socialists among you allow this socialist economy to prove the superiority that its ideology claims. Stop sending them goods. Let them stand on their own feet and then see what happens."

Much could be said about the bloody history of the U.S.S.R. —about Stalin's and Hitler's savage butchering of the Polish people. We could talk about what the U.S.S.R. did with the $11 billion America sent in Lend-Lease aid when they were fighting Germany. We could talk much about the evident treachery and lying that characterizes the history of the United States. Our late director of the FBI, J. Edgar Hoover, warned, "We are at war with communism and the sooner every red-blooded American can realize this, the safer we will be." But it appears that America's policy toward communism is one of containment, rather than victory.

After Lieutenant J. D. Hunter of Arlington, Virginia, was killed in Vietnam, President Johnson sent the boy's parents the usual letter of condolences. The young man's father answered the President's letter by saying that his son had been proud to serve in the U. S. Army but that he had complained to his father that his men were fighting a "no win" war. The grieving father wrote that anything short of a real victory would mean that he and his wife, along with thousands of other fathers, mothers, wives, brothers, and sisters, had had their loved ones sacrificed on an altar of political intrigue.

The Assistant Secretary of Defense answered the father's letter. He told Mr. Hunter that the United States was engaged in a limited war for limited objectives and that military actions had to be weighed accordingly. He explained that bombing operations in the North were constrained because of the limited political objectives in the South, and that the United States was not seeking to destroy the government of North Vietnam.

The anguished father wrote a final letter to the Defense Department in which he stated that his son was right when he told him that he and his men had been called upon to fight a no-win war. The father expressed his grievance that fighting a no-win war with limited political objectives meant that American soldiers were fighting a war with one hand tied behind their backs, and that that was a miserable way to fight a war.

The Vietnam War cost America the lives of fifty-six thousand of our fighting men, handicapped another three hundred thousand, and took billions of tax dollars. When James R. Schlesinger was Secretary of Defense, he proposed that we lost in Vietnam because we did not use the power we had. He made this comment: "The gravest problem for the Western world is without question the loss of vision, of moral stamina, of national purpose."

Americans have been fooled by the Communists long enough. It is time that key figures in our government begin to awaken to the fact that communism is a vicious attack upon what was once a free world. Communists have dedicated themselves to world conquest. I cannot forget the words of Dimitry Manvilsky, internationally known Soviet leader, who said in his lecture to the Lenin School of Political Warfare in Moscow in 1930, "War to the hilt between communism and capitalism is inevitable. Today, of course, we are not strong enough to attack. Our time will come in twenty or thirty years. To win we shall need the element of surprise. The bourgeoisie (the capitalist nations) will have to be put to sleep. So we shall begin by launching the most spectacular peace movement on record. There will be electrifying overtures and unheard-of concessions. The capitalist countries, stupid and decadent, will rejoice to co-operate in their own destruction. They will leap at another chance to be friends. As soon as their guard is down we shall smash them with our clenched fist."

Liu Chao-chi, a former president of Communist China, said in his book *How to Be a Good Communist*, "What is the fundamental duty of us Communist Party members? As everybody knows, it is to establish communism, to transform the present world into a communist world."

The goal of international communism has never changed. In 1973, speaking to a meeting in Prague, Czechoslovakia, Leonid Brezhnev stated: "We are achieving with détente what our predecessors have been unable to achieve with the mailed fist. . . . Trust us, comrades, for by 1985, as a consequence of what we are now achieving with détente, we will have achieved most of our objectives in Western Europe. We will have consolidated our position. We will have improved our economy. And a decisive shift in the correlation of forces will be such that, come 1985, we will be able to exert our will wherever we need to."

In 1977, *The Communist Daily World* recorded Y. Krasin quoting Brezhnev as saying, "Détente does not in the slightest abolish or alter the laws of the class struggle. International détente and the class struggle are two sides, two organically interconnected aspects of the dialectics of social progress in the epoch of transition from capitalism and socialism." We have only to look at what has happened or is happening in countries like Vietnam, Laos, Cambodia, Mozambique, Angola, southwestern Africa, Rhodesia, Ethiopia, and Afghanistan to understand what the Communists are after. Richard F. Staar, senior fellow at the Hoover Institute, Stanford University, and editor-in-chief of the Yearbook on International Communist Affairs, reports that communist movements exist in ninety-nine countries with a total membership claimed to be in excess of seventy-one million.

When communism takes over a nation, the first thing that happens is that the churches are shut down, preachers are killed or imprisoned, and Bibles are taken away from the people. Communists are expert deceivers. In Moscow today we see little churches that are merely there as window dressing to fool people as to communist intentions. There is in the Soviet Union today no religious freedom, no freedom of speech, no freedom of the press.

As we have already stated, Alexandr Solzhenitsyn spent eleven years in a Siberian prison camp. On July 9, 1975, Solzhenitsyn was asked to address the AFL-CIO. He was introduced by George Meany with these words: "We heed this voice not because it speaks for the left or the right or for any faction, but because it hurls truth and courage into the teeth of total power, when it would be so much easier and more comfortable to submit and to embrace the lies by which that power lives. What is the strength of his voice? How has it broken through to us when others have been stilled? Its strength is art. Alexandr Solzhenitsyn is not a crusader, he is not a politician, he is not a general, he is an artist, and by his art he illuminates the truth. It is, in a sense, subversive. It is subversive of hypocrisy, subversive of delusion, subversive of the 'big lie.' No man in modern times, and very few in all of history, have demonstrated as drastically as Alexandr Solzhenitsyn the power of the pen, coupled with courage, to free men's minds."

Solzhenitsyn made these comments to the AFL-CIO: "The communist ideology is to destroy your society. That has been their aim for 125 years and has never changed; only the methods have changed . . . the primary, the eternal concept is humanity. And communism is antihumanity.

"Do we really have to wait for the moment when the knife is at our throats? Couldn't it be possible, ahead of time, soberly to assess the worldwide menace that threatens to swallow the whole world? I was swallowed myself. I have been in the dragon's belly, in the red-burning belly of the dragon. He wasn't able to digest me. He threw me up. I have come to you as a witness to what it's like there, in the dragon's belly."

In the second volume of his *Gulag Archipelago*, Solzhenitsyn says that the prison camps held up to fifteen million inmates at a time. He estimated that from the Revolution to 1959 a total of fifty-six million prisoners died in those camps. The godless Communists have killed additional millions since that time. In November 1979 Solzhenitsyn's wife, Natalia, warned eighteen hundred people at Dartmouth College, "Your oblivion to the reality of the suffering in today's world is dangerous."

While he was Secretary of the Treasury, William E. Simon, acting as leader of the U.S. delegation, and John K. Tabor, acting Commerce Secretary, were received by Leonid Brezhnev during a joint U.S.-U.S.S.R. commercial commission in Moscow for its fifth annual session. In his book A *Time for Truth*, William Simon talks about his days in Russia. He speaks of being treated as an honored guest and of being "treated splendidly in our royal cocoon." He then tells this moving story: "Somewhere outside that cocoon, in some other dimension of reality, we knew that there was an oppressed populace. Somewhere outside it, we knew, citizens were illclad, illhoused, illfed, and unfree—some being torn from their families and homes and hurled into prisons and insane asylums for the crime of disagreeing with our jovial hosts. But none of this was visible in our opulent nest. Only the most pleasurable sights and sounds had been allowed to filter into that artificial world prepared for us by the lords of the Kremlin. Soviet society itself had little or no reality.

"When our 'agreed statement' was handed to the press, we

prepared to depart. We exchanged our formal compliments, made our farewells, and boarded Air Force Two. Still caught up in our official roles, we continued to discuss the ramifications of East-West trade. Then, abruptly, the roar of the motor broke into our conversation, and as the plane taxied down the runway, we all fell silent. After a moment or two Air Force Two lifted off. We heard the dull thump of the locking wheels. The ground fell away beneath us. We were no longer on Soviet soil! And everyone burst into applause.

"I'll never forget the moment of elation that possessed us all. It needed no translation. I knew exactly what the emotion was: a sense of oppression being lifted from all of us who had never known oppression. It felt, for a crazy moment, as if we were staging a great escape. I remember that sense of 'I can breathe again. I can talk again. I'm not being spied on anymore.' It was a sudden vanishing of all the menacing things that characterize the Soviet Union, the shadowy intrusions that you can feel but cannot see. Throughout all the long, co-operative working hours, underlying the jovial ceremonies, lurking beneath the flash of crystal, the flow of vodka, the unspoken awareness of unseen oppression had been with each one of us. We too had felt unfree. So all of us, seventy-eight dignified representatives of the United States of America, shouted and applauded like youngsters in sheer relief because we had emerged from that mammoth jail called the Soviet Union, because we were flying home, flying toward freedom. And at that moment that's all that 'home' meant to every one of us—blessed, blessed freedom.

"And it was then for the first time that I could put into words that sense of a deep, unnameable difference between the Soviet officials and myself. It was the difference between men who had never known freedom, and men who were born free. Most of them, I suspected, didn't even know that difference between us existed. They heard about it, they read about it, but they couldn't comprehend something they had never known. I was certain that they couldn't understand that rush of joy and relief that was racing through us like a powerful tide. I realized something disturbing: Those Soviet officials are men who do not *know* that they live in a dungeon. And as I realized that, I understood down to my very roots how important my liberty was to me, that the need for it was a part of my very identity. My God, I thought, without it, I would not be me!" (Simon, pp. 17, 18) Mr. Simon went on to explain that it is only when people confront political tyranny that they fully grasp the meaning and the importance of freedom.

Our forefathers knew the importance of freedom, and they did much to ensure that freedom to their posterity. We too must preserve our freedoms for our posterity. Communism is atheistic. When God is taken out of a society, all freedom is lost. It is time that Americans rise from positions of apathy and realize the seriousness of the very implications of taking God out of our society. It is communistic to destroy the concept of God. We have already taken prayer and Bible reading out of our public schools. Madalyn Murray O'Hair is now proposing that God's name be removed from the Pledge of Allegiance and "In God We Trust" be removed from our currency. With the removal of God from a society, there is a removal of liberty.

It is time Americans realized the severe attack currently being waged in America against our families. This nation's foundation is its homes. Karl Marx described "the hallowed co-relation of parents and child" as disgusting. Communists often remove children from their homes and take full responsibility for their education in order to indoctrinate them into the communist way. Parents and children in the Soviet Union are separated when homes are judged to be "unfit." The three most common reasons for this are (1) insanity of the parents, (2) alcohol or drug addiction of the parents, and (3) the practice of the Christian way of life or the teaching of Christian principles in the home. In her address at Dartmouth College, Natalia Solzhenitsyn said: "We are not allowed to teach our children. The laws oblige us to rear our children in the spirit of Marxism and communism." When the Communists established their "rules for bringing about revolution" in 1919, they said this: "Corrupt the young; get them away from religion. Get them interested in sex. Make them superficial. Destroy their ruggedness."

It is time that we listened to Alexandr Solzhenitsyn when he speaks of the West being on the verge of collapse. He indeed spoke the truth when he said, "Friends, I have not come to tell you comfortable things, but I have come to tell you the truth." We have only to look at our daily newspaper to realize that the Soviet Union is now stronger than the West, and thus cares little about what the West has to say. Thousands of Christians are being tortured in Russia today and in other Communist countries. They are sentenced to prison terms and sent to insane asylums for charges of "antisocial activities" (which include religious activities) and for influencing children's minds with books containing "nonsensical ideas on reality."

The February 4, 1980, issue of *Newsweek* tells of the exile of the Soviet Union's most prominent political dissenter, fifty-eight-year-old physicist and Nobel Peace Prize winner Andrei Sakharov, and his wife. While going across town to attend a weekly seminar, Sakharov was stopped by Soviet police and taken to the state prosecutor's office. Less than an hour later, his wife received a phone call telling her that he had been arrested. Within hours, they were both banished to Gorki, a military-industrial city 250 miles east of Moscow. Gorki is off-limits to foreigners. Sakharov and his wife were sent there for an indefinite period of "internal exile."

Newsweek reported, "The Kremlin's intent was to stifle Sakharov's prestigious voice at home and abroad, and to deal a crippling blow to the struggle he had led for human rights and political freedoms in the Soviet Union. 'They have eliminated the main figure in the movement,' a worried Moscow scholar said last week. 'The message is clear: The Soviet Government has decided that it will tolerate no more opposition.'" Is it only because of their world reputation that men like Mr. Sakharov and Mr. Solzhenitsyn were not killed by the Soviet Union?

The January 23, 1980, issue of the Washington *Post* makes these statements: "For all the immediate political implications of Mr. Sakharov's fate, it is useful to step back a pace and ask a basic question: What kind of country is it that denies a natural place and a decent life and ultimately the right of residence to

patriotic citizens who are, by any reasonable standard, adorn-
ments to their society? People like Andrei Sakharov and Alexandr Solzhenitsyn, not to speak of hundreds, thousands of
lesser-known victims of political persecution and exile, would be
and are recognized as outstanding individuals in many other
lands. In their own land they are officially reviled. It is tragic for
them, and for their countrymen."

The February 22, 1980, issue of *Christianity Today* reports
that, since the Soviet invasion of Afghanistan, religious persecution has increased in the Soviet Union. A report of the arrest of
Russian Orthodox priest Dimitri Dudko, one of the most prominent activists for religious freedom in the Soviet Union, is
given. The report quotes part of a letter Dudko wrote early in
January saying, "It seems that 1980 will be a very difficult year
for all of us. Some have already been seized. I have been summoned to interrogation as a witness, and maybe yet as one who
is accused."

The report reveals that Dudko was arrested at his parish
church in Grebnevo outside of Moscow on January 15, 1980,
and taken to Lefortovo Prison. Dudko's apartment (there are
no property rights in a communist country) and church were
searched for twelve hours after his arrest, and everything of a
religious nature was confiscated. Homes of several of his church
members were also searched. Dudko had been warned about his
preaching during the seventies and had been transferred to
different cities several times. He had been harassed and searched
before his January 15 arrest. Although Dudko suffers from
thrombophlebitis, prison authorities have not accepted the
bandages and mineral water Dudko's wife has tried to get to
him.

Several days before his arrest Dudko had written a letter containing the following: "If anything happens to me, let this [let-
ter] be my message from behind prison walls. . . . It is quite
clear now why the authorities put away Father Gleb [Yakunin—
the leader of the Committee for the Defense of Believers'
Rights in the U.S.S.R.]—they want to silence dissenting voices
[within the church] as far as possible. . . . They do this—

grievous as it may be to say so—by the hands of the church leadership. The directives are issued in the name of the patriarch, but they are signed by the senior administrator of the Moscow patriarchate, Metropolitan Alexi, who is extremely obedient to the Soviet authorities. Sound the alarm: 'Silence and compromise are not tactical steps, they are betrayal.' "

We must wonder how many other voices have been "silenced" in the Soviet Union.

Why are we as Americans so apathetic to the threat of communism? Why have we ignored it for so long? Can any of us forget Dr. Thomas Dooley, the young American doctor who gave his life while establishing hospitals to help the people of Indochina? Dr. Dooley wrote three books. In his book *Deliver Us from Evil*, Dr. Dooley includes detailed descriptions of atrocities carried out by the Viet Cong. In one instance he describes what happened to seven children who were punished for conducting secret classes on religion. Dr. Dooley writes: "Two Viet Minh [communist] guards went to each child and one of them firmly grasped the head between his hands. The other then rammed a wooden chopstick into each ear. He jammed it in with full force. The stick split the ear canal wide open and tore the eardrum. The shrieking of the children was heard all over the village. Both ears were stabbed in this fashion. The children screamed and wrestled and suffered horribly. Since their hands were tied behind them, they could not pull the wood out of their ears." (Dooley, p. 175)

The teacher who had taught the children about Jesus Christ was tortured by the communist guard. His tongue was pulled out with a pair of pliers and cut off. He was left to drown in his own blood. After these victims were brought to Dr. Dooley's hospital for treatment, he wrote: "The purpose of this book is not to sicken anyone or to dwell upon the horror . . . but I do want to show what has come upon these people of the Delta. And justice demands that some of the atrocities we learned of in Haiphong be put on record. . . . Early in my Haiphong stay I was puzzled not only by the growing number but by the character of communist atrocities. So many seemed to have religious significance. More and more, I was learning that these punishments were linked to man's belief in God." (pp. 176, 181)

On February 22, 1962, J. Edgar Hoover accepted an award from the Freedom Foundation at Valley Forge. On that day, he made these comments: "The basic answer to communism is moral. The fight is economic, social, psychological, diplomatic, strategic—but above all it is spiritual." (*None Dare*, p. 234)

On Sunday morning, April 29, 1979, President Jimmy Carter and Pastor Georgi Vins walked up the steps of the First Baptist Church in Washington, D.C. The crowds and the television cameras pressed in upon them. Just forty-eight hours before that time, Georgi Vins had been in a prison camp in Russia, where he had expected to serve the remaining five years of his sentence. He was released from the prison camp as part of a prison exchange for two convicted Soviet spies.

Now he was attending his first worship service in five years. Georgi Vins was the secretary of the Counsel of Evangelical Christian and Baptist Churches in the U.S.S.R. and had been in a labor camp in the bitter cold of Yakutia, an area of eastern Siberia where the temperature often reaches sixty degrees below zero. He had been arrested in 1974 and sentenced to five years in the camp to be followed by five years in exile because of his activity as a preacher and a pastor. He had worked outdoors doing manual labor, sustained by a meager diet, and had had no medical care.

At the church service, George Vins had been asked to pray. It was the first time in his life he had prayed in public without fear of being interrupted by the police. Georgi Vins' unusual release ended three generations of persecution for the Vins family. Georgi Vins had served his first imprisonment between 1966 and 1969. At his later trial he said: "I insist that here in our country a campaign of annihilation is being waged against Christians. Since you have refused to obtain the facts, I can tell you that from 1929 to 1945, 25,000 Christians were imprisoned and 22,000 died in the camps. From 1945 to 1974, 20,000 were imprisoned and 6,000 were excluded from higher education.

Since 1929, 10 million books have been confiscated. These are the main points indicating that even today Christians are being physically annihilated in the camps and prisons." (Jane Ellis [trans.], *Georgi Vins: Prisoner of Conscience*, p. 276)

Communists know that in order to take over a country they must first see to it that a nation's military strength is weakened and that its morals are corrupted so that its people have no will to resist wrong. When people begin to accept perversion and immorality as ways of life, as is happening in the United States today, we must beware. This should be a danger signal and a warning to our country. Our enemies know that when we are weak morally, and when we have lost our will to fight, we are in a precarious position for takeover.

Communists seek to discredit the authority of the Word of God. Today in America we find the Bible being questioned by many of our people. Let us again regard the wisdom of one of our Founding Fathers, John Adams, who said, "Statesmen may plan and speculate liberty, but it is religion and morality alone upon which freedom can securely stand. A patriot must be a religious man."

Preachers in this country must stand up and call sin by its right name, and America's citizens must send to Washington politicians who care more about their country than anything else. These must be politicians who are not willing to sell their souls and abandon their consciences for a vote.

William Penn once said, "Men must be governed by God or they will be ruled by tyrants." It is our choice today in America which way we will go. We will either experience revival or ruin. A decisive question was asked by Thomas Jefferson many years ago: "Yes, we did produce a near-perfect republic, but will they keep it, or will they, in the enjoyment of plenty, lose the memory of freedom?"

Let us weigh heavily the words of Alexandr Solzhenitsyn: "I am not a critic of the West. I repeat that for nearly all our lives we worshiped the West. We do not admire it, we worshiped it. I am not a critic of the West. I am a critic of a fact which we can't comprehend: How can one lose one's spiritual strength, one's willpower, and possessing freedom not value it, not be willing to make sacrifices for it?" (from a speech given at BBC, March 1, 1976, reprinted in *The Canadian Review*)

A FALTERING NATIONAL DEFENSE

If ever there was a time for a strong national defense, it is today. In the face of a menacingly swift spread of communism around the globe, we find that for more than fifteen years now, the United States has been severely declining militarily. By militarily disarming our country, we have actually been surrendering our rights and our sovereignty and, as the Soviets would soon like to see—our freedoms and our liberties.

We must face the facts: America is in serious trouble today; she has, both economically and militarily, lost her prominence among the nations of the world. Now that America is in such a weakened position and at the threshold of destruction or surrender, our leaders are finally realizing what many have tried to point out for years—that the Soviets are liars and cheaters; that they are determined to conquer our free country and to infiltrate the American people with godless communism. It is time that we as Americans realized that our "peaceful intentions" are acts of stupidity, and that the lives of our citizens are at stake.

The Russians have been delighted with the course we Americans have taken. Instead of displaying national unity and godliness among our people, we have taken a course that leads to destruction by permitting a godless society to emerge in America. Our improper priorities have led us down the road to weakness. We are sowing corruption in our land and are reaping instability in our nation. Our faltering defenses are yet another evidence of this.

While we know that Russians understand only force, we have been busy taking God out of our society in general and our schools in particular, instead of thinking about protecting our people. Now our young people are reaping the consequences of America's sins. And at the Kremlin we are viewed with derision.

Ten years ago we could have destroyed much of the population of the Soviet Union had we desired to fire our missiles. The sad fact is that today the Soviet Union would kill 135 million to 160 million Americans, and the United States would kill only 3 to 5 per cent of the Soviets because of their antiballistic missiles and their civil defense. Few people today know that we do not have one antiballistic missile. We once had $5.1 billion worth of them, but Ted Kennedy led a fight in the Senate and had them dismantled and removed. From 1971 to 1978 the Soviets outspent the United States by $104 billion for defense and an additional $40 billion for research.

Earlier I quoted verses 1 through 6 of Chapter 13 of the Book of Romans in the Bible. Rulers should be ministers of God to the people for good. In the verse, "he beareth not the sword in vain," we find the acknowledgment that those in places of authority, officials in Washington, have the right to bear the sword. The bearing of the sword by the government is correct and proper. Nowhere in the Bible is there a rebuke for the bearing of armaments. A political leader, as a minister of God, is a revenger to execute wrath upon those who do evil. Our government has the right to use its armaments to bring wrath upon those who would do evil by hurting other people. Good citizens show their subjection to governmental powers by paying taxes and by showing honor to those in high places because those "ministers of God" attend continually to providing them safety; that is, they should be continually providing them safety. Thus we see that the role of government is to minister justice and to protect the rights of its citizens by being a terror to evildoers within and without the nation.

We are now being told by top military experts that the Soviet Union will consider itself totally impervious to any threat from America by the year 1985.

Scientists of the Peace Research Institute meeting in Switzerland agreed that 1985 could be the year the world would experience a holocaust, due to the tremendous atomic proliferation presently occurring around the globe. As was earlier quoted, Leonid Brezhnev stated in a speech to East European Communist Party leaders in 1973 in Prague, Czechoslovakia that by 1985 the Soviet Union's position will be consolidated to the point that she will be able to exert her will wherever needed.

America's "no win" policy and her lack of nerve to confront the spread of communism have mainly come from the ranks of official Washington, not from the grass-roots public in America. William Simon points out that in his years as Secretary of the Treasury, in close to four hundred Capitol Hill subcommittee appearances, he always had one disagreeable message, and that was that our government in general and our Congress in particular were responsible for both the economic and energy crisis and for the dangers associated with them. Mr. Simon points out in his book A *Time for Truth* that the OPEC nations' oil embargo dramatized to Americans for the first time that this country had lost its energy independence.

Speaking recently to some members of the American Conservative Union, I found that the United States' industrial machine in national defense apparatus is kept alive by an increasingly vulnerable jugular of oil imports, transported over sealanes. Thirty to 40 per cent of the oil we use comes to the United States via an eight-thousand-mile route on the open sea. Recently the massive Soviet naval buildup combined with startling Soviet geopolitical gains in Africa, the Middle East, and the Caribbean have served to increase the possibility that the Soviets can. at will, cut off America's vital oil lifeline. This means that the economies of the Western world could effectively be thrown into turmoil, bringing the industrial machine to a halt and rendering the United States' defenses impotent.

I was shown the primary sea route for the transport of Middle Eastern oil to the United States, which cuts a large swath from the Persian Gulf, around the Cape of Good Hope, and up through the Atlantic to refineries in the United States. This sea route passes at least nine Soviet naval ports, anchorages, and bunkering installations. A second sea route for the oil supplies, from the Suez Canal through the Mediterranean and across the Atlantic to our shores, runs an obstacle course containing at least five such Soviet naval bases. A third route, for the transport of our crude oil from the Alaskan North Slope to refineries on the Eastern Seaboard, requires that tankers pass through the Panama Canal. Of course, we know that this vital strategic corridor was handed over to Panama's Marxist dictator recently. It is today increasingly susceptible to Soviet influence and could pose a further threat to our oil lifeline. Soviet trollers are often used for paramilitary purposes, and we now find that these trollers infest these sealanes.

Our lifeline, and I use that with a double meaning, must be bolstered through a vigorous effort to bring our national defenses to the place they must be. National survival is now the issue. Our leaders must be made to see that it is their responsibility to preserve, protect, and defend our nation, whatever the risk to themselves or to their careers. It is now time that emergency action be taken to increase American military preparedness.

Liberal politicians have too long minimized the communist threat with words of "détente" and "mutual assured destruction." The acronym for mutual assured destruction is "mad." That is exactly what the defense strategy in this country is today. With mutual assured destruction, we have virtually no defense and an overwhelmingly unacceptable offense. Former Secretary of Defense Robert McNamara, who is now the president of the World Bank, formulated this policy. It is this man who started our gradual unilateral disarmament. We need leaders of moral courage today who know that there is safety only in strength, not in weakness.

It is clear today that we have not acknowledged or heeded the urgent warnings of some of our key military experts. In his August 1978 *Reader's Digest* article "Let's Not Torpedo Our Navy," Jay William Middendorf II, former Secretary of the Navy, said: "Indeed, so severe is the decline that I fear we are fast approaching a time of testing such as the United States has never had to endure. Unless we move fast on a naval rebuilding program, I am convinced that the next ten years will see the end of the U.S. ability to deter and prevail, with all the grave consequences that implies for free people everywhere.

"There has been an alarming shift in the balance of naval power . . . the Soviet Navy now is more than triple the size of our fleet and its overall effectiveness is increasing."

In the September 10, 1979, issue of *U.S. News & World Report*, in an interview with General Robert H. Barrow, commandant of the U. S. Marine Corps, entitled, "Are the Marines Obsolete? Their Chief Speaks Out," General Barrow answers the question, "Are amphibious ships being kept up to date?" with these words: "No, not in numbers, and this is of deep concern to us. In 1967, we had 162 amphibious ships. Today, although some of them are better ships, we have only 66. There are at present none on the drawing board and approved for building. By the 1990s, we face block obsolescence in amphibious ships. We don't need more marines. We just need sufficient ships to be able to go wherever that place is that no one can probably foresee at this time."

General Lewis W. Walt was assistant commandant of the Marine Corps from 1968 to 1971. He served in combat during World War II, the Korean War, and Vietnam, winning two Navy Crosses, two Distinguished Service Medals, the Silver Star Medal, two Purple Hearts, and numerous other decorations. In his book *The Eleventh Hour*, published in 1979, he gives us concise and accurate information regarding the military strength of the United States. He is frank and truthful. "The facts are these," he states in the first part of his book. "The United States has been brought, by its own civilian leaders, to a position of military inferiority to the Soviet Union. At this moment, you and your loved ones stand exposed to physical destruction. The option of whether you shall live or die rests primarily with the hardened men who occupy the Kremlin. . . . No generation of Americans has ever before been so recklessly placed at the mercy of so pitiless and powerful an enemy." (pp. xi, xii)

General Walt outlines his belief that in a short time the Soviet Union may force the United States into a decision of surrender, a handing over of the American people "to an oligarchy of tyrants whose viciousness and brutality have no match in the long, bloody history of man's cruelty" (p. xii), or the terrible decision of fighting a war America cannot win. General Walt has written, "Today the U.S. has no civil-defense program, no antiballistic missiles, and no appreciable defense against even a bomber attack. . . . This stripping of our defensive forces has been a deliberate policy move of our civilian defense officials. They believe that by baring our population to the Soviet sword we demonstrate our peaceful intentions. The error in their thinking was to believe that the Soviet Union would follow our example. The Soviets have reacted in an ominously opposite manner. While we cut back, they built, until today they have the world's most extensive air-defense and civil-defense systems." (pp. 3, 4)

General Walt reiterates what I have already clearly shown regarding the intentions and the deceitfulness of the Soviet Union. "If you are shocked about our weakness, don't blame yourself. This tragic and dangerous state of unbalance has been kept from the American people. The national news media have refused to consider it news. The political leaders whose folly or apathy created the danger have engaged in a deliberate effort to disguise the true situation. Your military leaders have been silenced by orders from their civilian superiors. Those who have retired to speak out have been stone-walled by the press and ridiculed by the politicians and academic strategists.

"This calculated act of unilateral disarmament in the face of a hostile and powerful enemy is one of the most irresponsible acts of government in the history of mankind." (pp. 4, 5)

General Walt agrees that it is our political leaders who have placed us in a vulnerable position. He agrees that as we have disarmed, we have also drifted politically farther from the concepts of free enterprise and limited government. He believes that there has been a "collapse of courage" in the United States because we as a nation have been adopting a materialistic set of values. He states that our political leaders watch communism growing in our world and do nothing about it because they are afraid. People stand and watch as their fellow citizens are attacked, and they do not interfere because of fear.

We have seen that moral decay always precedes political turmoil, economic instability, and military weakness in a country. General Walt makes this observation of history: "If you will take your choice of any history book and start with ancient Egypt and read on into modern times, you will see that no great nation has ever existed any longer than the supremacy of its military power. When the military power of Athens declined, the Golden Age of Greece came to an abrupt halt. Carthage fell to Rome, and when Rome became too weak militarily, the closest thing to world government the West has ever seen collapsed before a military onslaught. In each case, the decline of military power resulted from moral decay and lack of will on the part of the people and their leaders." (p. 83)

Recently Dr. Jack Van Impe visited the headquarters base of the Strategic Air Command. This is the center from which a nuclear war would be directed. While at the base, Dr. Van Impe learned some important facts that he conveyed to me. SAC is the United States Air Force's long-range strike force of combat aircraft and intercontinental ballistic missiles. SAC contributes to the deterrents of war through its ability to respond to threats endangering the security interest of the United States. Since 1946, the SAC base had always been considered indestructible because it was located forty-six feet underground and could withstand nuclear blast and nuclear radiation for at least a full month. Now this has changed, Dr. Van Impe was told. Russia can destroy the base with a direct hit. Therefore SAC has three KC-135 aircraft in the air operating twenty-four hours a day in case the ground base is destroyed. If this were to occur, the horrible missile war would be directed from the heavens. Both Russia and America have each other's coastal areas surrounded with nuclear-laden submarines. The Russians will be able to strike our cities from either the Atlantic or the Pacific whenever they decide to make the first strike attack. *Jane's Fighting Ships*, the authoritative British publication, along with British intelligence, has informed our leaders that this is the eventual goal of the Russians: a "Pearl Harbor" nuclear attack. If and when it happens, Americans would have exactly fifteen minutes to prepare.

A very respected man among our military experts is Major General George J. Keegan, Jr., who was a former chief of Air Force Intelligence. General Keegan has probably examined more thousands of pages of Soviet documents and pictures of Soviet-deployed missiles and other weapons than any other living person outside the Soviet Union. He speaks with great authority. After examining every major Soviet weapons system he has found that not only quantitatively, but also qualitatively, they are vastly superior to those of America's. General Keegan predicts that no later than 1985 the Soviet Union will consider itself to be totally impervious to any threat from America.

Recently, former Air Force Secretary Thomas C. Reed projected that the Soviet Union will soon run out of oil. He based his projection on three intensive studies that have been made by the intelligence forces of this country. Needing oil for their great war machine, and having no currency acceptable to the OPEC exporters, Reed says, "By the end of 1981 the Soviets will set in motion the events leading to resolution of our world conflict in the spring of 1982. . . . They will choose this spring to accommodate evacuation from their cities and initial recovery if it comes to that. They will hope to avoid nuclear confrontation, but if it comes, they will not blink."

Today we find that many young people have been absorbed by America's no-fight and no-win policy. In a December 24, 1979, *Newsweek* article entitled, "Marines on Guard," I read, "In 1900, fifty U.S. marines defended the American Legation in

Peking for eight weeks against the Boxer rebels. It was in the best leatherneck tradition of fighting this country's battles, from the Halls of Montezuma to the shores of Tripoli. But in recent months, Marine embassy guards offered only token resistance while U.S. outposts in three countries were besieged. One marine has been killed, eight are held hostage in Iran and two freed hostages have voiced sympathy for their captors' cause."

General Walt says: "It is fashionable in some segments of our society today to devalue heroism, and one of the ways this is done is to assert that heroic acts are merely acts of insanity. I have seen too much heroism to accept such cynicism. . . . A nation is a reflection of the values of the individuals who make up that nation. We still have freedom and independence in this nation because a majority of our individual citizens have always in the past valued those two things enough to fight for them and die for them. We will remain free and independent only so long as this remains true." (p. 29)

Recently one of the staff writers of our local newspaper wrote a story entitled, "Area Students' Views Mixed on Return of Draft." It gave views of modern-day students concerning the return of the draft. Of course, there were both pro and con views. A few days after the story came out, I was privileged to read a letter from a man in Lynchburg who answered one of the young men's remarks that he was glad that he would soon be twenty-six and not have to worry about the draft. This man made several comments, including these: "Our youth of today must remember one thing for certain. You are living in a great country. You all have had wonderful opportunities and have lived in almost luxury for your life. Stop and remember why? All because people before you had to and did make sacrifices. As you realize, you may have to do so in the near future. You, our youth of today, will do yourself proud and make others proud of you. . . . We fought our war and I have few regrets and even now when Old Glory passes by a lump comes in my throat and my eyes grow misty for I remember so many that gave so much and wonder why others are not too concerned."

As a preacher of the Gospel, I must speak out against evil. Evil forces would seek to destroy America because she is a bastion for Christian missions and a base for world evangelization.

Alexandr Solzhenitsyn has well pointed out that communism is more than a political viewpoint—it is an atheistic religion. I must speak out against godless communism, which would seek to destroy the work of Christ that is going out from this base of America.

Most of our leaders have been blinded by the intention of the Communists because these leaders are in spiritual darkness. In the Bible in the book of Ephesians (4:18) we read, "Having the understanding darkened, being alienated from the life of God through the ignorance that is in them, because of the blindness of their heart."

When we turn our backs on God, we turn our backs on freedom. The Bible says that where the Spirit of the Lord is, there is liberty. We cannot expect to long be a free nation when we turn our backs on God. We have reviewed our political and economic trouble and now see the seriousness of our military position. But there is hope. God will again bless us if we will turn back to Him as individuals and as a nation. There is power in the name of Jesus Christ, and it is the only power that can turn back godless communism. If God is on our side, no matter how militarily superior the Soviet Union is, they could never touch us. God would miraculously protect America. The destiny of America awaits our choice as to what we will do with God.

THAT MIRACLE CALLED ISRAEL

One of the most encouraging things I see in the world today is God's continued blessing on the tiny nation of Israel. Even with the problems of runaway inflation, stormy sessions in the Knes- et (Israel's parliament), and a determined effort by all of her neighbors to annihilate her, Israel still stands as shining testi- mony to the faithfulness of God. Israel is a bastion of democ- racy in a part of the world that is politically unstable and fre- quently characterized by near lunacy. Yet God is faithful and Israel remains a free nation.

Any man or woman who takes the time to read the Bible will find that it is more up to date than our newspapers. It is filled with prophecies regarding the Jewish people. The Bible clearly prophesied that after more than twenty-five hundred years of dispersion, the Jewish people would return to the land of Israel and establish the Jewish nation once again. On May 14, 1948, at 4:30 P.M., Israel officially became a nation again, the only na- tion in the world to ever be so dispersed and then regathered.

In his book *Abraham to the Middle East Crisis*, Dr. Fred- erick G. Owen writes of that day: "Early that morning Great Britain's flag, the Union Jack, was hauled down. During that sunny day a multitude gathered at a roped-off, guarded section of Rothschild Boulevard in Tel Aviv (the new capital). The chief Rabbi leaders along with many representatives of the world press awaited. At exactly 4:00 P.M., David Ben-Gurion called the meeting to order. The assembly rose and sang the Jewish National Anthem, 'Hatikvah,' while in an adjoining room the Palestine Symphony Orchestra played. The music had hardly ceased when Ben-Gurion rose and read in a firm voice in Hebrew the Declaration of Independence of the new nation, Israel. The entire assemblage rose and applauded, and many of them wept." (pp. 315–16)

The history of the Jewish people is one of much suffering and persecution. The Old Testament Scriptures time and again say the Jews disobeyed God, and because of this, God allowed them to be taken into captivity by their enemies. Moses had warned the people that if they did not obey the laws of God, they would be punished. The Jews did not listen to Moses, and dispersion, captivity, and persecution were the results. Because of their disobedience, they became despised by nations and were overthrown time and again.

In 586 B.C., Nebuchadnezzar and the Babylonians conquered Jerusalem and took the people captive to Babylon. After seventy years of captivity, a remnant of the Jewish people returned to their land to rebuild the Temple in the city of Jerusalem. Later Seleucid King Antiochus Epiphanes profaned this rebuilt Jewish Temple. Jews were massacred by the thousands during the Roman occupation of Palestine.

The Jewish people suffered continually. The plague of the "Black Death" that spread through Europe was blamed on the Jews. Thousands of Jewish people were slaughtered, and there was a complete extermination of two hundred Jewish communities. Many of the Jewish people fled to Poland. Deuteronomy 28:37 was being fulfilled: "And thou shalt become an astonishment, a proverb, and a byword, among all nations whither the LORD shall lead thee." For a short time the Jews prospered. In the eighteenth century, however, much of eastern Poland became part of the Russian Empire, and things changed for the Jewish people. Persecution came again—this time from czarist authorities. This persecution became unbearable in the nineteenth century. The word *pogrom* was adopted by the czars as organized massacres of the Jewish people. Soldiers went through Jewish settlements, burning and murdering. The Jews fled westward and arrived in the United Kingdom and in the United States.

The Jewish people have known nothing but suffering. In every nation in which they have gone, social and economic sanctions have been brought against them. In many countries to which they immigrated the Jews could not own land. Their property was confiscated, and they were expelled from England and France. In some countries, Jews had to be identified by wearing a certain sign. In some areas they had to live within designated boundaries. The history of the Jewish people has been one of ridicule, hate, and horror.

Although they have suffered greatly and have endured the persecutions brought against them, the Jewish people remain. All those who have persecuted the Jews have had tragic ends. Frederick the Great once said, "No nation ever persecuted the Jew and prospered." God has kept His promise to Abraham, the father of the Jewish race: "And I will make of thee a great nation, and I will bless thee, and make thy name great; and thou shalt be a blessing: And I will bless them that bless thee, and curse them that curseth thee. And in thee shall all families of the earth be blessed." (Gn. 12:2–3)

It is now evident that the dispersion of the Jews did not last forever. These scattered people have clung to the words of their prophets who foretold that they would ultimately return to their land and there someday prosper again. How the Jews have endured as a people is a miracle of God. Dr. Jack Van Impe relates this story in his book *Israel's Final Holocaust*: "Queen Victoria asked her Jewish Prime Minister, Benjamin Disraeli, 'Can you give me one verse in the Bible that will prove its truth?' He replied, 'Your Majesty, I will give you one word— Jew! If there was nothing else to prove the truth of the Bible, the history of the Jews is sufficient.' "

In Jeremiah 31:10 we read, "Hear the word of the LORD, O ye nations, and declare it in the isles afar off, and say, He that scattered Israel will gather him, and keep him, as a shepherd doth his flock." Prophecy began to be fulfilled when quite suddenly the Jewish people started immigrating back to their homeland. By 1914 there were about a hundred thousand Jews in Palestine in the area of Jerusalem. Then World War I erupted. A positive result of the war was Britain's help to the Jewish people. A British general freed Jerusalem from the Turks, and the Jews rejoiced.

But then came Adolf Hitler. Hitler blamed the Jews for all the ills of society. Shortly after the Führer took office, the persecution of the Jews began in 1933. By 1938, twenty-five thousand Jews were in concentration camps for no reason. They were tortured unmercifully. The gruesome Nazi atrocities to the Jews continued through World War II. Before Hitler's defeat, more than six million Jews had died in his death camps and his portable killing units. Shortly after Israel officially became a nation, President Truman issued a statement making the United States the first country to recognize the State of Israel. When David Ben-Gurion, Israel's first Prime Minister, was broadcasting Israel's thanks to the United States for the recognition of their statehood, his speech was interrupted by an explosion. Israel's bloody war of independence began immediately after the establishment of her statehood. During eight months of war with the Arabs, 6,000 Israelis were killed. The fighting ended in January 1949, and during this time the Jews had increased their territory by six hundred miles. When the final armistice was signed, they gained 21 per cent more land than had been originally given to them in the United Nations partition.

In the eighteen months after the doors of immigration were opened, 340,000 Jews arrived in their homeland. By June 30, 1953, their population had doubled. The prophesied return of the children of Israel to Palestine had finally happened! In Ezekiel 37:12 the prophet declares: "Thus saith the Lord God: Behold, O my people, I will open your graves, and cause you to come up out of your graves, and bring you into the land of Israel."

In Isaiah 43:5–6 we read these words: "Fear not, for I am with thee: I will bring thy seed from the east, and gather thee from the west; I will say to the north, Give up; and to the south, Keep not back: Bring my sons from far, and my daughters from the ends of the earth." They did indeed come from all parts of the world. They left homes and fortunes to go back to their biblical "home." The prophecy in Jeremiah 32:42–44 had come true: "For thus saith the LORD: Like as I have brought all this great evil upon this people, so will I bring upon them all the good that I have promised them. And fields shall be bought in this land, whereof ye say, It is desolate without man or beast; it is given into the hand of the Chaldeans. Men shall buy fields for money, and subscribe evidences, and seal them, and take witnesses in the land of Benjamin, and in the places about Jerusalem, and in the cities of Judah, and in the cities of the mountains, and in the cities of the valley, and in the cities of the south: For I will cause their captivity to return, saith the LORD." They were bruised and bleeding, but finally the Jews were back in their own land. Yet even after the rebirth of their nation, fighting was not to be ended for the Jews.

Although at Israel's inception she had been surrounded by fifty million Arabs, she had God's promise, "Therefore all they that devour thee shall be devoured; and all thine adversaries, every one of them, shall go into captivity; and they that spoil thee shall be as spoil, and all that prey upon thee will I give for a prey. For I will restore health unto thee, and I will heal thee of thy wounds, saith the LORD; because they called thee an Outcast, saying, This is Zion, whom no man seeketh after." (Jr. 30:16–17)

In 1956 Israel quickly conquered the Gaza Strip. Major powers intervened to bring about a cease-fire in order to save Egypt from complete collapse, but tensions continued to mount between 1956 and 1967.

Egypt's then President, Gamal Abdel Nasser, claimed that it was his intention to destroy Israel, to push her into the sea, and to annihilate her citizens. On Israel's nineteenth anniversary of independence, May 14, 1967, Egyptian forces moved into the Sinai. It was broadcast over the radio that Egypt was prepared to plunge into total war and to put an end to Israel. The United

Nations peace-keeping force stationed in Israel was removed, and the Arabs announced over the radio that there was no longer an emergency force to protect Israel. Nasser declared that they would not accept coexistence with Israel. On May 30 it was announced that the armies of Egypt, Jordan, Syria, and Lebanon were poised at the borders of Israel, and standing behind them were the armies of Iraq, Algeria, Kuwait, and Sudan. Nasser closed the crucial Israeli port of Eilat on the Gulf of Aqaba as an overt act of war, and so the war was on.

The rest is history now, and can be explained by a miracle of God. There is no way that the tiny nation of Israel could have stood against the Arabs in a miraculous six-day war had it not been for the intervention of God Almighty. In only six days the Arabs had retreated, and Israel had captured all of Jerusalem. The entire city was in Jewish hands for the first time since A.D. 70. Russians stood in disbelief as they realized that they had suffered a loss of three billion dollars' worth of military aid to the Arabs in a six-day period.

On October 6, 1973, Israel was again engaged in war. It was called the Yom Kippur War because most of the Jews had been in their synagogues observing Yom Kippur when Egypt attacked the Sinai Peninsula, and Syria attacked the Golan Heights. Eleven Arab nations attacked Israel. Israeli military forces suffered severe casualties. Again, however, within a few days, things were turned around. The Jews gained all strategic positions, threatened Damascus, and headed for Cairo. With two major Arab nations in serious trouble, Russia called for peace. Although not with the spectacular results of the 1967 war, Israel again had been victorious in withstanding her enemy's attempts at annihilation.

The last book of the Bible, the Book of Revelation, contains prophecy regarding future events. Israel plays a significant role in that prophecy. This tiny nation will once again be attacked by her enemies, led by the great Russian armies and her Arab allies, but as the prophet Ezekiel prophesied in Ezekiel 38 and 39, Russia will be defeated and Israel once again will be spared by the hand of God. If the Russians would only read what God has in store for them and believe it, they may find themselves falling on their knees, forsaking their godlessness, and crying unto the God of Israel for forgiveness. No, God is not finished with the nation Israel.

But He may be finished with those nations that persecute Israel. As God promised in Genesis 12:3: "And I will bless them that bless thee, and curse him that curseth thee." Every nation that has ever persecuted the Jews has felt the hard hand of God on them. Every nation that has ever stood with the Jews has felt the hand of God's blessing on them. I firmly believe God has blessed America because America has blessed the Jew. If this nation wants her fields to remain white with grain, her scientific achievements to remain notable, and her freedom to remain intact, America must continue to stand with Israel.

There are some very distressing developments presently in American-Israeli relations. I see a growing willingness to accept as reputable and civilized the murderers of the PLO. There is an increasing tendency to allow our need for oil to blind us to our greater need for God's continued blessing. If America allows herself to be blackmailed by the oil cartel and trades her allegiance to Israel for a petroleum "mess of pottage," she will also trade her position of world leadership for a place in the history books alongside of Rome. We cannot allow that to happen.

The Jews are returning to their land of unbelief. They are spiritually blind and desperately in need of their Messiah and Savior. Yet they are God's people, and in the world today Bible-believing Christians in America are the best friends the nation Israel has. We must remain so.

Part II

MORALITY—
THE DECIDING FACTOR

I believe the 1980s will be a decade of destiny. During the crucial years of the 1980s it will be determined whether we continue to exist as a free people. It is now past time for the moral people of America to fight against those forces that would destroy our nation. No other nation on the face of the earth has been blessed by God Almighty like the people of the United States of America, but we have taken this for granted for too many years.

It is time that we faced reality. We are in trouble as a nation. We are very quickly moving toward an amoral society where nothing is either absolutely right or absolutely wrong. Our absolutes are disappearing, and with this disappearance we must face the sad fact that our society is crumbling.

I cannot keep silent about the sins that are destroying the moral fiber of our nation. As a minister of the Gospel, I have seen the grim statistics on divorce, broken homes, abortion, juvenile delinquency, promiscuity, and drug addiction. I have witnessed firsthand the human wreckage and the shattered lives that statistics can never reveal in their totality.

With the dissolving of our absolutes, America now has a high crime rate that costs the taxpayer $2 billion a year. In the past 10 years violent crimes have increased 174 per cent in America. Murder is up 129 per cent. Aggravated assault is up 139 per

cent. A serious crime is committed every 3.5 seconds. One robbery is committed every 83 seconds. One murder is committed
every 27 minutes.

Drug addiction and alcoholism are in pandemic proportions.
Suicide is growing at a frightening pace. More than 400,000 heroin addicts live in the United States (60,000 in California
alone), and 22 million Americans smoke marijuana. The No. 1
drug and health problem is alcohol, and there are more than 9
million alcoholics in the United States. Retail sales of alcohol in
one recent year totaled $32.5 billion.

We have teen-agers who are experimenting with sex in the
most vile form, while teen-age pregnancies, incest, and sexual
child abuse are rampant problems. Gonorrhea is now contracted
by more than 2 million Americans each year. It is the most
common infection recorded by public-health officials, and it is
increasing so rapidly among the nation's young people that
medical authorities are desperately searching for a vaccine
against it. About 65,000 women become infertile each year because of its infection.

Dr. Harold M. Voth, M.D., made this statement at the Eagle
Forum on October 23, 1977: "It comes as no surprise to me
that suicide is a national symptom. These youngsters are lost
and are filled with anguish and finally, overcome by despair,
they terminate the most precious gift of all—life itself. It is
heartbreaking to listen to the outpourings of the young who see
what life has to offer but who cannot grab hold and make their
own lives go forward. The causes lie within them, and those dis-
turbances were created by imperfect family life. Loneliness is
becoming a national illness. People are not just lonely because
they are alone. They are lonely because they are empty inside,
and that comes from not having had good family life as children."

According to a recent study undertaken by The Johns Hopkins
School of Hygiene and Public Health, nearly two thirds of U.S.
females (63.3 per cent) have premarital sexual intercourse by
19 years of age. It is predicted that teen-age pregnancies are expected to escalate in the 1980s. Early in 1979 the Stanford Re-

search Institute estimated annual welfare costs at $8.3 billion, including all cash-support payments and food outlays by the federal, state, and local governments to households containing teenaged mothers or women who first become pregnant in their teens.

A thriving new industry floods into the nation's homes through pornographic literature and television programs. Film producers and magazine writers now exploit innocent little children in an attempt to make money from child pornography. It is a fact that more than 20 million sex magazines are sold at our American newsstands every year. The United States will soon be the pornographic capital of the world with 780 X-rated theaters.

America's families are in trouble. America's homes are the stabilizing factors in our society, yet the family is disintegrating at an alarming rate. Nearly 1 out of 2 marriages is ending in divorce, as the divorce rate is now 46 per cent. According to the United States Census Bureau more than 1.3 million unmarried couples are living together.

Two thousand American children die annually from child abuse (over 70 per cent from injuries inflicted by stepfathers—the result of divorce). *Each day* more than 4,000 unborn babies are destroyed by abortion (over 1 million annually). The IRS has made abortion clinics "charitable" organizations, therefore exempt from taxes.

Sin has permeated our land. The Bible states that the pleasures of sin are but for a season. (Heb. 11:25) Those men and women in our United States who are indulging in the grossest of permissive and sexual sins are under the judgment of God. Their pleasure will be but for a very short season. Issues that have to do with the very health and perpetuity of this republic must be dealt with. Solomon wrote in Proverbs, "Righteousness exalteth a nation; but sin is a reproach to any people." (Pr. 14:34) The strength of America has been in her righteousness, in her walk with God. Now we see national sins that are permeating our nation, and we find that our citizens are without remorse, without regret or repentance, and we are not far from judgment of God upon this great nation of ours. With our erosion from the historic faith of our fathers, we are seeing an erosion in our stability as a nation. We have already shown that we are economically, politically, and militarily sick because our country is morally sick.

Now let us take a look at those personal moral decisions individuals make that determine their life course and ultimately that of our nation.

FAMILY—THE BASIC UNIT

There are only three institutions God ordained in the Bible: government, the church, and the family. The family is the God-ordained institution of the marriage of one man and one woman together for a lifetime with their biological or adopted children. The family is the fundamental building block and the basic unit of our society, and its continued health is a prerequisite for a healthy and prosperous nation. No nation has ever been stronger than the families within her. America's families are her strength and they symbolize the miracle of America.

Families in search of freedom to educate their children according to religious principles originally settled this land. Families in search of religious freedom, determined to work and enjoy the fruits of their labor, tamed this wild continent and built the highest living standard in the world. Families educating their children in moral principles have carried on the traditions of this free republic. Historically the greatness of America can be measured in the greatness of her families. But in the past twenty years a tremendous change has taken place.

There is a vicious assault upon the American family. More television programs depict homes of divorced or of single parents than depict the traditional family. Nearly every major family-theme TV program openly justifies divorce, homosexuality, and adultery. Some sociologists believe that the family unit, as we know it, could disappear by the year 2000. Increased divorce and remarriage have broken family loyalty, unity, and communications. We find increased insecurity in children who are the victims of divorced parents. Many of these children harden themselves to the possibility of genuine love, for fear that they will be hurt again. Their insulated lives make them poor future candidates for marriage, and many young people have no desire to marry whatsoever. But I believe that most Americans remain deeply committed to the idea of the family as a sacred institution. A minority of people in this country is trying to destroy what is most important to the majority, and the sad fact is that the majority is allowing it to happen. Americans must arise and accept the challenge of preserving our cherished family heritage.

I quote again from the Washington *Post* poll of December 16, 1979, "Americans' Hopes and Fears About the Future": "To be alone—those are dreadful words to most Americans, expressed repeatedly in this era supposedly dedicated to self." I recently read that one of our leading political commentators said that loneliness will be a major political issue in the 1980s. God said in the Book of Genesis that it was not good that man should be alone. God made men and women with the need for fellowship and the desire for a family life.

The home was the first institution established by God. God's program cannot be improved. In the Book of Genesis in the Bible we find these words: "And the LORD God caused a deep sleep to fall upon Adam, and he slept: And he took one of his ribs, and closed up the flesh instead thereof; And the rib, which the LORD God had taken from man, made he a woman, and brought her unto the man. And Adam said, This is now bone of my bones, and flesh of my flesh: She shall be called Woman, because she was taken out of Man. Therefore shall a man leave his father and his mother, and shall cleave unto his wife: And they shall be one flesh. And they were both naked, the man and his wife, and were not ashamed." (Gn. 2:21–25) Nothing is more right than a man and a woman joined together in holy wedlock. As a family, they are in submission to the Lordship of Jesus Christ—the most heavenly thing on earth.

A commentator from one of the major networks once asked me, "What right do you Baptists have to promote your ideas about the family being the acceptable style for all of humanity?" I replied that it was not Baptists who started the family; it was God Almighty, and He is not a Baptist. God made a help-meet for man. The family is that husband-wife relationship that God established in the Garden of Eden, later producing children. God gave Adam authority and dominion over the creation and told him to multiply and replenish the earth. The family is that basic unit that God established, not only to populate but also to control and contain the earth. The happiest people on the face of this earth are those who are part of great homes and families where they are loved, protected, and shielded. When I have been out having a long, hard day, often in a hostile environment, it is great to walk into my home, to close the front door, and to know that inside the home there are a wife and children who love me. Home is a haven to which I run from the troubles of this world, a place of security and warmth, where each member has the knowledge of belonging. Most of the people who are leading the antifamily efforts in America are failures in the family business because they have not committed their lives to Jesus Christ and so do not know His perfect plan for their lives.

The single most important influence on the life of a child is his family.

The strength and stability of families determine the vitality and moral life of society. Too many men and women, trying to protect their own sinfulness and selfishness, are for the desires of self-gratification destroying the very foundation of the family as we know it.

In the war against the family today, we find an arsenal of weapons. The first weapon is the cult of the playboy, the attitude that has permeated our society in these last twenty years. This playboy philosophy tells men that they do not have to be committed to their wife and to their children, but that they should be some kind of a "cool, free swinger." Sexual promiscuity has become the life style of America. The cult of the play-

boy is more than just a revolution of dirty magazines. It represents a life style that ultimately corrupts the family. Men are
satisfying their lustful desires at the expense of family.

The second weapon against the family is the feminist revolution. This is the counterreaction to the cult of the playboy.
Many women are saying, "Why should I be taken advantage of
by chauvinists? I will get out and do my own thing. I will stand
up for my rights. I will have my own dirty magazines." Feminists are saying that self-satisfaction is more important than
the family. Most of the women who are leaders in the feminist
movement promote an immoral life style.

In a drastic departure from the home, more than half of the
women in our country are currently employed. Our nation is in
serious danger when motherhood is considered a task that is
"unrewarding, unfulfilling, and boring." I believe that a
woman's call to be a wife and mother is the highest calling in
the world. My wife is proud to be called a housewife. She is
dedicated to making a happy and rich life for us and our three
children. She does not consider her life work of making my life
happy and that of loving and shaping the lives of our precious
children inconsequential or demeaning. Women who choose to
remain in the home should never feel inferior to those working
outside, but should know they are fulfilling God's command for
the home.

We have been living in a distorted and decaying society
where women are made to feel a loss of self-esteem and a loss of
status when they choose to be full-time housewives. Women are
finding today that they feel they must justify themselves if they
choose to remain in the home. Edith Schaeffer, in her book
What Is a Family? points out the glory and the seriousness and
responsibility of being a full-time housewife. Answering the
question, "What is a family?" she says: "A formation center for
human relationships—worth fighting for, worth calling a career,
worth the dignity of hard work." She says, "The family is the
place where the deep understanding that people are significant,
important, worthwhile, with a purpose in life, should be learned
at an early age. The family is the place where children should

learn that human beings have been made in the image of God and are therefore very special in the universe." (p. 69) She says: "The environment in a family should be conducive to the commencement of natural creativity, as natural as breathing, eating, and sleeping. A balanced, created person can come forth, developing and branching out in a wide number of areas, if some amounts of imagination and care are used. The first requirement is a dignity of attitude toward the family. This dignity involves accepting the seriousness and excitement of having your own home be a very specific creativity center. Given one, two, three, or more new little beings, one at a time, adopted or born to you, you have an opportunity to develop a growing, changing, constantly better environment for budding and blossoming creativity . . . someone has to have time to give to this." (p. 58)

It is sad that we find in our major magazines articles such as that in the July 9, 1979, *U.S. News & World Report* entitled, "Full-time Homemaking Is Now 'Obsolete,'" It says: "Shirley Johnson, the Vassar economist, figures that for each additional $1,000 a woman earns, the chance of divorce increases by 2 per cent." A January 15, 1979, *U.S. News & World Report* article entitled, "Working Women Joys and Sorrows" states, "Women are swelling the work force at a rate of almost 2 million every year—a phenomenon that is beginning to transform everyday life in the United States. From astronaut to zoologist, nearly every occupation has been invaded by women, who are pouring into the job market almost twice as fast as men. More than half of our country's 84 million women, including a majority of mothers with school-age children, now work or seek jobs. So dramatic is the shift from homemaking to careers that Eli Ginzberg, head of the National Commission for Manpower Policy, describes it as 'bigger than the atomic bomb or nuclear power.' Ginzberg predicts that the desire of women for jobs ultimately may alter the lives of every American: 'It changes the relationship of men to women; it changes the relationship of mothers to children.'"

Edith Schaeffer knows the security and love a family can give to each of its members. She says, "Family bridges the centuries and is not meant to be represented by splintered, shattered, broken human counterparts. Togetherness in sickness and in health is to be 'till death do us part' . . . it is while we are in the land of the living that the family is meant to care for each other, and to be a real shelter—from birth to old age." (p. 118)

Many women today say that they must work for economic reasons. Although inflation has placed a financial burden on the family, we are overly concerned about materialistic wealth. Many Americans consider it more important to have several cars in the driveway, a beautiful house, and two color television sets than to have a stable home environment for their children.

Men and women are seeking easy divorces. The October 15, 1979, *U.S. News & World Report* said that demographers estimate that 45 per cent of infants born in 1980 will live in one-parent families for at least part of their childhood. A person's character is determined by the pledges and promises he or she makes. A man or woman who does not keep his or her word can hardly be a good example to children, but thousands of men and women who have made a pledge of marriage, an eternal pledge of marriage, are breaking that promise in front of impressionable children.

Young people are living together today because they have observed parents who thought little of the eternal commitment they made to each other in their marriage vows. Couples living together cannot experience, however hard they try, the intimacy, security, and genuine love of a stable marriage in a relationship that is anything less than 100 per cent commitment. Parents are failing to teach their children a sense of commitment to relationships. Only marriage fulfills basic human needs for security and love.

An article by Judy Mann entitled, "We're a Lot Freer, But Is It So Good?" in the January 4, 1980, Washington *Post* states, "So what's ahead? What's ahead for the eighties for the baby-boom generation, the generation that gave us the free-speech movement, free sex, free dope, free Vietnam, the generation that liberated homosexuals, women and finally men? . . .

"As the seventies came around, we rejected homemaking and plunged into careers. Women who went to work knew they were spending a lot less time with their children than mothers who did not. Parents came up with the theory that it wasn't the quantity of time we spent with our children that counted but the quality. People who challenged this were attacked as anti-feminists.

"We focused on day care for children as the single greatest worry of working mothers, and everyone assumed we meant day care for little kids. For a few years we did. But what of the teen-agers who come home now from junior high school and high school to empty houses all around the neighborhood? Listen to the working mother of two teen-age daughters: 'I'm a single parent. I have to work. I can't be here every afternoon. There's no way I can know everything that goes on.'

"We're in something of a fix. How should we teach our children about the sanctity of marriage when we're in the process of divorcing a second or third spouse? How do we tell them drugs are dangerous and they should stay away from them when they can get pot in our dresser drawers? How do we expect them to excel in the public schools when we come home from work too tired to help them study?

"The baby-boom generation seems to have survived its social experiments and we've had a lot of fun but something is happening to our children and attention must be paid. The warning signals—illiteracy, teen-age suicides, burnouts, people who are unemployable—are all around us, sending us signals that while we may have created a better world for ourselves, it is not a safer one for our children.

"This is not the stuff of marches, of protests. We are adults now. This time we are the parents. We can't take over the high-school administration building in an effort to get dope out of the restrooms and learning back into the classrooms. We have to be cautious, mature, thoughtful, resourceful, and persuasive. We who challenged and discarded the standards and life styles of our parents now have the far trickier task of fashioning new standards for our children, searching for mutually acceptable guidelines between the freedoms we enjoy as adults and the freedoms they want for themselves as children. And somehow, both the fathers and mothers are going to have to realize that it takes more than a little quality time to raise children: It takes large quantities of high-quality time.

"Whether we do it through more part-time work for fathers and mothers, through more flexitime, through parental leave of absence, through the thirty-hour work week, parental co-operatives, and other forms of sharing child-raising responsibilities, we now need to free more of our time to raise our children.

"In the eighties, the baby-boom generation is finally going to have to grow up."

The answer to stable families with children who grow up to be great leaders in our society and who themselves have stable homes will not come from, as Judy Mann states, more part-time work for fathers and mothers, or parental leaves of absence, or thirty-hour weeks, or parental co-operatives and other forms of sharing childraising responsibilities. It will come only as men and women in America get in a right relationship to God and His principles for the home. Statistics show that couples who profess a born-again relationship have much happier, healthier marriages. In a January 22, 1979, *U.S. News & World Report* interview with Dr. Robert B. Taylor, specialist in family medicine, entitled, "Behind the Surge in Broken Marriages," Dr. Taylor says: "We find that couples who are actively religious tend to have more stable marriages. Worshiping together and attending church activities help develop strong couple bonds that are very hard to break." The Bible gives men and women God's plan.

Scripture declares that God has called the father to be the spiritual leader in his family. The husband is not to be the dictator of the family, but the spiritual leader. There is a great difference between a dictator and a leader. People follow dictators because they are forced to do so. They follow leaders because they want to. Good husbands who are godly men are good leaders. Their wives and children want to follow them and be under their protection. The husband is to be the decisionmaker and the one who motivates his family with love. The Bible says that husbands are to love their wives even as Christ also loved the church and gave Himself for it. A man is to be a servant to his family while at the same time being a leader. A husband and father is first of all to be a provider for his family. He is to take care of their physical needs and do this honestly by working and earning an income to meet those needs. Then he is to be a protector. He is to protect them not only from physical harm but from spiritual harm as well. He is to protect them from television programs and from magazines that would hurt them. Child abuse involves much more than physical abuse. We have little children today who are growing up in homes where mothers and fathers literally hate each other. Those children are living in a constant perpetual hate war that is destroying them. A father has a God-given responsibility to lead his family in their worship of God. A father is to be a godly example to his wife and children; he must be consistently living a good life style before his family. He is to pray with his family and read to them from the Word of God. A man cannot do these things if he does not know Jesus Christ as his Lord and Savior. The Bible says, "But as many as received him, to them gave he power to become the sons of God, even to them that believe on his name." (Jn. 1:12) The love of God is available to every man, and God has made an offer to us and asked us to receive the gift of salvation. Until men are in right relationship with God, there is no hope for righting our families of our nation. Because we have weak men we have weak homes, and children from these homes will probably grow up to become weak parents leading even weaker homes.

Dr. Harold M. Voth, M.D., senior psychiatrist and psychoanalyst at the Menninger Foundation, Topeka, Kansas, has said, "The correct development of a child requires the commitment of mature parents who understand either consciously or intuitively that children do not grow up like Topsy. Good mothering from birth on provides the psychological core upon which all subsequent development takes place. Mothering is probably the most important function on earth. This is a full-time, demanding task. It requires a high order of gentleness, commitment, steadiness, capacity to give, and many other qualities. A woman needs a good man by her side so she will not be distracted and depleted, thus making it possible for her to provide rich humanness to her babies and children. Her needs must be met by the man, and above all she must be made secure. A good man brings out the best in a woman, who can then do her best for the children. Similarly, a good woman brings out the best in a man, who can then do his best for his wife and children. Children bring out the best in their parents. All together they make a family, a place where people of great strength are shaped, who in turn make strong societies. Our nation was built by such people."

The Threat of Government to the Family

Since the family is the basic unit of society, parents have the responsibility of rearing their family. Families reared in the correct way contribute significantly to the success of a constitutional government. It should be in the home where Christian character is formed and where adherence to moral law is taught, encouraged, and enforced. Our government is trying to enact laws that I feel are contrary to the traditional American family. The Domestic Violence Prevention and Treatment Act (H.R. 2977) is a bill that has passed in the House and is pending hearing in the Senate. The bill originated after HEW created the Office of Domestic Violence (ODV) as part of the Administration for Children, Youth, and Families. If H.R. 2977 is passed it would appropriate sixty-five million dollars to the ODV, which would enable this new bureaucracy to develop and implement federal programs targeted toward the families. The ODV would inevitably supervise the conduct of the local and community programs that are already established to deal with the problems of domestic violence. The plans of this new bureaucracy are to "prevent" domestic violence. Dr. Murray A. Straus, who is the director of the Family Violence Research Project at the University of New Hampshire, suggests that we should "Gradually eliminate physical punishment as a mode of childrearing . . . eliminate the husband as 'head of the family' from its continuing presence in the law, in religion . . . and [in] family life." If H.R. 2977 is passed the federal government could become directly involved in the area of husband-wife relationships and other intrafamily relationships. The Domestic Violence Prevention and Treatment Act could establish a federal bureaucracy to intervene in matters relating to husband and wife. Admittedly, there is in our country a problem with domestic violence, but it is an inappropriate response to legislate a federal bureaucracy to take care of this problem.

Pending in the Senate is another bill, S./ 1722. Included in this bill is the means for preventing the federal government from prosecuting any form of pornography. There would be no way that a family could protect itself from the onslaught of this type of material. Currently there is a bit of protection, although it is weak. But this new criminal code reform would eliminate that totally. Should this bill pass, the federal government could not intervene in the importation of pornography, nor could it intervene in the interstate transportation of pornography. The mail would be allowed to carry virtually anything. This new criminal code reform would legalize marijuana. There would be no penalty attached to the possession of marijuana, and only the sale of marijuana in large quantities would be a misdemeanor. This bill would also make it impossible to prosecute anyone for the transportation across state lines of a girl or a woman unless it could be shown that there was a connection with a prostitution ring. Under this law the death penalty would be completely repealed. Women could sue their husbands for rape.

It is our own government that has attacked the family's role as a primary educator of children. The Internal Revenue Service is now seeking to control private and Christian schools. The HEW has undertaken the redrafting of textbooks to purge traditional moral concepts. Court decisions have all but mandated the replacement of religion with secular humanism. Almost insurmountable financial obstacles are placed before parents who wish to educate their children in nonpublic schools. The Department of Education has been created at the request of the

National Education Association, which believes that the state and not the family has the primary responsibility to educate children. Ironically, the government is attacking the one institution that holds it together.

I am against federally funded day-care centers that would bring the age of mandatory school attendance down to two years old. This would get children away from their parents and under the early influence of public education.

As outlined in the chapter on communism, communism has no use for the family. Communists believe in taking children away from the family and raising them separately so they can indoctrinate them with government loyalty. How I fear this will happen to our own children.

Not only has the United States Government threatened its family, through acts of commission, but also it attacks the family in acts of omission. The most notable example of government malfeasance in its family obligations is in the area of defense. As a result of our government's unilateral disarmament, mutual assured destruction, and the acceptance of Soviet military superiority, our American government is providing its families far less protection from nuclear attack than is the Soviet Union providing its families. Reliable Intelligence experts, like Lieutenant General Daniel O. Graham, U.S.A. (Ret.), and Major General George Keegan, U.S.A.F. (Ret.), report that in the event of a nuclear exchange, no fewer than ten Americans would perish for every Soviet life placed at risk. The reason is simple: The Soviet Union has established a strong offensive military posture combined with a strong civil defense, antiaircraft defense, and anti-missile defense, whereas the United States has lagged far behind in each of these categories.

Recently our President instituted the White House Conference on Families, which is to be a national discussion focusing on American families. Our President stated that the purpose of the White House Conference on Families is "to examine the strengths of American families, the difficulties they face, and the ways in which family life is affected by public politics." The conference is guided by a forty-one-member National Advisory

Committee (with only one prolife member) that has adopted a process of taking the White House conference to the people. The conference activities include seven major national hearings, input from state conferences and national organizations, three White House conferences in June and July of 1980, and a national task force to bring together a report of findings and recommendations. An implementation period will attempt to translate recommendations into realities. The hearings were designed to be opened to the public and to give families an opportunity to discuss their concerns, ideas, successes, and problems relating to contemporary family life. Our President's mandate is to "reach out, not only to scholars and to experts, but [also] to many thousands of Americans around this country who know from their experience what makes a family strong."

Jim Guy Tucker, who is the chairman of the White House Conference on Families says that he is looking forward to the next two years with "enthusiasm and determination to strengthen and support our most precious resource—families." That is odd, since the people appointed to head the national conference have already mapped an agenda that proposes to sanction homosexuality for couples, expand day care, create new government programs to regulate families, and federal funding for abortion. A problem concerning the White House conference regarded the definition of the family. It was finally decided that any persons living together constituted a family. This could mean two homosexual men or two lesbian women living together. The new definition was described as better reflecting "the differences in structure and life style." It is time that the moral majority across this country insists that the rights and duties of the family are independent of government and of bureaucracy. I agree with the proposal from the National Pro-Family Coalition that the definition of a family is: "A family consists of persons who are related by blood, marriage, or adoption." When a man and a woman come to a marriage altar and are legally and spiritually united, a family has been born. When children are born or adopted into that union the family is being enlarged. And that is simply what a family is. You cannot re-create what God has established. God did not make a mistake when He created Adam and Eve and brought them together to become one flesh. Now our government is spending three million dollars on these White House families conferences, which are headed by antifamily people seeking to redefine what a family is.

Antifamily forces in the White House Conference on Families were dealt a severe setback in November 1979 when the first of the state conferences was held in Fredericksburg, Virginia. Profamily forces mounted, and hundreds of conservatives throughout the state, upon hearing of the potential danger of the conference, showed up to frustrate liberal forces who had hoped to dominate the conference. Of twenty-four delegates to the White House Conference on Families elected at the Virginia Conference, twenty-two were endorsed by the profamily coalition in what one Richmond newspaper called "a stunning victory by conservatives." Rules were quickly changed to prevent this from happening again. Chairman Tucker announced that no more delegates would be elected by the public.

I respect the decision of Governor Forrest H. James, Jr., who has decided that his state of Alabama will not participate in this year's White House Conference on Families. The governor's wife, Bobbie, wrote in a letter to Chairman Jim Guy Tucker that as a sacred trust to the people of Alabama, their state would not participate in any conference that did not establish traditional Judeo-Christian values concerning the family, which she stated was the foundation of our nation under God. Mrs. James also conveyed in her letter to Mr. Tucker that terminology used in White House guidelines (such as "family stereotypes," "differences in structure and life style," and the instructions that state delegations be selected without regard to "sexual orientation") were offensive to her and her husband and did not reflect either the law of the land or the basic concepts of most Alabamians.

Liberals at that conference claimed that the answer to the problems of American families is additional spending and bureaucratic intervention in family life. In commenting on the

Virginia meeting, Congressman John Ashbrook (R., Ohio) said, "The people of Virginia rose up and defended their families against the legions of social mechanics and tax-financed intervention professionals." The conference organizers were visibly upset by the outcome of the Fredericksburg conference and engaged in exchanges with profamily advocates. Congressman Ashbrook's concept of the family was proposed by the National Pro-Family Coalition. It includes:

Definition of Family—A family consists of persons who are related by blood, marriage, or adoption.

Primacy of the Family—The family is the most important unit in society. The strength and stability of families determine the vitality and moral life of society. The most important function peformed by the family is the rearing and character formation of children, a function it was uniquely created to perform and for which no remotely adequate substitute has been found. The family is the best and most efficient "department of health, education, and welfare."

Children's Rights—Any enumeration of children's rights must begin with the right to life from the moment of conception. We reject public policies or judicial decisions that embody the children's-liberation philosophy: that children have rights separate from those of their family and/or parents. Advocacy of children's rights that does not begin with advocacy of the right of the child to be born is reflective of moral and intellectual bankruptcy.

Parental Rights—God has given to parents the right and responsibility to rear and form the character of their children in accordance with His laws. Parental rights are primary, unless, by the standards of common law, the parents have been shown to be unfit to discharge their parental duties. We are unalterably opposed to government policies and judicial decisions that permit or promote government-funded "services" of counseling, contraception, and abortion to minor children without parental knowledge and consent.

Child Abuse—As the child has the right to protection from the moment of conception, through every stage of development, the government, acting for the common good, should take prudent and appropriate action to protect the life and safety of any child threatened. Actions should be taken at the state and local levels, with due regard for the rights of the child and the parents concerned.

Education—Parents have the primary right and responsibility to educate their children according to the philosophy of their choice without government interference or financial penalty.

Families and the Media—We expect the communications media to exercise restraint, discretion, and taste in their programming. There is grave concern that traditional family values are increasingly attacked, denigrated, twisted, and ridiculed in the media. We also support strong national, state, and local laws that restrict the dissemination of pornographic materials.

Religious Freedom—We believe that the rights of parents to rear their children according to their religious beliefs is a fundamental order of God and nature. It must not be undermined or counteracted, directly or indirectly, implicitly or explicitly, by any government action.

Government Programs and Policies—We endorse Senator Paul Laxalt's Family Protection Act and the family-protecting approaches embodied in it, an approach that encourages family, community, and local initiative to support families. We recognize that solutions to family problems will not be found in a proliferation of government programs. We reject the unfounded assumption that bureaucrats or "human services personnel" know better than parents what is best for their families.

The purpose of the Family Protection Act is to counteract disruptive federal intervention into family life in the United States and to encourage restoration of family unity, parental authority, and a climate of traditional morality. The Family Protection Act, S./ 1808, was introduced in the United States Senate on September 24, 1979. There are thirty-eight separate concepts in the Family Protection Act dealing with such things as education, taxation, welfare, domestic relations, and the guarantees provided by the First Amendment. Everything in that bill supports traditional values, encourages families to stay together, upholds parental authority, and reinforces traditional husband-and-wife relationships.

Senator Jesse Helms told me recently that he received letters from people who are sorely troubled by their inability to have any impact on the political decisions that are bringing our country closer and closer to collectivism. Senator Helms says he tries to impress upon these people that the most enduring contribution they can make to our country and to our political system is to work for the security, stability, and welfare of their families. "This is the unit that God has ordained as basic to human life and happiness," says Senator Helms. "We must restore and preserve the family as the focus of our personal and social well-being and the strongest defense we have against the totalitarian state."

"Your grandpa would shake his head and sigh that the younger generation is going to hell in a handbasket." Thus begins an article by William Rasberry entitled "Children Without Character" in a December 31, 1979, issue of the Washington *Post*. In his article, Rasberry quotes professor Edward A. Wynne, associate professor of education at the University of Illinois, who has compiled statistics revealing a steady increase in adolescent conduct that can be described as either other-destructive or self-destructive. Wynne reveals these statistics: Deaths by homicide of white males aged 15 to 19 increased from 2.7 per 100,000 in 1959 to 7.5 per 100,000 in 1976—an increase of 177 per cent. Between 1950 and 1976, the annual suicide rate for young white males rose from 3.5 per 100,000 to 11.9 per 100,000—an increase of 260 per cent. In addition, there is statistical evidence of major increases in the youthful abuse of illicit drugs and alcohol, in sexual promiscuity, in illegitimacy, and in venereal disease. Wynne says that these statistics reveal a steady increase in those acts demonstrating a lack of what is traditionally called "good character."

Wynne believes that the failures in the lives of children have intensified continuously over the past twenty to thirty years and produced a generation of "self-centered, withdrawn, unsympathetic, irreligious, unpatriotic, and characterless young people." Wynne asks, "The growing decline of youth character raises the central question of social continuity: Is our society rearing adults who can keep the country going?" He believes that the answer is "No." He says, "It's a good deal harder to inculcate simple morality when we keep telling our children, by precept and example, that morality is relative. It's difficult to engender patriotism when we no longer take for granted that America is a special place, or that its institutions and its guiding principles are based on something other than making a dollar. . . . In the end, the survival of any society depends on its ability to create successive groups of mature adults who are committed to its major traditions." Wynne believes that the blame can be attributed to the way we run our schools. His synopsis is partially correct, but most of the blame must be placed on godless parents who are rearing children in godless homes and in a godless society.

We live in a materialistic society full of tension and false values. Public educational systems are full of corruption. Vehicles of the media such as movies, television, radio, and publishing promote sensationalism, violence, crime that pays, sex, and permissiveness without accountability. The permissive society in which we live today is neglecting absolutes. Children learn from society that truth is not eternal, and that they can lie to get ahead. They are taught that there is no God and no hereafter. But aside from all these, the major problem still stems back to the home. Since a child is an extension of the family in which he is reared, the problem with our youth must trace back to their upbringing. The Bible states in Proverbs 22:6, "Train up a child in the way he should go, and when he is old, he will not depart from it." The sad fact is that today parents are not willing to take time with their children to love, encourage, and guide them. Millions of children are desperately looking for guidance, discipline, and love.

God holds parents responsible for the spiritual development of their children. Parents are responsible for establishing a home in which there is Bible reading, prayer, church attendance, holy living, and clean language and behavior. Parents must heed the admonition God gave Israelite parents as recorded in Chapter 6 of the Book of Deuteronomy in the Bible:

And thou shalt love the LORD thy God with all thine heart, and with all thy soul, and with all thy might.

And these words, which I command thee this day, shall be in thine heart:

And thou shalt teach them diligently unto thy children, and shalt talk of them when thou sittest in thine house, and when thou walkest by the way, and when thou liest down, and when thou risest up.

Parents fail their children when they do not effectively discipline them. Children must be taught and disciplined consistently. Discipline is not just punishment, nor is it merely scolding; it is the complete application of corrected behavior in a disobedient child. Discipline never succeeds until it becomes correction. In this day and age there is much talk about child abuse. We are confusing child abuse with discipline, which is necessary if we are to raise healthy children. Training includes both instruction and discipline. We read in Ephesians 6:4, "And, ye fathers, provoke not your children to wrath, but bring them up in the nurture [discipline] and admonition [instruction] of the Lord." The Bible clearly emphasizes, "Spare the rod, spoil the child."

For the past two decades psychologists have told parents not to spank their children. The result has been the most rebellious and irresponsible generation of young people who have ever lived in America. Now those same psychologists are saying that parents should spank and discipline their childrren. Let the admonition of Scripture stand, "Foolishness is bound in the heart of a child; but the rod of correction shall drive it far from him." (Pr. 22:15) Children actually loathe the tolerance of their parents in our "anything goes" society. To children permissiveness is a mark of parental unconcern. There is no love in permissiveness. Proverbs 29:15 states, "The rod and reproof give wisdom; but a child left to himself bringeth his mother to shame." And Proverbs 13:24 states, "He that spareth his rod hateth his son; but he that loveth him chasteneth him betimes." I do not believe in beating a child in anger. In love, a parent must correct his child to teach him the lessons of life. Parents who do not correct their children actually hate them; they do not love them. When children are not corrected they grow up with a distorted view of right and wrong.

In a September 10, 1979, *U.S. News & World Report* interview with General Robert H. Barrow, commandant of the United States Marine Corps, entitled, "Are the Marines Obsolete? Their Chief Speaks Out," General Barrow was asked, "Is it more difficult to train marines today than it was twenty years ago?" He replied, "Oh yes indeed. If I may talk about something that troubles me about our country: It's the family. I see serious problems in that great institution called the American family. I don't know what the causes are—whether it's high mobility, the great quest for material things, disinterest in religion, or what. But not many families have disciplined children, and that's where it all starts." In answer to the question, "If the real problem is in the home, then why do you place such emphasis on recruiting high-school graduates?" he answered, "If he has the diploma, the recruit probably comes from a stable home where there is love, concern, and encouragement for him to want to finish high school. And, conversely, very often the fellow who has dropped out has probably come from a home that is chaotic—broken, even though the mother and father may be there." In answer to the question, "Overall, is the caliber of today's recruits better or worse than in the past?" General Barrow answered, "Well, they're better than many of those we should not have been taking in during the early years of the all-volunteer force. But we have a hard time trying to develop discipline in some of these youngsters today. Not everyone takes to it as well as they may have a generation or two ago.

"In our society, the emphasis on discipline has been too much on the verb and not enough on the noun. Too many think of discipline in terms of punishing, as opposed to behaving in accordance with the rules, mores, and laws that set standards of human behavior." And last, in answer to the question, "What happens when you take these people into a tough boot camp and start giving them Marine Corps-style discipline?" he answered, "Most of them grab it like they have a vitamin deficiency. They want it! That's a surprise, but they really do. Despite some inadequacy of background, they have a thirst for discipline."

On February 14, 1977, the United Nations General Assembly unanimously passed a special resolution establishing 1979 as the International Year of the Child (IYC). This movement did not end on the last day of 1979. It is a continuing movement to promote the principles it was designed to initiate. Many people have been deceived by the IYC, thinking that its primary purpose was to alert people about child abuse and child neglect. Many thought that the IYC would help children. A deeper look at the roots of this movement shows a darker side. In 1959 the United Nations passed a resolution called the "Declaration of the Rights of the Child," which was not implemented at that time. The UN declared 1975 to be the International Women's Year, and designated 1976 through 1985 as the International Women's Decade. In 1976 the United Nations named 1979 to be the International Year of the Child, with UNICEF as the agency in charge of implementation. The Women's International Democratic Federation (WIDF) is a socialist organization that is responsible for the International Women's Year. WIDF held the first international seminar in preparation for IYC on October 2, 1977, in Prague, Czechoslovakia. In feminist Betty Friedan's account of the World Conference for Women in Mexico City, she says, "I had a curious luncheon invitation from a woman involved with the old-time Communist Women's group, the International Federation of Democratic Women. . . . They said, did I know, by the way, it was they who introduced the resolution to make 1975 International Women's Year? I hadn't known that. . . ." (Friedan, p. 345)

WIDF claims credit for IWY and a major role in the IYC

proclamation. Through these UN declarations, international social planners gained access to a worldwide network of governments. At the first international seminar in preparation for IYC
in Prague, Czechoslovakia, featured speaker, Marie Kabrhelova,
chairwoman of the Czechoslovak Women's Union, said, "Long
before the representatives of all the peoples of the world
in the UN decided to adopt the Declaration of the Rights of
the Child and its ten principles, the socialist countries had
gained vast experience in applying the ideas contained in the
declaration in everyday life. Socialism, the new social order, initiated sixty years ago by the Great October Socialist Revolution,
which in such a decisive way influenced the development of
mankind and the whole world, has always considered its main
duty to be to secure peace and to devote all-round care to the
young generation. All the rights of the new generation to a har-
monious, healthy, and universal development of all children and
young people are laid down in the constitutions of all socialist
countries. They are also included in the draft of the new constitution of the Soviet Union, which was the first country in
history to solve all the important problems of the young generation in such an inspiring way." (East Berlin: *Women of the
Whole World, Journal of the Women's International Democratic Federation,* No. 1 [1978], p. 23)

We have already clearly pointed out that the goal of communist countries is to take children away from their parents and
have them reared by the government so that they can be indoc-
trinated with communist principles.

Five million dollars in United States taxpayer money was
used to hold state and national IWY conferences. President
Carter designated 1979 as the International Year of the Child
by executive order; 1980 was authorized as the White House
Conference on Children, and 1981 was authorized as the White
House Conference on Families by executive order. The IWY
and the IYC are inseparably connected because they have the
same world leaders and the same philosophy. Resolutions
passed at the national IWY meeting in Houston in 1977
revealed goals of "reproductive freedom" (abortion); "sexual

preference" (homosexuality); "nonsexist" education (at all levels); and federally funded development centers for all children. Resolutions passed at the Houston IWY were presented to the President and our Congress. If implemented, they will completely restructure the society in which our children must live. Feminists state repeatedly in their writings that their goal is to "restructure existing institutions."

IYC leaders are not solely concerned with neglected and abused children. Let me state some of their goals as found in the White House Conference on Children, report to the President, 1970, pages 65, 66, and 278. Children should be "liberated," "the real solution requires a fundamental change in the value commitment, and the actions of the persons who control the public and private sector of our common life—parents, and those whose decisions determine the life styles of other human beings." Then, "Day care is a powerful institution . . . a day-care program that ministers to a child from six months to six years has over eight thousand hours to teach him values, fears, beliefs, and behaviors." We would here ask, "Do we want our children taught the values and beliefs of social planners who formulated this movement?" Socialism rejects God and anything that has to do with eternal life. Feminist Gloria Steinem said, "By the year 2000 we will, I hope, raise our children to believe in human potential, not God." (*Saturday Review of Education*, March 1973)

The New York *Times* reported, "The creation of a national program of early childhood education reaching every youngster in the country, starting at three years of age . . . has emerged as a top priority among American teachers . . . the Child and Family Services Act of 1978 . . . is considered by education groups to be the opening wedge in their attempt to establish a universal education program beginning with [the] three-year-old." That bill did not become law, but it will be raised again.

Principle 10 in the 1959 UN Declaration of the Rights of the Child states: "The child shall be protected from practices which may foster racial, religious, or any other form of discrimination."

I could produce many more examples verifying that the goal of IYC leaders is to "liberate" children not only from traditional morals and values, from parental authority, from practices that may foster religious principles, but also from nationalism, patriotism, and from capitalism. They even promote liberation from "militarism," but their major goal is disarmament, a theme that runs through their literature, an example being: "There is much that is necessary for the welfare of the child, but the highest priority is a world at peace . . . [there] must be an end to the arms race." (*Women of the Whole World*, No. 1 [1978], p. 13) Permeating literature on the children's issue, we find that there is the desire to establish a new international economic order that would replace all capitalist economies with socialism.

The goals of IYC are: (1) Give children the "right" to sue their parents in retaliation for "unjustified" discipline, unwanted "indoctrination," and/or "inadequate parenting." Such a case is currently under way in Boulder, Colorado. (2) Children would get a minimum wage for performing household chores. (3) Children would have the "right" to choose their own parents. A child could move out of his home and select where and with whom he would like to live. (4) Minor female children would be given the "right" to have abortions on demand without parental consent or knowledge. (5) The federal government would supervise all "family planning." Parents would virtually be licensed to be parents. The care of children would be taken away from the parents and put into the hands of the government. (6) Legislation would be passed that would legalize homosexual marriages and homosexual adoptions. (7) There would be an equal rights amendment for children. (8) The federal government would assume all responsibilities concerning the rearing of children. It is shocking that our elected representatives have already proposed, debated, and passed various congressional acts such as the Comprehensive Child Development Act of 1971 and the Child and Family Services Act of 1975.

The Swedish Parliament voted 259 to 6 on July 1, 1979, making it illegal for Swedish parents to discipline their children by spanking. This seems like a very shocking act, but the United States is fast cascading down the same road. Last May 1979 the U. S. National Commission on the IYC hailed Sweden as one of two countries "most advanced" in its recognition of children's rights. When the state accepts ultimate responsibility for a child's welfare, it indoctrinates that child with secular humanistic values. There is at this current time H.J. Res. 109, which states that it would "grant children additional rights equivalent to the rights now possessed only by adults." For instance, "the right to be consulted on all matters which concern one's psychological and physical well-being; the right to be represented by skillful legal counsel as an individual having rights and interests independent of any rights and interests that the parents or guardians of the child may have."

A pastor friend recently told me about a girl from Sweden with whom he had had contact. She turned in her parents for spanking her. She was taken from her family and put with another family that the state chose for her and said would be a much better family. Her new father raped her and today she is broken and grieved. She told my friend that she was too young to make a decision as to whether she should stay with her family or have another family. This same thing can happen in America if we do not stand up now as moral Americans and as godly mothers and fathers and be informed as to the issues and fight against what is wrong and what is godless. There are many cases right now in the United States of children who are taking their parents to court and too many decisions are being decided against traditional morality. In January 1978, where a little eight-year-old boy testified in a Cook County court in Chicago that he wanted to stay with his father rather than return to California to live with his mother, he gave reasons that his mother's alcohol and drug abuse and another person named Janice who shared his mother's bed were not "good." The little boy's father was a Sunday school teacher in the Salvation Army. When the little boy was asked why he preferred living with his father, he stated that he got to go to church and do fun things. When his mother took the stand she alleged that the child was "under great religious mind control." She was awarded temporary custody of the little boy, and later the decision was made permanent by a California court.

We must not be duped by the proponents of IYC who would like to fool us with good intentions of this movement. How can supporters of legalized abortion, IYC proponents, say that they are for children's rights, when a child's primary right is the right to life? We do not hear much about the Preamble to the Declaration of the Rights of the Child that was written twenty years ago that states: "Whereas the child, by reason of his physical and mental immaturity, needs special safeguards and care, including appropriate legal protection, before as well as after birth . . ." And Principle 4 states: "He shall be entitled to grow and develop in health; to this end special care and protection shall be granted both to him and to his mother, including adequate prenatal and postnatal care. . . ." I see the ultimate goal of IYC as governmental control of the minds and lives of our children. The Bible declares that parents are to instruct their children and bring them up in the discipline and instruction of the Lord. Children do not belong to the state. They do not even belong to parents. Children belong to God. Parents have been given the responsibility of rearing those children in the nurture and admonition of the Lord.

I am deeply grieved by child abuse. Any man who would beat his wife or his children is nothing more than an animal. Any woman who would hurt her children does not deserve the title of mother. But "children's rights" are not the answers to child abuse. "Child neglect" and "child abuse" are terms used only to cover the true intention of the proponents of the IYC. Only a revival across America will help to get rid of child abuse and child neglect. Not only is the IYC antifamily, but it is anti-God and anti-American as well. I repeat: The family is the most important unit in society. The strength and stability of families determine the moral life of society. The most important function performed by the family is the rearing and character formation of children. God established the family, and moral Americans must see that it is protected. If the home were to go, there would be nothing to hold this country together. Communism could easily take over.

Children are a heritage of the Lord, and they deserve the very best that their parents can give them. They deserve a well-educated, imaginative, full-time mother. Children deserve to be considered more than second-class citizens for whom surrogate mothers, nursery schools, baby-sitters, or housekeepers are considered to be all that they need. The greatest investment a mother can ever make is in the lives of precious children.

I like what the Eagle Forum has established as children's needs. These include:* (1) To have the love of a mother and a father who understand their different roles and fulfill their different responsibilities. (2) To have the care of a mother who makes mothering her No. 1 career, at least in the all-important preschool period. (3) To live in an economic system that makes it possible for husbands to support their wives as full-time mothers in the home, and that enables families to survive on one income instead of two; that gives preference to the wage earner who is the principal financial support of three or more dependents (because other preferences disadvantage children most); and that respects the dignity of marriage by not imposing heavier income taxes on married couples than on unwed couples. (4) To have his father's name if born of a legitimate union of husband and wife. (5) To know about the happiness and lasting rewards of premarital chastity followed by a monogamous lifetime commitment in marriage, "for better or worse, in sickness and in health, till death do us part." (6) To know about the social and psychological cost of promiscuous conduct: venereal disease, illegitimate pregnancies, marriage failure, and emotional disorders. (7) To have sex education taught by parents, churches, or others who believe in the Ten Commandments. (8) To attend schools where moral standards are taught and discipline is enforced so that person and property are safe and a learning environment is maintained. (9) To be taught

* The pronouns "he" and "his" refer to both the male and the female child.

the basic tools of reading, writing, and arithmetic so that he can eventually achieve his full potential as a self-supporting citizen. (10) To be taught from textbooks that honor the traditional family as the basic unit of society, woman's role as wife and mother, and man's role as provider and protector, and that do not offend the parents' religious or moral values. (11) To have gender differences respected in gym classes, athletic practices, in competition, restrooms, and locker facilities. (12) To have an education that respects gender identity so that the child will be able, upon maturity, to develop a lasting heterosexual relationship. (13) To know that he was created by a loving and just God who watches over everyone and has given each of us the opportunity for eternal life. (14) To know that the United States of America, in the words of our Declaration of Independence, is founded on the "self-evident" truth that each child is "created" by God and "endowed" by his "Creator" with "certain unalienable rights." (15) To be given the opportunity to develop a good conscience by being taught that some things are right and other things are wrong, and that civilization and social order depend on public support of a moral code of conduct. (16) To know about the rewards that come from the daily asking of God's blessing on our lives and activities. (17) The right to life, even if that life is inconvenient or burdensome to others, and to have the help of parental love to overcome handicaps and obstacles. (18) To have society take whatever means are necessary to eliminate the use of minors in pornographic or sadistic materials; to eliminate the solicitation of minors by drug peddlers, homosexuals, or prostitutes; and to eliminate child abuse and child incest. (19) To live in a society in which individuals can enjoy the fruits of their own labor and initiative, rather than having them confiscated and redistributed by a government that takes over all economic and political decisionmaking. (20) To have pride in his nationality because: "Breathes there the man with soul so dead who never to himself has said, 'This is my own, my native land.'?"

These twenty needs are guidelines for godly, concerned parents who are concerned with the future of America.

THE FEMINIST MOVEMENT

I believe that at the foundation of the women's liberation movement there is a minority core of women who were once bored with life, whose real problems are spiritual problems. Many women have never accepted their God-given roles. They live in disobedience to God's laws and have promoted their godless philosophy throughout our society. God Almighty created men and women biologically different and with differing needs and roles. He made men and women to complement each other and to love each other. Not all the women involved in the feminist movement are radicals. Some are misinformed, and some are lonely women who like being housewives and helpmeets and mothers, but whose husbands spend little time at home and who take no interest in their wives and children. Sometimes the full load of rearing a family becomes a great burden to a woman who is not supported by a man. Women who work should be respected and accorded dignity and equal rewards for equal work. But this is not what the present feminist movement and equal rights movement are all about.

The Equal Rights Amendment is a delusion. I believe that women deserve more than equal rights. And, in families and in nations where the Bible is believed, Christian women are honored above men. Only in places where the Bible is believed and practiced do women receive more than equal rights. Men and women have differing strengths. The Equal Rights Amendment can never do for women what needs to be done for them. Women need to know Jesus Christ as their Lord and Savior and be under His Lordship. They need a man who knows Jesus Christ as his Lord and Savior, and they need to be part of a home where their husband is a godly leader and where there is a Christian family.

The Equal Rights Amendment strikes at the foundation of our entire social structure. If passed, this amendment would accomplish exactly the opposite of its outward claims. By mandating an absolute equality under the law, it will actually take away many of the special rights women now enjoy. ERA is not merely a political issue, but a moral issue as well. A definite violation of holy Scripture, ERA defies the mandate that "the husband is the head of the wife, even as Christ is the head of the church" (Ep. 5:23). In 1 Peter 3:7 we read that husbands are to give their wives honor as unto the weaker vessel, that they are both heirs together of the grace of life. Because a woman is weaker does not mean that she is less important.

I deeply respect Mrs. Phyllis Schlafly. Mrs. Schlafly is a conservative activist. She is a lawyer and has an extensive background in national defense. At services in the Thomas Road Baptist Church, Lynchburg, Virginia, Mrs. Schlafly made these comments: "The more I work with the issue of ERA, the more I realize that the women's liberation movement is antifamily. The proof came in November 1977 when the conference on International Women's Year met in Houston. It passed twenty-five resolutions which show very clearly what the feminists are after. They are for the Equal Rights Amendment, which would take away the marvelous legal rights of a woman to be a full-time wife and mother in the home supported by her husband. They are for abortion on demand, financed by the government and taught in the schools. They are for privileges for lesbians and homosexuals to teach in the schools and to adopt children. They are for the government assuming the main responsibility for child care because they think it is oppressive and unfair that society expects mothers to look after their babies. All their goals and dogmas are antifamily. They believe that God made a mistake when He made two different kinds of people.

"They believe that we should use the Constitution and legislation to eliminate the eternal differences and the roles that God has ordained between men and women. They want to require all laws and regulations and all schools to treat men and women exactly the same. They want to do it with federal control. That is what Section 2 of the Equal Rights Amendment would do. Another dogma of the women's liberationists is that you have no right to make a moral judgment between what is right and what is wrong. They want to give the homosexuals and the lesbians the same dignity as husbands and wives. They want to give the woman who has an illegitimate baby the same dignity as the one who has had one in holy matrimony. The Equal Rights Amendment, uses the word 'sex,' not the word 'woman.' ERA puts sex into the Constitution—a mandate that one could never make a reasonable common-sense difference of treatment between male and female, or between good sex and bad sex. ERA would do this with the power of the federal government. Moral Americans have beaten ERA forces for seven years. Then the proponents passed their unfair time extension. They are trying to use the power of the federal government to force the unratified states to switch from no to yes. Meanwhile, they are trying to use the courts to deny states the right to switch from yes to no. We must continue to fight against the ERA and to win this battle for God, for the dignity of women, and for the institution of the family."

Phyllis Schlafly, one of the most knowledgeable people I know, continued to outline the ERA movement. The next several paragraphs are a synopsis of her presentation.

The Equal Rights Amendment offers women nothing in the way of rights or benefits that they do not already have. In the areas of employment and education, laws have already been enacted to protect women. The only thing the Equal Rights Amendment would do would be to take away rights and privileges that American women now have in the best country in the world. Let us look at some of the women who are the leaders in the feminist and ERA movements.

Betty Friedan, founder of the National Organization for Women (NOW), made this statement in a NOW-ERA fund-raising letter: "The ERA has become both symbol and substance for the whole of the modern women's movement for equality. . . . I am convinced that if we lose this struggle we will have little hope in our own lifetime of saving our right to abortion. . . ." Betty Friedan states that a feminist agenda for the eighties must call for "the restructuring of the institutions of home and work." As has already been stated, Gloria Steinem, editor of *Ms.* magazine, made this statement: "By the year 2000 we will, I hope, raise our children to believe in human potential, not God. . . ." Dr. MaryJo Bane, associate director of Wellesley College's Center for Research on Women, made this statement: "We really don't know how to raise children. . . . The fact that children are raised in families means there's no equality . . . in order to raise children with equality, we must take them away from families and raise them. . . ."

Humanist Manifesto II, signed by Betty Friedan, contains this statement: "No deity will save us, we must save ourselves. Promises of immortal salvation or fear of eternal damnation are both illusory and harmful." In the notes from the Second Year Women's Liberation we find these comments: "We must destroy love . . . love promotes vulnerability, dependence, possessiveness, susceptibility to pain, and prevents the full development of woman's human potential by directing all her energies outward in the interests of others." In the document *Declaration of Feminism*, we find this: "Marriage has existed for the benefit of men and has been a legally sanctioned method of control over women . . . the end of the institution of marriage is a necessary condition for the liberation of women. Therefore, it is important for us to encourage women to leave their husbands and not to live individually with men . . . we must work to destroy it [marriage]." In her speech in Houston, Texas,

Gloria Steinem made this comment: ". . . for the sake of those who wish to live in equal partnership, we have to abolish and reform the institution of legal marriage."

The Equal Rights Amendment sounds deceptively simple. It contains only three sentences: "Section 1: Equality of rights under the law shall not be denied or abridged by the United States or by any state on account of sex. Section 2: The Congress shall have the power to enforce, by appropriate legislation, the provisions of this article. Section 3: This amendment shall take effect two years after the date of ratification." When ERA went to the floor of the House and Senate, a number of congressmen and senators tried to insert amendments. When ERA went to the floor of the Senate, Senator Sam Ervin proposed nine separate clauses as amendments to ERA. Every one of these clauses was defeated on a roll-call vote. They included such provisions as, "Except it won't require us to draft women. Except it won't require us to send our young women into military combat. Except it won't take away the rights of working women. Except it won't take away the rights of wives, mothers, and widows. Except it won't take the right to privacy of men or women, boys or girls. Except it won't interfere with laws which are based on physiological differences." Every one of these clauses was defeated.

ERA came out of Congress on March 22, 1972, and went to the states with a clause setting a time limit of seven years for ratification. In the first twelve months, thirty states passed it, most of them without any hearings or debates on the issue. When concerned women became involved and went to their state legislators and ERA was thoroughly examined, states began to realize that they had made a mistake in passing the ERA. In the next six years, five more states passed ERA, but five others rescinded passage. As the time limit neared expiration, proponents of the ERA asked Congress for a time extension. This was exactly like a losing football team demanding a fifth quarter in order to give them time to catch up, and furthermore providing that only the losing team may carry the ball. We are now in the three-year extension, which is actually illegal. The power move evidenced by this extension has been unprecedented in the history of our Constitution.

Let us examine the Equal Rights Amendment. In the first section we find that the word "sex," not "women," is put into the Constitution. It is not clarified what meaning of sex is ascribed here. "Equality of rights" is an undefined term. There is no judicial history for that term. ERA applies only to governmental action, laws, and regulations. Their terms are vague and undefined. Thus one of the major defects of the ERA is that it is a blank check to the U. S. Supreme Court to tell Americans what it means after it is ratified. It is probable that the ERA would require sex-neutral words to be put in all our laws—words like person, taxpayer, spouse, and parent. If we look at our Constitution today we find that it is the most beautiful sex-neutral document ever written. It does not talk about men and women, male and female. The U. S. Constitution uses only words such as person, citizen, resident, inhabitant, etc. Women have every constitutional right that men have. Employment laws are already sex-neutral. ERA has nothing to do with equal pay for equal work.

Our country has fought in nine wars, and has had a draft for thirty-three years of this century. No woman in America has ever been drafted or sent into military combat. The draft act has always read: "Male citizens of age eighteen must register." This is an example of a sex-discriminatory law. There is an exemption to females. This is the American way. We have laws that exempt women from military combat duty. There is one for the Army, one for the Navy, and one for the Air Force. In November 1979, the House Armed Services Committee held four days of hearings on the women's liberation proposal to repeal the laws that exempt women from military combat duty. There were women who held jobs in the Pentagon who said, "Women want their career advancement to be generals and admirals and to be assigned to combat duty." Men like Admiral Jeremiah Denton, who spent seven years in a POW camp in Vietnam, spoke about what it means to be in combat. Should the ERA pass, the Constitution would compel us to force women to serve in the military and to go into combat zones. The ERA is an amendment to the Constitution, which is the supreme law of the land, and if ERA goes into the Constitution it would immediately wipe out the laws that exempt women from military combat. The military would have to obey the Constitution.

The women's liberation movement is seeking to require sex integration of every aspect of all school systems. This would mean that there could be no more all-men's or all-women's schools or colleges. All classes and dormitories would have to be coed. All sports programs would have to be coed. There could be no single-sex fraternities or sororities, no Girl Scouts, Boy Scouts, YMCA, YWCA, or Campfire Girls. There could be no Girls State or Boys State. There could be no mother/daughter and father/son school events. Under ERA it would be unconstitutional to have any of these things because they "discriminate on account of sex." ERA not only would apply to public schools, but it would also extend to all private schools and colleges whether or not they receive public money.

The Founding Fathers who established our great nation separated the power of government between the federal government and the states, and then again between executive, legislative, and judicial branches. We have maintained great freedom under this system. Under this distribution of power between the states and the federal government, a large area of law has been retained at the state level. Many of the laws at the state level have traditionally made differences of treatment based upon sex, and they are the type of laws that would be subject to ERA. These laws include: marriage, divorce, child custody, adoptions, homosexual laws, incest laws, prison regulations, and insurance rates. These are all laws that traditionally have made some type of difference of treatment based on sex. Section 1 of ERA would prohibit any common-sense difference of treatment based on sex. Section 2 would shift the total decision-making power over these laws to the federal government. Under Section 1 of the ERA they would be forced to make these laws sex neutral. There could never be a law that says a husband should support his wife. Laws such as this were not designed to discriminate against one's sex. They merely defined responsibilities designed for the purpose of keeping the family together. Not only would ERA make state laws sex neutral, but it would also shift the final decision-making power to the federal government.

In summary, we conclude that there are no exceptions to Section 1 of the Equal Rights Amendment. ERA proponents voted down and eliminated all clauses that would have preserved women's exemption from the military, draft, and wartime combat duty; that would have preserved the rights of wives, mothers, and widows to be financially supported by their husbands benefits; that would have preserved protective health and safety laws for working women; that would have preserved the right of privacy in school and public restrooms, hospitals, and prisons; that would have preserved the rights of legislatures to pass laws against abortion, and homosexual and lesbian privileges. Section 2 of the Equal Rights Amendment would mean federalizing vast powers that states now have, including marriage and divorce, child custody, prison regulations, and insurance rates. Section 2 would mean that federal courts and the federal bureaucracy would make all final decisions regarding marriage, divorce, alimony, abortion, homosexual and lesbian privileges, and sex integration of police and fire departments, schools and sports, hospitals, prisons, and public accommodations.

It is ironic that ERA and feminist proponents do not talk about the display of printed or pictorial materials that degrade women in a pornographic, perverted, or sadistic manner. In fact, *Playboy* magazine hosts ERA parties and contributes heavily to their campaigns. In Illinois alone, *Playboy* gave five thousand dollars to help ratify ERA. The check was personally presented by Christy Hefner, the daughter of the magazine's publisher. In Florida a fund-raising event was held for the ERA. The honored guest was Marguex St. James, President of COYOTE (Call Off Your Old Tired Ethics), an organization of prostitutes. Marguex St. James said, "Give me two weeks and a dozen girls in any state capital, and I will deliver ERA on a silver platter."

Brigadier General Andrew J. Gatsis, who is now retired, entered the military in 1939 as a private. He was a professional combat infantryman for thirty-six years. A West Point graduate, he served in several wars, including the Korean War, where he personally led a counterattack on Christmas Day 1952. He also served in the Vietnam War. He is one of the most highly decorated officers in the United States armed forces. Speaking to an Eagle Forum workshop on March 23, 1979, he made these comments about the drafting of women into combat: "I have served as an infantry commander in three separate combat tours, all at the fighting level. I have personally participated in hand-to-hand combat and have seen men fight and die on the battlefield. I have had women in my command, have observed their performance firsthand, and have had to contend with the disruptive effect on military discipline and combat efficiency brought about by the women's liberation movement, a movement fully supported and promoted by the top *echelons* of our government.

Proponents of the ERA are continuing efforts to reduce combat effectiveness through the goals of ERA by preparing the American public to accept the idea of drafting women and placing them into combat units. They are using the all-volunteer force as a mechanism for misleading Americans into thinking war and combat roles are natural to women.

"I would like to say there are some women, certainly in the minority, who like the military, who like to live and work with men, and have given an excellent performance in certain noncombat positions such as clerks, telephone operators, computer technicians, supply supervisors, nurses, and the like. World War II is ample proof of this. However, these rules do not satisfy the objective of the women's movement, which is to make women equal with men in all sectors of military activity regardless of the damage and effect it has on fighting spirit or combat efficiency. In fact, avid supporters of ERA have little concern for our defense posture and are willing to weaken or sacrifice it if it conflicts with the goals they seek.

"I must tell you that the top command structure of our military forces, the Pentagon, is saturated with ERA proponents, and under the complete control of avid supporters of the women's liberation movement. Members of various women's organizations such as NOW (National Organization for Women) have been placed in key manpower positions of authority who formulate and direct policies concerning U.S. military readiness posture. The result and outflow is that U.S. readiness revolves more around enhancing the women's liberation movement than it does meeting the military capability of a potential Army.

"In spite of the effort to propagandize the American public with the great success of the all-volunteer force and its large component of women, the plan has backfired. The myth that women do as well as men, and even better in some cases in the all-male traditional roles, is beginning to show up for the falsehood it is. The military services are unable to get sufficient soldiers to enlist or stay in the jobs that require those skills. Women are finding out how tough this training is and that they will spend considerable time in the fields. As a result, they are avoiding nonglamorous career management fields such as air defense, artillery, paint mechanics, linepole climbing, and the like, causing large overstrength in the medical and administrative fields.

"In a desperate attempt to overcome this shortage in the combat support areas, the Army is now experimenting with the program that offers special bonuses, free education, and a reduced time of service from three to two years, to encourage them to accept unnatural roles. In addition, just recently, they began to lower the score for entrance into the military from a score of 50, which is the national average, to 31 for women. This approach is also failing, for approximately 50 per cent of women enlistees are not finishing their tour of service.

"To convince the American public that women could perform all jobs in the military as well as men, one of the greatest psychological-warfare efforts ever devised was launched through the national and major news media. The first step was to order a series of tests and evaluations to substantiate predrawn conclusions that women are fit to fight on the battlefield. When the studies came back showing that women as a whole were inadequate in this area, the studies were sent back for re-evaluation.

"The next move was to have senior civilian defense officials and military leaders hail the sex-integrated all-volunteer force as a great success. Today even top defense officials have to admit it is a dismal failure, as they cannot meet recruiting goals and the quality is low. Having seen their plan shattered within the last year, these same officials have begun to redirect their efforts to a strategy that calls for the draft of women. Recently, the Secretary of Defense, Harold Brown, asked the House Armed Services Committee to register women as well as men for the draft. Very shortly thereafter, all chiefs of the four military services— Army, Navy, Marines, and Air Force—went before the Senate Armed Services Subcommittee for personnel and manpower and recommended that women be required to register for the draft.

"If the draft is ever implemented, and ERA is ratified, all barriers will be removed from placing women in combat roles. The proponents of ERA will tell you that this will never happen and only a very few women will be put in combat, since all military assignments are based on the soldier's physical profile and his trained skill. Even though these are the rules, anyone who has ever been in combat knows a large number of people are always improperly assigned, due to the fact that pipeline replacements do not flow even—it's a very complex system—replacements never arrive when needed, and the nature of casualties is never so predictable that one can requisition the proper type and exact number to fill the job vacancy required. The normal procedure is to reach into the locally available noncombat resources for replacing combat shortages.

"For example, after my company had been thrown off of its positions by a large Communist Chinese attack one early morning, we were left with only 42 men out of 197. Since there were no combat-type replacements at hand, I was forced to muster my noncombat-type personnel, such as clerks, cooks, and vehicle drivers for the counterattacking force needed to eject the enemy from Hill 266. The point to be made is that, when the situation is critical, noncombat qualified women who are locally available in support units will be used.

"Let me comment what placing women in combat roles will mean to them and to military combat effectiveness. The combat environment is an ugly one. For the ground soldier, it is characterized by drudgery, indignity, and anonymous horrors. It calls for a toughness that women do not normally possess, for battle is primitive, vicious, brutal, and exhausting. It is coupled with depression and crippling fatigue, which together create terror in the soldier's heart and make him wonder as he sees the night coming down if he will see the edge of dawn. His feelings fluctuate from despair to extreme hate and bitterness, which tend to bring forth his most animal instincts.

"If he is fighting in the Mekong Delta, he must endure living in mosquito-infested paddies, immersed in filthy waters up to his waist and armpits for continuous periods of twenty-four to forty-eight hours, where he is subjected to fungus, bacterial infections, and immersion foot. The skin breaks out with tiny red scale vesicles on the foot and other parts of the body. The feet become swollen and top layers of dead white skin come off in silver-dollar patches. These conditions are aggravated by body leeches, which the soldier must also endure. The loss rate for male casualties in this kind of operation averaged 50 per cent in my command.

"If he is fighting in the hills of Korea, he is subject to bitter cold, frostbite, and diseases such as the plague resulting from living in rat-infested bunkers. If his mission turns to the Middle East or Africa, he suffers from filth, relentless heat, and the dryness of the desert. In the highlands of Vietnam, he's plagued by bamboo viper snakes, torrential rains, jungle rot, malaria, and the like. In Europe it is the deluge of mud, the slime of dripping dugouts, and the weariness of continuous marches along the hot, dusty road.

"These are only some of the daily environmental living conditions of the ground combat soldier, let alone the nightmares of mortal combat. These are not the kinds of conditions in which we wish to place anyone. But can we, as civilized people, even begin to entertain the thought of sending our women into such an environment against their will?

"To survive these conditions and to function effectively at the same time against a determined enemy, it is mandatory that the individual soldier be in top physical condition with the long-term inborn stamina that will not wane after long grueling hours of trudging toward the objective. It is a kind of strength that keeps the soldier fit to fight after he reaches the enemy, regardless of the obstacles he must overcome before contacting them.

"The concerted drive to convince the public that women can do as well as men in combat is at its height today. Listen to the statement made by our Secretary of the Army, Clifford Alexander, who has never been in combat and has only had six months of active military service in the Army National Guard as a private first class: 'There are few things that men can do that women can't. By law, they don't fight. My personal opinion is contrary to what the law says.' The Army chief of staff says, 'I see no reason why women cannot serve effectively in combat roles further to the rear.'

"All kinds of tests—field tests, training tests, and readiness tests—have been conducted over and over again showing conclusively that women are not fit for combat and that by nature they are smaller, physically slower, physically weaker particularly in upper-body strength to throw a grenade effectively, dig a foxhole, hack a path through the thick jungle with a machete, fight an enemy soldier with a rifle butt and a bayonet, pull oneself through a long, narrow tunnel with heavy demolitions to flush an enemy sniper out of his hiding place. Yet the power of the women's liberation movement prevails in the U. S. Army, and these results are not accepted. They counter by saying, 'Women may be weak in these areas, but they are better educated and score better in aptitude tests.' There is some truth to this since all females must have a high-school education to qualify for the service. But the difference lies in the fact that education is not the ingredient that wins battles for the combat soldier. It is simple tactical plans, guts, stamina, and brutal physical force that bring victory.

"What is so ironic about all of this is that most of the motivated volunteer female soldiers do not want to go into combat; it is the women liberationist leaders who will never have to go who are pushing so hard for this.

"I only wish those who push for placing women in combat could see it as I have. Are they ready to see their daughters and wives exposed to the wrath of the enemy because they could not dig in the hard ground in time for protection? Should they have to hear the screams of burning human torches trapped in the entanglements of barbed wire after napalm cans are exploded along the main line of resistance? Must they become the victims of suffocation in a covered position resulting from burned-out oxygen due to white phosphorus? Are we really ready to have them face the cold, steel bayonet of the male enemy soldier? Or be horribly mangled in a trapped minefield that no one can penetrate? Think of that young eighteen-year-old moist-eyed girl with homesickness, looking at the faded twilight; she believes the sky is lost forever. Do they need to hear that dreaded noise of incoming artillery beating like a kettle drum, which is like two steel needles pressing on the eardrums? Have they thought about what our women would suffer as prisoners of war at the hands of the enemy who uses the pressure water-hose technique of blowing one's stomach up like a balloon to gain military information? And what a trump card our enemy would have in blackmailing the United States while holding a large number of women prisoners! How can we reconcile our moral perceptions of women with these immoralities of war? No one who has seen real combat could believe that our congressmen and governmental leaders would talk about drafting women and placing them in combat, yet they are doing this very thing today."

Hidden away throughout all the bureaucracies there are hundreds of little advisory committees that are supposedly there to represent the view of the people. One of them within

HEW is called the Secretary's Advisory Committee on the Rights and Responsibilities of Women. This is a panel that directly advises the Secretary of HEW on what women of America want. The panel is made up of twelve very aggressive, self-proclaimed feminists. The head of this group was asked if there were other viewpoints in America besides the feminist viewpoint, to which she replied, "Oh no. I'm confident we represent all American women." The input of those twelve women is recognized by top government.

Need I say that it is time that moral Americans became informed and involved in helping to preserve family values in our nation? Now it is not too late. But we cannot wait. The twilight of our nation could well be at hand.

THE RIGHT TO LIFE

Life is a miracle. Only God Almighty can create life. God said, "Thou shalt not kill." Nothing can change the fact that abortion is the murder of life.

Sitting in an airport in Washington, D.C., recently, I picked up the January 9, 1980, issue of the Washington *Post*. There I read horrifying statistics in an article entitled "Legal Abortion Seen in 30 Per Cent of Pregnancies." That article reported the grave fact that in 1978 nearly 30 per cent of all pregnancies in the United States were terminated by legal abortions. A family-planning perspective study estimated that there were 1,374,000 legal abortions in 1978. About one third of the abortions were obtained by teen-agers, and about three quarters were for unmarried women. Last year more than 1.5 million little babies were murdered in America. Experts estimate that between 5 million and 6 million babies have been murdered since January 22, 1973, when the U. S. Supreme Court, in a decision known as *Rowe* v. *Wade*, granted women an absolute right to abortion on demand during the first two trimesters of pregnancy—that is, the first six months of pregnancy—and an almost unqualified right to abortion in the last trimester, the last three months of pregnancy, for health reasons including psychological, social, and economic well-being. No other major civilized nation in history has ever been willing to permit late abortion except for the gravest of medical reasons. Abortion stands as an indictment of murder against America for killing unwanted babies.

Human life is precious to God. Jesus Christ died upon the cross for every man and woman who has ever lived and who ever will live. In the past, America was known for her honoring and protecting the right of a person to live. No one will disagree that the state exists to protect the lives of its citizens. From the days of Hammurabi, civilized people have always looked upon abortion as one of the vilest of crimes. Now, in our society, we are losing respect for the sanctity of human life. America has allowed more lives to be killed through abortion than in all our wars and traffic accidents. Only a perverted society would make laws protecting wolves and eagles' eggs, and yet have no protection for precious unborn human life.

Equally ironic, there is a great debate going on regarding capital punishment. Today in America we kill babies and protect criminals. The death penalty is a deterrent to crime. In the Book of Romans in the Bible we find in Chapter 1 that God has given government the responsibility and authority to punish by death: "For rulers are not a terror to good works, but to the evil. Wilt thou then not be afraid of the power? . . . If thou do that which is evil, be afraid; for he beareth not the sword in vain. . . ."

Recently I received this letter: "Dear Dr. Falwell, I just viewed your telecast on abortion. I am so ashamed that in April of 1973 my baby became a part of the unwanted generation that you spoke of. At the time I could only think of ridding myself of this problem, and over the years, even though knowing it was wrong, I convinced myself that I would do the same thing again if I had to live it over. I had a saline abortion, but the doctor told me nothing of what would really happen other than simply expelling the fetus. Listening to your program today, that problem that I had became a helpless baby, not a fetus. I claimed God's promise in 1 John 1:9 that if I confessed my sin God is faithful and just to forgive my sin and to cleanse me from all unrighteousness. I only pray that my baby is with Christ and that maybe someday I can be the mother in heaven that I should have been on earth. Do you think that could at all be possible? By the way, Dr. Falwell, five years later, in 1978, God gave my husband and me the assurance that He had forgiven. He gave us a baby daughter. A confirmation of God's forgiveness to me is that the doctor said I might never have children. Please continue to do what you are doing. Emphasize that God is a God of forgiveness." The letter is signed, "A forgiven mother."

In Genesis 9:6 we read, "Whoso sheddeth man's blood, by man shall his blood be shed; for in the image of God made he man." And in Psalm 139:13–16 the psalmist says, "For thou hast possessed my reins; thou hast covered me in my mother's womb. I will praise thee; for I am fearfully and wonderfully made: Marvelous are thy works; and that my soul knoweth right well. My substance was not hid from thee, when I was made in secret, and curiously wrought in the lowest parts of the earth. Thine eyes did see my substance, yet being unperfect; and in thy book all my members were written, which in continuance were fashioned, when as yet there was none of them." Scripture refers to man being made in secret as in the mother's womb. These particular verses refer to the development of the embryo. "All members being written down" speaks of all parts of the baby's body. In Luke 1:39–44 we read, "And Mary arose in those days, and went into the hill country with haste, into a city of Juda; and entered into the house of Zacharias, and saluted Elisabeth. And it came to pass that when Elisabeth heard the salutation of Mary, the babe leaped in her womb; and Elisabeth was filled with the Holy Ghost: And she spake out with a loud voice, and said, 'Blessed art thou among women, and blessed is the fruit of thy womb. And whence is this to me, that the mother of my Lord should come to me? For, lo, as soon as the voice of thy salutation sounded in mine ears, the babe leaped in my womb for joy.'" Medical experts affirm that a child is alive before birth. Life begins at conception. Sophisticated equipment enables doctors to measure signs of life in the early stages of fetal development. The Bible clearly states that life begins at conception.

In reality, life began with God, and since Adam it has simply passed from one life cell to another. That is what the Apostle Paul referred to in the Bible when he said, regarding marriage, that two shall become one flesh. When the male sperm and the female egg merge, human life is passed on, and the mother and father become one in that little baby in the womb. Life is a miracle, and no one on this earth has the right to abort it. Scientists now agree that at the moment of conception a new and unique human individual is created.

From the moment of conception any further formation of the individual is merely a matter of time, growth, and maturation. This is a growth process that continues throughout each of our entire lives. At three weeks, just twenty-one days after conception, a tiny human being already has eyes, a spinal cord, a nervous system, lungs, and intestines. The heart, which has been beating since the eighteenth day, is pumping a blood supply totally separate from the mother's. All this occurs before the mother may even be aware of new life within her. By the end of the seventh week we see a well-proportioned small-scale baby with fingers, knees, ankles, and toes. Brain waves have been recorded as early as forty-three days. By eleven weeks all organ systems are present and functioning. The eighteen-week child is active and energetic, flexing muscles, punching, and kicking.

Dr. Thomas L. Johnson, professor of biology and embryology at the University of Virginia, observes that an "individual organism (the zygote) cannot be a part of the mother . . . it has an entirely different set of chromosomes . . . it is a separate and unique life." In reply to the statement that life begins as the infant leaves the mother's womb, Dr. Johnson says that the moment of birth is not a moment of magic when a potential being is transformed into an actual being. The unborn child is merely moving from a required aquatic environment to a required gaseous environment so that it can develop into its next stage of life.

How are abortions done? I am not a doctor, so I must rely on doctors who have written about the methods to give me the information. The most popular of the abortion methods is called the suction aspiration method. It is used in 80 per cent of all abortions up to the twelfth week of pregnancy. Anesthesia is given to the mother but not to the child. The mouth of the womb, the cervix, is dilated. Sometimes it is damaged because during pregnancy the cervix is closed tightly to protect the baby. A suction *curet*, a hollowed tube with a knifelike edge tip, is inserted into the womb. A strong suction twenty-eight times stronger than that of a vacuum cleaner tears the baby to pieces, drawing those pieces into a container. Great care must be used to prevent the womb from being perforated. Photographs record recognizable parts of a baby's body that were sucked out of the womb.

The second of the popular methods of abortion is called the saline injection, or simply salt poisoning. Though outlawed in Japan and other countries due to its risk to the mother, this procedure is widely used in the United States after the baby is sixteen weeks old. A concentrated salt solution is injected into the amniotic sac. The baby breathes and swallows the solution and dies one to two hours later from salt poisoning, dehydration, hemorrhages of the brain and other organs, and convulsions. The baby's skin is often stripped off by the salt solution. The mother goes into labor and a dead or dying baby is delivered twenty-four to forty-eight hours later.

Another method of abortion is called hysterotomy. This is similar to the Caesarean section, though its purpose is to kill rather than to save the child. Hysterotomy is used if the saline or prostoglanden method has failed, or when a tubal ligation is to be done at the same time. Almost all of these babies are born alive. The abdomen and womb are opened surgically; the baby is lifted out; the cord is clamped, and the child usually struggles for a while and then dies. Some babies, if not encouraged to die, may survive this operation and are subsequently adopted. Others move, breathe, and some even cry before they die.

A D&C abortion utilizes a sharp loop-shaped steel knife. The uterus is entered through the vagina, and the cervix is stretched open. The surgeon cuts the body of the tiny baby to pieces and slices the placenta from the inside walls of the uterus. Bleeding is usually profuse. Operating nurses must reassemble the parts of the baby to make sure that the uterus is empty, as the mother could become infected if parts are left behind.

Reading about these methods is unnerving. But it must be done in order to understand the seriousness of abortion. Abortion is not birth control nor family planning. It is murder according to the Word of God. And it was sadly the decision of our U. S. Supreme Court that gave free license to the murder of 5 million to 6 million babies since January 22, 1973. America has the blood of all those babies on her hands.

Bernard N. Nathanson, M.D., was cofounder of the National Association for Repeal of Abortion Laws (now the National Abortion Rights Action League). From February 1971 to September 1972, he was director of the Center for Reproductive and Sexual Health, the largest and busiest abortion clinic in the world. In 1973, when the Supreme Court handed down its decision on the right to abortion, Dr. Nathanson was Chief of Obstetrical Services at St. Luke's Hospital in New York City. It was in that position that he dealt with the fetus as an intrauterine patient. Very sophisticated equipment was used to monitor the fetus. Dr. Nathanson found that what appeared on the monitors was the same for the fetus as for an infant. Today he makes the statement that he has "in fact presided over sixty thousand deaths." Newspapers and magazines featured Dr. Nathanson's turnabout. One major newspaper with an article entitled "Abortion Leader Recants" tells of doctors losing their nerve while operating—of doctors plagued with nightmares and drinking problems.

Dr. Nathanson has recently released a book entitled *Aborting America*. Dr. Nathanson includes in his book an article he submitted and that was published in the *New England Journal of Medicine* in their November 28, 1974, issue. I here quote from that article, entitled "Deeper into Abortion."

"In early 1969 I and a group of equally concerned and indignant citizens who had been outspoken on the subject of legalized abortion organized a political action unit known as NARAL, then standing for National Association for Repeal of

Abortion Laws, now known as the National Abortion Rights Action League. We were outspokenly militant on this matter and enlisted the women's movement and the Protestant clergy into our ranks. We used every device available to political-action groups such as pamphleteering, public demonstrations, exploitation of the media, and lobbying in the appropriate legislative chambers. In late 1969 we mounted a demonstration outside one of the major university hospitals in New York City that had refused to perform even therapeutic abortions. My wife was on that picket line, and my three-year-old son proudly carried a placard urging legalized abortion for all. Largely as a result of the efforts of this and a few similar groups, the monumental New York state abortion statute of 1970 was passed and signed into law by Governor Nelson Rockefeller. Our next goal was to assure ourselves that low-cost, safe, and humane abortions were available to all, and to that end we established the center for reproductive and sexual health, which was the first—and largest—abortion clinic in the Western world.

"Some time ago—after a tenure of a year and a half—I resigned as director of the Center for Reproductive and Sexual Health. The center had performed sixty thousand abortions with no maternal deaths—an outstanding record of which we were proud, we are proud. However, I am deeply troubled by my own increasing certainty that I had in fact presided over sixty thousand deaths.

"There is no longer serious doubt in my mind that human life exists within the womb from the very onset of pregnancy, despite the fact that the nature of the intrauterine life has been the subject of considerable dispute in the past. Electrocardiographic evidence of heart function has been established in embryos as early as six weeks. Electroencephalographic recordings of human brain activity have been noted in embryos at eight weeks. Our capacity to measure signs is daily becoming more sophisticated, and as time goes by, we will doubtless be able to isolate life's signs at earlier and earlier stages in fetal development.

"We must courageously face the fact—finally—that human

life of a special order is being taken. And since the vast majority of pregnancies are carried successfully to term, abortion must be seen as the interruption of a process that would otherwise have produced a citizen of the world. Denial of this reality is the crassest kind of moral evasiveness." (pp. 164–65)

As a secular physician, Dr. Nathanson agrees that "abortion undermines the integrity of the family, which was already reeling from other assaults. The Supreme Court reinforced this with its 1976 follow-up ruling, *Planned Parenthood* v. *Danforth*, in which it threw out statutes in Missouri requiring a husband's consent for abortion, or requiring consent of the parents of an unwed mother under age eighteen. Then in *Bellotti* v. *Baird* (1979), the Court threw out the Massachusetts law that required parental consultation or notification, allowing a judge to grant permission. I resent these rulings. The medical profession officially opposed such a policy when abortion was first liberalized." Dr. Nathanson also states, "The state, through the decree of the Supreme Court, has become a willing party to the dissolution of the family on the consent question. On abortion, it has taken an adversary position on the formation of new families. And it takes an adversary position against the family as the stabilizing unit within society. Pregnancy and childbirth are cohesive in their effect on the family, while sex, apart from the family and childbearing, is never socially cohesive; on the contrary, it is a chaotic force." (pp. 256–57)

In a final chapter of his book, Dr. Nathanson concludes, "Having come this long way, through the abortion crusade of the late sixties and my own reconsideration of the late seventies, I am compelled to report that the revolution we undertook was a seductive and ultimately poisonous dream. It all appeared so certain at the time. Now, in the light of the best data from my profession, and weighing the philosophical choices left us by those data, that old certainty—as with many other of our cherished certainties—has vanished forever. In its place a new conviction has arisen, that human life is a continuum that can only be broken for the most serious of reasons." (p. 250)

If we as a nation become completely seared in our conscience and hardened in our attitude toward the life of unborn babies, what will be next? What about infanticide? How long will it be before we decide that a little baby that may be retarded should be done away with rather than allowed to live for the good of that child? No one person or state has the right to decide whether another human being should be allowed to live. What about euthanasia? Some old people become burdens and are placed in nursing homes and forgotten. A great deal of money is needed to "maintain" this care. How long will it be before America decides that it is more merciful to do away with old people than to let them live.

Francis A. Schaeffer, along with Dr. C. Everett Koop, sixty-two-year-old surgeon-in-chief of the Children's Hospital in Philadelphia, has recently released a movie and book entitled *Whatever Happened to the Human Race?* These men asked this question: "Once the uniqueness of people as created by God is removed and mankind is viewed as only one of the gene patterns which came forth on earth by chance—there is no reason not to treat people as things to be experimented on and to make over the whole of humanity according to the decisions of a relatively few individuals. If people are not unique, as made in the image of God, the barrier is gone. . . . Since life is being destroyed before birth, why not tamper with it on the other end?

"Will a society which has assumed the right to kill infants in the womb—because they are unwanted, imperfect, or merely inconvenient—have difficulty in assuming the right to kill other human beings, especially older adults who are judged unwanted, deemed imperfect physically or mentally, or considered a possible social nuisance?" (p. 89)

On February 10, 1980, Dr. Mildred F. Jefferson was a guest on the "Old-Time Gospel Hour" television broadcast. Dr. Jefferson is a surgeon on the staff of Boston University Medical Center. She is a remarkable woman who serves in key roles on many medical boards and committees. She is a diplomate of the American Board of Surgery and has received numerous honors and awards.

Dr. Jefferson made these comments regarding abortion: "Many people try to hide behind the confusion of not knowing what happens before a baby is born. But we do not have to be confused. We in medicine and science have a different name for every stage of the development of the baby, but it does not matter at all whether you know those names or not. When a young woman has not had much opportunity to go to school and she becomes pregnant no one has to tell her that she is going to have a baby.

"I became a doctor in the tradition that is represented in the Bible of looking upon medicine as a high calling. I will not stand aside and have this great profession of mine, of the doctor, give up the designation of healer to become that of the social executioner. The Supreme Court Justices only had to hand down an order. Social workers only have to make arrangements, but it has been given to my profession to destroy the life of the innocent and the helpless.

"Today it is the unborn child; tomorrow it is likely to be the elderly or those who are incurably ill. Who knows but that a little later it may be anyone who has political or moral views that do not fit into the distorted new order. To that question, 'Am I my brother's keeper?' I answer 'Yes.' It is everyone's responsibility to safeguard and preserve life. A child is a member of the human family and deserves care and concern.

"We are in a great war for the hearts and minds of our people, for the moral future of our country, and for the integrity of a nation. It is a war that we must win. When we win, that victory will not be for ourselves but for God, for America, and for all mankind."

Once abortion is legalized it follows that this leads to genetic manipulation. A scientist who looks through a microscope says in essence, "Well, I'll take this reproductive cell because it looks a little better and a little stronger, and I'll eliminate these others." Once genetic manipulation is accepted this eventually leads to the acceptance of elimination. Why not eliminate people who are not quite up to par, who have physical defects, who are elderly and no longer useful, who are critically ill? We find that corruption at the bureaucratic level is not alleviating potential problems.

At the federal level, those in charge at HEW (or, as it is now known, the Department of Human Resources and the Department of Education) have an enormous amount of leeway in how they can change our lives. The whole area of test-tube babies is now being debated in Congress. The decisions on that are being made in the bureaucracy by the National Institutes of Health. The will of the people has no way of being heard except as letters are written to the National Institutes of Health. There have already been experiments of crossing human and frog reproductive material in one university in this country. Corporations now have patents on new life forms they are planning to create once they can get the test-tube-baby phenomenon legalized. But it is not even Congress, where we as citizens could have some impact, that is making the decision. It is the bureaucracy; it is the National Institutes of Health.

Dr. Carolyn Gerster is a physician in active practice with her husband, specializing in internal medicine and cardiopulmonary diseases. She has her medical degree from the University of Oregon Medical School in Portland. She spent two years as a medical officer in the United States Army, at which time she was stationed in France and Germany. Dr. Gerster was the co-founder and first president of the Arizona Right to Life Committee and is now the national president of the National Right to Life Committee, Inc. She is the mother of five sons and a communicant of the Episcopal Church. At an Eagle Forum meeting on March 23, 1979, Dr. Gerster spoke on medical experiments being made on human beings. Following are her comments:

"I was asked to become a member of the American College of Physicians many years ago. It's an honorary society of internal medicine. I was very proud right up until the day that the society gave the James D. Bruce Award for Medical Research to Dr. Saul Krugman for the following experiment. Dr. Krugman had taken living hepatitis virus MS2 and injected this living virus into 25 retarded children in Willowbrook Home for Retarded in upstate New York. This was defended on the basis that conditions were so bad at Willowbrook that the children would probably get hepatitis anyway. This is so typical of the anti-life mentality. The obvious human solution was to clean up the conditions at Willowbrook not to inject retarded children with living hepatitis virus. . . .

"In June 1973, *Medical World News* carried a story on an experiment that had been reported by Dr. Peter Adams, an assistant professor at Case Western Reserve in Cleveland. Dr. Adams, in conjunction with physicians from Finland, had completed an experiment in which 12 babies born alive by hysterotomy abortion up to 20 weeks were decapitated. Their heads were cut off and a tube was placed in the main artery feeding the brain and put on a heart/lung machine. These 12 little heads were kept alive much like the Russians kept the decapitated dogs' heads alive in the 1950s. The purpose of the experiment was to collect data on carbohydrate metabolism in the brain. This was financed by NIH (National Institutes of Health)—your tax dollars at work; you paid for that experiment.

"The most dangerous word in the Court's decision was the word 'meaningful.' They could not say that the unborn was not a living human being, that would have been scientific nonsense. 'Life begins at conception' is not a Catholic dogma. It's not a religious dogma. The fact that life begins at conception is found on page 55 of *Arey's Developmental Anatomy* and is in every embryology text used in every medical school. It is a biological fact and no more repealable than the law of gravity. What the Court was saying in essence was 'Is this life meaningful?' Is this a 'person' in the whole sense of the word? When you start categorizing and making a value judgment of human life, you're in trouble. 'Non-personhood' can easily be extended to other dependent individuals."

It is a known historical fact that the German Medical Society used abortion to eliminate babies who might have genetic defects. Expectant couples even had to report for a required genetic study. If genetic difficulties, such as diabetes, epilepsy, mongolism, insanity, etc., were found, the unborn was killed. Hitler killed 275 Germans in this way. After Hitler came to power, he announced that Jews had genetic defects. The story is history from there. It began with abortion and ended with one man deciding who should be eliminated.

Recently I read about a family who feels much differently than the average person about disabled children. In *Family Weekly* of November 18, 1979, in an article entitled "Blessed Are the Givers: The DeBolts and Their Adopted Family," a moving story tells about Bob and Dorothy DeBolt, who have twenty children, fourteen of whom are adopted. Let me tell you about some of their adopted children. One is a girl named Karen, who is the first congenital quadruple amputee to be adopted in the United States. Tich and Anh are two Vietnamese boys whose spinal cords had been severed by artillery fire. Sunee is a Korean Caucasian girl with shiny black hair and brown almond-shaped eyes who is paralyzed from the waist down by polio. Wendy, a Korean girl, was adopted when she was blind and battered. Phong, a Vietnamese child, saw his mother and father killed in a bombing raid. J.R. is a blind paraplegic. Twe and Ly are two Vietnamese girls who survived a terrible plane crash during Operation Babylift. Many of the DeBolt adopted children are blind, crippled, or both. "A co-operative spirit is everywhere apparent in the DeBolt household," says the article. "The children, normal and 'special' alike, all have chores. After breakfast they scrape their own plates and put them in the dishwasher. But with all the rules, regulations and demands, there is one word that permeates all household activity—and that's 'love.'" The DeBolts see the effect of caring for their special children as nothing but a positive influence on their own children. "They are embarrassed to make mountains out of molehills when they see their siblings make molehills out of mountains," Mrs. DeBolt explained to a visitor. The DeBolts have started Aid to Adoption of Special Kids (AASK). This is a nonprofit organization in Oakland, California, whose primary function is to recruit parents willing to adopt children with special needs. AASK publicizes the existence of Crippled Children's Services, a national organization that will pay for all medical care related to an adopted child's handicap. Dorothy

DeBolt is fond of saying, "There is nothing quite like seeing a child get another chance."

But in America today we find millions who are not even getting the first chance. How tragic it is that our own government is spending millions of taxpayer dollars each year to fund abortions. Statistics in a *Phi Delta Kappan* September 1979 issue indicated that according to the National Center for Health Statistics teen-age pregnancies, which are the primary causes of school dropouts among girls, are increasing steadily. If present rates continue, more than one third of today's 14-year-old girls will be pregnant at least once by the time they are 20, and one fifth by the time they are 18. The trend is costing federal, state, and local governments as much as $8.3 billion a year in welfare and medical expenses, the Stanford Research Institute reports.

It has always been a tradition that graduates of American medical schools, at the time of their commencement, have taken the Hippocratic Oath. In their book *Whatever Happened to the Human Race?* Schaeffer and Koop point out, "The Declaration of Geneva (adopted in September 1948 by the General Assembly of the World Medical Organization and modeled closely on the Hippocratic Oath) became used as the graduation oath by more and more medical schools. It includes: 'I will maintain the utmost respect for human life from the time of conception.' This concept of the preservation of human life has been the basis of the medical profession and society in general. It is significant that when the University of Pittsburgh changed from the Hippocratic Oath to the Declaration of Geneva in 1971, the students deleted 'from the time of conception' from the clause beginning, 'I will maintain the utmost respect for human life.' " (p. 17) It is time that medical students as well as every other person in our United States put those words "from the time of conception" back into their thinking. It is time that men and women put God at the center of all things rather than humanism, which puts man at the center of all things. We must make a decision. We can be a nation mightily blessed by God, or we can be a nation characterized by words such as those engraved on a tombstone pictured in Schaeffer and Koop's book, *Whatever Happened to the Human Race?* which reads, "To those who were robbed of life, the unborn, the weak, the sick, the old, during the dark ages of madness, selfishness, lust, and greed for which the last decades of the twentieth century are remembered." (p. 119)

Legalists, legislators, and members of the judiciary must begin to display some moral conscience to protect the rights of those who do not have the ability to defend themselves. I admire the courage the Catholics have shown down through the centuries in standing against abortion. There have been times when they have had to stand alone.

Let us as parents teach our children the seriousness of sin, and let us everywhere become prolife in everything we do. Let us talk life, and talk anti-abortion. Let us get involved in organizations that are promoting prolife. At present there is a human-life amendment being proposed to the Constitution. The amendment says: "Section 1. With respect to the right to life, the word 'person' as used in this article and in the fifth and fourteenth articles of amendment to the Constitution of the United States applies to all human beings irrespective of age, health, function, or condition of dependency, including their unborn offspring at every stage of their biological development. Section 2. No unborn person shall be deprived of life by any persons, provided, however, that nothing in this article shall prohibit a law permitting only those medical procedures required to prevent one death, the death of the mother. Section 3. The Congress and the several states shall have power to enforce this article by appropriate legislation."

If we expect God to honor and bless our nation, we must take a stand against abortion. I do want to say to those millions of mothers who have had abortions that God is a God of forgiveness. No one has to live under a terrible weight of guilt that even secular psychiatrists and psychoanalysts say women are experiencing after an abortion. The blood of Jesus Christ, God's Son, cleanses us from sin. I am not trying to put a heavy weight of guilt on the doctors, nurses, and the hospitals that have performed abortions. But I am saying, let us stop it, and stop it now. We as a nation must take a Bible position on morality and begin to teach it everywhere, beginning in our homes, in our schoolrooms, in our communities, and in our states. We must teach children from kindergarten on up how precious life is and how important it is to preserve life.

HOMOSEXUALITY

Not too many years ago the word "homosexual" was a word that represented the zenith of human indecency. Without exception it was a word that was spoken with contempt. This is no longer true. In fact, there is a movement for legislation that would deem homosexuals as "normal." Homosexuality is now presented as an alternate life style. Hundreds of thousands of men and women in America flagrantly boast their sin and march in public view. They are an indictment against America and are contributing to her downfall.

History proves that homosexuality reaches a pandemic level in societies in crisis or in a state of collapse. The sin of homosexuality is so grievous, so abominable in the sight of God, that He destroyed the cities of Sodom and Gomorrah because of this terrible sin. The Old Testament law stated, "Thou shalt not lie with mankind, as with womankind: it is abomination" (Lv. 18:22); and "if a man also lie with mankind, as he lieth with a woman, both of them have committed an abomination: They shall surely be put to death." (Lv. 20:13) We are no longer under that law because of Christ's sacrificial death on the cross. However, God still abhors the sin of homosexuality, and it will not go unpunished. New Testament references to homosexuality include Romans 1:26–28, which says: "For this cause God gave them up unto vile affections; for even their women did change the natural use into that which is against nature:

And likewise also the men, leaving the natural use of the women, burned in their lust one toward another; men with men working that which is unseemly, and receiving in themselves that recompense of their error which was meet. And even as they did not like to retain God in their knowledge, God gave them over to a reprobate mind, to do those things that are not convenient." These people knowingly rejected God's revealed truth. Thus God "gave them up to uncleanness through the lust of their own hearts, to dishonor their own bodies between themselves." (Rm. 1:24) When it speaks of women changing the natural use into that which is against nature, it is speaking of lesbians. And likewise the men here, homosexual men, leaving the natural use of the women burned in their lust one toward another, God calls it unseemly. It is hard to imagine the things that men do with men and women do with women; God calls it unseemly. Because these men and women did not like to retain God in their knowledge, God gave them over to a reprobate mind to do those things that are not convenient. Romans 1:30 tells what happens to them "who knowing the judgment of God that they which commit such things are worthy of death not only do the same but have pleasure in them that do them."

In 1 Corinthians 6:9, 10 in the Bible we are told that neither the "effeminate, nor abusers of themselves with mankind . . . shall inherit the kingdom of God." Those who "defile themselves with mankind" are again mentioned in 1 Timothy 1:9, 10. Romans 1 clearly states, "For the wrath of God is revealed from heaven against all ungodliness and unrighteousness of men who hold the truth in unrighteousness."

Jesus Christ loves every man and woman, including homosexuals and lesbians. Only He has the power to forgive and cleanse people guilty of this terrible sin. But this does not mean that we should accept their perversion as something normal. A person is not born with preference to the same sex, but he is introduced to the homosexual experience and cultivates a homosexual urge. It is innocent children and young people who are victimized and who become addicts to sexual perversion.

I have read letters from ex-lesbians and ex-homosexuals who

admit that sometime in their life they had a bad experience with either a male or female that triggered their entrance into a homosexual or lesbian relationship.

Homosexuals have come out of the closet. Once homosexuality was considered a hideous thing that no one talked about, but now in San Francisco the citizens jokingly call their city Sodom and Gomorrah. Homosexuality is reprobate and an abomination—a sin against the human body and against nature. In God's divine plan He "created man in his own image, in the image of man created he him; male and female created he them. And God blessed them, and God said unto them, 'Be fruitful and multiply and replenish the earth.'" (Gn. 1:27, 28) Heterosexuality was created by God and is endorsed by God.

We would not be having the present moral crisis regarding the homosexual movement if men and women accepted their proper roles as designated by God. God's plan is for men to be manly and spiritual in all areas of Christian leadership. God's Word says, "Watch ye, stand fast in the faith, quit you like men, be strong." (1 Co. 16:13) In the Christian home the father is responsible to exercise spiritual control and to be the head over his wife and children; "for the husband is the head of the wife, even as Christ is the head of the church." (Ep. 5:23) Women are to be feminine and manifest the "ornament of a meek and quiet spirit, which is in the sight of God a great price." (1 Pt. 3:4) In the Christian home the woman is to be submissive; "wives, submit yourselves unto your own husbands, as unto the Lord." (Ep. 5:22) Homosexuality is Satan's diabolical attack upon the family, God's order in Creation.

Homosexuals are no longer a quiet minority, but a very vocal minority who are demanding to be accepted as a legitimate minority.

Homosexuality is a symptom of a sin-sick society. Militant homosexuals march under a banner of "civil rights" or "human rights." The homosexual issue has nothing to do with the issue of equal rights for differing groups. Our Constitution holds that all men are created equal, but laws were made to deal with unequal behavior. If homosexuality is deemed normal, how long will it be before rape, adultery, alcoholism, drug addiction, and incest are labeled as normal? The root sin of homosexuality is actually rebellion against God. The basis of all sin is a rejection of God. When describing homosexuals in Romans 1:21 it says, "when they knew God, they glorified him not as God." The result of men's and women's rejection of God is corrupt behavior that not only destroys individual lives but also destroys national life.

As male leadership in the family falters and as female leadership takes over out of desperation, young people will gain their sense of security from their mother rather than from their father. In many homes the father is either absent or is too busy to care for his family; many times the father is vicious and cruel when he is there, and there is no loving example of any kind to follow. The homosexual crisis is really spawned by the family crisis that is now going on. Male leadership is vital to stability in the family. Dr. Voth, senior psychiatrist and psychoanalyst at the Menninger Foundation in Topeka, Kansas, says, "One of the most fundamental functions of parenting is to evoke, develop, and reinforce gender identity and then proceed to shepherd the developing child in such a way as to bring his psychological side into harmony with his biological side, and thereby develop a solid sense of maleness or femaleness. The quality of maleness or femaleness is intimately woven into the over-all fabric of personality. Human beings are not biologically bisexual, despite what the gay liberationists would have us believe. The human spirit is greatly impaired when childhood development does not lead to fully developed masculinity or femininity. Fully masculine men and feminine women are by definition mature, and that term implies the ability to live out one's abilities. These include the capacity to mate and live in harmony with a member of the opposite sex and to carry out the responsibilities of parenthood. Mature people are competent and masterful; not only can they make families but they can take hold of life generally and advance it, and in particular they can replace themselves with healthy children who become healthy men and women. The fate of mankind depends on the durability of the heterosexual relationship." (Eagle Forum)

Homosexuals cannot reproduce themselves, so they must recruit. One has only to read an American newspaper to find sordid instances of homosexual exploitation of young boys and girls. Why must they prey upon our young?

There is at this moment in Congress a gay-rights bill, H.R./ 2074, which, if passed, would establish homosexuals in America as a bona fide minority like women, blacks, Hispanics, etc. Every employer, station owner, pastor, and private-school administrator would be forced to employ a minority of homosexuals commensurate with the population in their area. At this moment they have fifty-one cosponsors of the bill in the House of Representatives.

The feminist movement is unisexual. Feminists desire to eliminate God-given differences that exist between the sexes; that is why they are prohomosexual and lesbian. In fact, it is shocking how many feminists are lesbians.

In the December 2, 1979, New York *Times*, there is an article entitled, "Lesbian Homes for Child Homosexuals." This article tells about the New Jersey Department of Human Services, which stated that it had in the past four years placed five to ten homosexual teen-agers with behavioral problems in foster homes headed by lesbians. The article said, "Ann Burns, an officer of the agency, said such placements were made only for children who considered themselves homosexuals and are considered such by social workers, and whose parents are unable and unwilling to care for them because of their homosexuality." (p. E6)

The October 12, 1979, Washington *Post* contains an article entitled, "50,000 Marchers Turn Out for Gay Rights Demonstration." It reports, "The turnout of an estimated 50,000 marchers here Sunday shows that gay rights are a 'matter of national concern,' says a congressman who wants to extend this Civil Rights Act to protect homosexuals.

" 'I think most Americans are ready for it,' Republican Ted

Weiss, New York, said Sunday before addressing the marchers, including many lesbians and gay men, massed on the mall at the foot of the Washington Monument.

"Weiss' bill has spurred Rep. Larry McDonald, D-Ga., to introduce a resolution that would put Congress on record as opposing any special legal status for homosexuals. It has not been acted on."

Arley Scott, vice president of the National Organization of Women (NOW), told the crowd of gay demonstrators in Washington, D.C.: "America, you see us [gays] in your offices, schools, in your government, in Congress, and I dare say in the White House. We are twenty million strong in this nation. We are moving from gay pride to gay politics." During that demonstration, many of us Christians were joined in fervent prayer for our land and for these people.

I believe that like other persons who have problems and need a change of life style, homosexuals require love and help. We cannot allow homosexuality to be presented to our nation as an alternative life style. It will not only have a corrupting influence upon our next generation, but it will also bring down the wrath of God upon America. I love homosexuals as souls for whom Christ died; I love homosexuals, but I must hate their sin. Christ would say "No" to the homosexual life style, but He would say "Yes" to them as persons to be offered love and deliverance. God's love cannot be separated from His holiness. We have a staff of Christian psychologists at our ministry who deal with homosexuality and other moral problems.

I am against the flaunting of homosexual life style before impressionable children. This is detrimental to the basic tenet of Christian society, the home. The home must be protected, and America must turn around before she suffers the wrath of God.

TELEVISION

There can be no doubt that television is the most powerful medium in the world today. Television is a molder of attitudes, of behavior, and of taste. It can be a powerful medium for good or for bad. Any medium that is captivating, that is psychologically powerful in the sense that it can capture the mind, the attention, and the imagination of people can be used for a great deal of harm. Television is an ethical issue, and it is time that moral Americans think through what television is really saying to the family.

The average day on television begins with the morning news, which sets the pace for what we think about the world. Almost all of our priorities are determined for us by where and upon what the news is focused. After the morning news there are the light variety programs. Usually a host or hostess is interviewing various guests. People sing or talk about different issues of life. Inevitably someone tells a dirty joke. The guest says something controversial and the host, who is looked on as either a father image or a mother image in American society, laughs at the dirty joke, and usually makes a comment with sexual overtones. The impression the viewer often receives is that everybody thinks dirty. Sometimes even the good people on television occasionally laugh at a dirty joke or a suggestive remark. Next come the talk shows. Every imaginable kind of situation is discussed on a talk show, good things as well as eccentric things.

You will find lesbians discussing how wonderful it is to live together and to rear their own kind of a family. You will find homosexuals talking about a "beautiful" homosexual marriage relationship. You will notice, however, that rarely has a talk-show guest been living in that kind of a sinful relationship for years. Several years ago I watched a talk show featuring two women who were living together in a homosexual relationship. They were presenting how wonderful that relationship was. I later found out that both those women had committed suicide. But I did not find this out through television. No one ever came back on that talk show and spoke about these women; it was announced in the papers in an obscure article. No one on the talk show told the result of what had happened in these women's lives.

Game shows fill a large portion of daily programming. There is much excitement and, over-all, materialism is stressed and glorified. The game shows are obviously aimed at females, who predominate among daytime-television viewers. The housewife finds herself wishing that she could have a lot of the things people on the game shows are getting with little effort and no work. The game shows are followed by the soap operas, which are the epitome of immorality. The attractive men and women in soap operas bounce from one love affair to another, from one marriage to another—and the television show is permeated with men and women portrayed as emotionally troubled and upset and who cannot figure out why their lives are in such turmoil. Statistics tell us that twenty million American housewives regularly watch soap operas. The programs' influence on the moral nature, the moral viewpoint of that housewife is tremendous. Recently additional studies have shown that a large number of men are beginning to watch soap operas. In a recent secular book entitled *Remote Control*, authors Frank Mankiewicz and Joel Swerdlow have stated that without a doubt the soap opera (not X-rated movies, not prime-time television) has been the greatest single influence shaping morals in the American home. I have counseled many women involved in adultery who, when asked what they do in the afternoon, always answer the same:

"Oh I watch television." When asked what they watch, the answer is always the same: "the soap operas."

In the afternoon, television features reruns. Additional shows are followed by the evening news. And, of course, the news is very negative. It is, sadly, a realistic commentary on what is happening in our society today. The news is followed by evening prime-time television. Evening programs take on many forms. Situation comedies cause people to laugh at all kinds of situations, including immoral ones. When an illicit scene cannot quite be depicted because it might upset a censor, situation comedies can present it as a joke. Situation comedies cause people to laugh at adultery, at homosexuality, and at drunkenness. Some are especially designed to make fun of biblical moral issues. Anita Bryant has been the blunt end of almost every imaginable kind of joke in situation comedies simply because she has stood on the side of the family and the home and on the side of morality. Many preachers are portrayed as either dummies or as right-wing extremists and troublemakers.

Dramatic television programs deal with "real life" situations. The family-oriented programs are often telling you to accept divorce as a natural alternative, and to accept controversial life styles. Rarely is there a presentation of a godly life style.

We hear much about child abuse today. But moral Americans fail to realize that one of the greatest and most dangerous forms of child abuse is to pour dirty, filthy words and pictures into their minds; these words and pictures eventually ruin them and wreck them for life. This is what television is doing to many of our children.

Epics portrayed on television are sagas that continue generation after generation. So often the sin of one generation continues into another. The grandfather is involved in sexual immorality and the son becomes involved in sexual immorality. Viewers get the impression that everyone is sinful and that immorality is acceptable. Subconsciously they think, "Why should I straighten out my life? Why should I try to be godly and live a decent life?"

Recently, the CBS Television Network broadcast one of the

most offensive programs ever aired. *Flesh and Blood,* a two-part, made-for-television movie, centered on the relationship between a young boxer and his alcoholic mother who begin an incestuous affair. Cable companies are showing first-run movies without any editing. Graphic sex and violence may be seen right in the average American's living room.

The television erosion of the home is a dangerous threat. Television has become the largest baby-sitting agency in the world —the adviser and counselor for many children. This is where children are learning their moral values. Studies show that every home in America averages 6½ hours of television viewing a day. In 1979, A. C. Nielsen Company ratings stated that the average American watches 26 hours, 18 minutes of television a week. Moral Americans are becoming concerned and trying to select the programs their children watch. But many times, off-color previews for another program or suggestive advertisements will be shown.

Networks appear to be committed to getting people to watch their programs by the enticement of sexual immorality. Moral Americans must begin to ask themselves questions: What is this program really saying to me? What is its message? What is its philosophy? What life style does it present? Is that life style based on Bible standards? Without realizing it, parents are allowing the minds of their children and young people to become saturated with values that advertisers and producers are displaying merely to make money.

We must not underestimate the power of advertising. Advertising does much more than sell products. Most ads are not realistic, and they distort images of the family, children, young people, and adults. Frequently replete with sexual images, ads appeal to a person's need for love and security, for meaningful relationships, and for the need to be accepted in society. The philosophy behind advertising is an entire study in itself. Most people do not realize the discreet selling tactics hidden in advertisements, nor do they realize how much money is involved in advertising products.

Many people say that they do not even listen to advertisements, but the average person by the time he reaches midlife has been bombarded with fifty million advertising messages. It has been found that preschoolers between the ages of two and five spend 84 per cent of their waking hours in front of the television set. They see more than a thousand commercials every week. Subconsciously, children learn how to attain popularity, success, and what is necessary to be "normal" and "popular." Many of the messages in advertisements are hidden, and even though people think they are not being affected by them, subliminally they are. It is those people who say they pay no attention to ads who play right into the hands of the advertisers.

Realistically, you will never see the alcohol beverage industry using an alcoholic to push its products. Nor will you see cancer victims promoting tobacco. Only the beautiful and the sensual are used to market these and a myriad of other products, from aftershave to automobiles. By appealing to our sexual appetites, advertisers are able to make millions of dollars. As consumers we must become aware of these tactics and remind ourselves that the purpose behind advertising is making money and not teaching morality.

One of the more suggestive ads currently being aired shows a young, attractive single woman inviting a young, handsome male to her apartment to share the evening and a particular bottle of liquor. In addition to promoting the alcohol, the ad implies the evening together includes sexual permissiveness. Children should not be exposed to ads that condone a permissive life style.

Lorence K. Grossman, president of Public Broadcasting Services (PBS), made the statement that PBS' slogan, "A World of Difference," means "more powerful programming." Mr. Grossman made the statement, "I trust our viewers to decide for themselves between right and wrong, good or bad." By "more powerful programming" Mr. Grossman means topics dealing with immorality, homosexuality, narcotics, family breakups, violence, and many other topics. Television projects the model of secular humanism, which has no absolutes and no standards. Man's own standard is to satisfy himself—to eat, drink, and be merry. Impressionable children believe what they see and hear. They pattern their lives by what they see on television. By the time they are young people, they are trying to emulate what they have viewed for years. Dr. Rose K. Goldsen, professor of Sociology at Cornell University, says, "TV is more than just a little fun and entertainment. It's a whole environment, and what it does bears an unpleasant resemblance to behavior modification—on a mass scale." Television is brainwashing children, young people, and adults to accept an amoral life style.

In the November 18, 1979, issue of *The Daily Advance* of Lynchburg, Virginia, Gene F. Jankowski, president of CBS Broadcasting, when asked, "Do you think TV should set some sort of moral tone?" replied, "I believe that it would be completely wrong for television to set a 'moral' tone. That's the role of the church, the school, and the family. Television is on the cutting edge of societal change, but it should neither lead nor lag too far behind that change. As a broadcaster, a citizen, and as a father, I would object to TV having that role." The January 6, 1980, issue of the Washington *Post* reports that 98 per cent of all the homes in this country contain at least one television set (more homes have TV sets than have indoor plumbing).

Much of the news reporting on television is not completely truthful. The most sensational facts and stories are selected to get the highest ratings. The criteria for news seem to lie with the dramatic and the entertaining. Many times, reporting bears only a minimal resemblance to reality. General Lewis W. Walt makes some keen observations of news reporting in his book *The Eleventh Hour*. When he was I Corps commander in Vietnam, he often asked television crews why they did not tell the story of the Marines' Civic Action Program. General Walt was speaking of the help the Marines had given the Vietnamese in building or rebuilding hundreds of schools, churches, roads, and other public facilities. The Vietnamese people had been helped in planting and harvesting rice, in setting up orphanages and medical clinics, and had been helped to regain their confidence and pride. General Walt saw this as an important, heartwarming, and human side of the war. But he states that when he asked television crews about this, the answers were always the same. Thousands of feet of film had been shot and dozens of stories had been written about the Civic Action Program, but editors back in the States concentrated on the horror and the combat. One CBS cameraman told General Walt that for every hundred minutes of film he took, less than five minutes of it ever made the TV screen, and it was always the most dramatic and bloody part, quite often taken out of context. General Walt illustrates one story: "In 1968, the North Vietnamese made a blunder. It became known as the Tet Offensive. They made a massive attempt to assault the principal cities of South Vietnam and they suffered staggering losses without achieving their objectives. After the battles were over, Walter Cronkite, the CBS anchorman, came to South Vietnam for an on-the-spot report. A Marine lieutenant colonel was provided to take him on a tour of Hue, which had been a scene of heavy fighting.

"At that time, the city was completely cleared. There was no fighting going on at all. I was stunned, therefore, when I saw Cronkite on television, standing in Hue, microphone in hand, while in the background were the sounds of machine-gun fire and explosions, which apparently had been dubbed in by sound effects men.

"The Tet Offensive, which was both a strategic blunder and a military disaster for the North Vietnamese, was reported to the American people as a defeat for our forces and those of South Vietnam.

"Peter Braestrup, formerly of the Washington *Post* and one of the most perceptive and honest newsmen who reported the war, did a study of the media coverage of the Tet Offensive and came to the same conclusion. He has been rewarded for his efforts with ridicule.

"Dr. Ernest Lefever, a research fellow at the Brookings Institution, did an analysis of CBS Television's news in 1972 and 1973. The results of his study were published under the title *TV and National Defense* by the Institute for American Strategy.

"At one point in his book, Dr. Lefever writes: 'CBS Evening

News, as demonstrated in Chapter Five, was highly critical of the U.S. position on Vietnam . . . CBS newsmen advocated a speedy withdrawal with little regard for what happened to South Vietnam and deplored the U.S. bombings of military targets in the North. CBS Evening News promoted this perspective by direct expression of opinion from its own newsmen, by quoting others, and by the selection of news which was heavily critical of the Saigon government, while tending to apologize for or even to glamorize the Hanoi regime. There was a constant barrage of criticism against the U.S. military, not only in Vietnam, but across the board.'

"In another part of the book, Dr. Lefever analyzes CBS coverage of U.S. military affairs in 1972 and 1973, classifying for each year a number of different stories. In 1972, for example, CBS devoted twenty-three minutes and ten seconds of air time to racial discrimination and riots in the military; one minute to the U.S.-U.S.S.R. military balance. In 1973, CBS devoted thirty-three minutes of air time to corruption and misconduct in the military and zero time to the U.S.-U.S.S.R. military balance." (pp. 71, 72)

With reporting that is this inaccurate, the power of television must be noted. A book that becomes a best seller after it is published in paperback may sell two million to three million copies. If a movie is really a hit, it may be seen by some six million people. The largest daily newspaper in America goes to two million homes. But a television program that does not reach thirty million homes is a failure. Because of its broad coverage, therefore, people accept this medium as accurate. Many people are brainwashed by what they see on television. Many others emulate what they see.

A January 1976 UPI article reported that after a burglary the Chicago police found that a man had been lying in a pool of blood for ten hours. A neighbor had discovered him. He had been lying six or eight feet away from his three children aged nine, eleven, and twelve who had been watching television the whole time and had never noticed that anything was amiss. That sounds ridiculous, but it's the kind of obsession and total waste of time and absolute infusion of vulgarity, profanity, and violence that is entering the hearts and minds of boys and girls. It is hard to forget the report that came from San Diego County, California, of the nineteen-year-old boy who chopped his parents and his sister to death with an ax and then crippled his brother. The boy was a high-school honor student. He was an athlete who modeled the murder (by his own comment) after a made-for-television movie about Lizzie Borden, who allegedly murdered her parents with an ax in 1892. According to the book *Remote Control*, several teen-age murders have been inspired by violence on television. In 1973, a seventeen-year-old admitted memorizing every detail of a murder movie and reenacting the crime, which was a murder-rape.

I am concerned about excessive violence, but I am far more concerned about the invasion of illicit sex into prime time. The powerful influence of America's greatest medium is today almost totally shaping public opinion regarding the family, marriage, divorce, homosexuality, behavior, all moral issues, and liberal attitudes. Violence, vulgarity, and sex have become the major themes on television today. During the next few years, if the cycle continues and the trend is maintained, television will be nothing but one X-rated program after another. In fact, it is very difficult to find a program at night that you and your family can sit down and watch all the way through. I am not advocating doing away with the television set. I believe that television, radio, and the printed page are things we must not destroy but that we must redirect.

If we do not control television it will control us. The sinful and immoral condition of our society is the source of the despicable state of television. I believe that an indifferent moral majority in America is the cause. If moral Americans took their stand and said to the advertisers, "We will stop buying your products until you start making television fit for us to watch," something would happen. Pressure on the advertisers and on the networks to clean up television for decent family viewing will change the programming.

It is only pressure groups that can make networks and producers more sensitive to the needs of viewers. Consumer pressure was exemplified when more than a year ago Sears withdrew ads from two television programs. The Chicago AP carried the news: "Sears, Roebuck and Company said Friday it has withdrawn its advertising from the TV shows 'Charlie's Angels' and 'Three's Company' because the programs had 'episode caution' —too much sex.

"Sears Chairman Edward R. Telling said Sears 'has no desire or intent to become involved in any form of censorship . . . [but] in recent weeks we have become increasingly concerned by news reports that prime-time television for next fall will risk offending a large segment of the public.'"

A November 1979 staff report of the Federal Communications Commission concluded that the three major commercial television networks are so secure and so dominant that the FCC appears powerless to require them to respond to viewers' interest. This is true even though the FCC has the authority to regulate commercial network television. The staff report concluded that the grip of the networks is such that no viable fourth network could successfully compete with the existing three. The three major commercial television networks now have tied up the needed local stations as affiliates. The report stated, "So long as one accepts the existence of three, and only three, networks operating at any given time, there will be severe limitations on the use of the regulatory process to alter the programs which viewers can watch."

I believe in the media. I believe that television, radio, and the printed page are the principal ways in which we are going to spread the Gospel of Jesus Christ to the world. The Apostle Paul said, "I am not ashamed of the gospel of Christ: for it is the power of God unto salvation to every one that believeth." (Rm. 1:16) The Gospel is the death, the burial, and the resurrection of Jesus Christ in behalf of every lost sinner in every age. Television is a form of a media that can be used very positively.

PORNOGRAPHY

Charles Keating, Jr., founder of Citizens for Decency through Law, is an American lawyer, businessman, and chairman of the Board of American Continental Corporation. He is a good husband and father to six children. Several years ago Mr. Keating realized the terrible corruption that was resulting in our country from pornography. He has taken a firm stand against it at great personal risk to himself and his family—because of his stand, harm was brought to one of his children. On the television broadcast of the "Old-Time Gospel Hour," Mr. Keating said, "Pornography is evident everywhere. At Forty-fourth and Madison in New York City, what is frequently called the Minnesota Strip, you see young thirteen- and fourteen-year-old girls with blond hair and blue eyes degraded and enslaved in lives of prostitution as a result of pornography. At an SAE fraternity house on a Cincinnati campus on a bright, sunny day at noon my daughter was abducted at gunpoint. She was taken to a nearby woods and raped violently. This was indeed one of the greatest tragedies our family has ever suffered. But we agreed and my daughter courageously confirmed that even this could not make us back down on our stand against pornography.

"Venereal disease, gonorrhea, and syphilis rage in epidemic proportion beyond control in the United States in spite of all of our miracle drugs. But even worse than these evident signs of moral decay, is the conquest of the minds, the hearts, and the souls of our children and our young people by the pornographers. Pornography is the antipathy of the basic premise of America in regard to freedom. Pornography is enslavement. It is enslavement to lust and evil. . . . It is time we went into the courtrooms and prosecuted and stood before the Congress and the Senate of the United States and said, 'Gentlemen, the line must be drawn. We the people of this country will no longer stand for pornography.' "

The Bible states that as a man thinketh in his heart so is he. We read in the Gospels that that which comes into a man by way of his eyes and his ears is what defiles him. That which enters by the window of the eye and the window of the ear finds its lodging place in the hearts of men and women, in the intellect, and ultimately in the will. When a thought is sowed, an act is reaped. When an act is sowed time and again it will eventually reap a habit. When a habit is established, a character is built. Many men and women are being brainwashed and demoralized by pornography. What Americans once rejected they are now accepting. Some may call God a liar, but this does not change His character. Jesus Christ said, "Blessed are the pure in heart, for they shall see God." Those who laugh at a literal hell may someday experience it, for according to the Bible all adulterers, fornicators, homosexuals, and perverts who live and die without a new-birth experience will spend eternity there. (Rv. 21:8)

Perhaps Americans have not shown a strong opposition to pornography because they do not know the full extent of what it is and what it does to people. Webster's Dictionary defines pornography as "originally, a description of prostitues and their trade." The word came from *porne* (prostitute) and *graphein* (to write). Twenty-five years ago the word meant "writings, pictures, or any symbolic stimulus intended to arouse sexual desire." Now the word pornography goes on to include more than arousal of sexual drives. Pornography now includes in its meaning, "arousing sexual drives of deviations, perversions, and abnormal behavior."

There have always been filthy books because there have always been filthy minds. Most of these books dealt with illicit sex and erotic love outside Christian bonds. Traditionally, their publication and sale were banned in the United States. About 1955, *Playboy* magazine brought sex into American drugstores. This introduced a *"Playboy* philosophy." At first, their famous centerfold showed a nude woman, but not all her body was revealed. With competition from other pornographic magazines, women were displayed in more and more revealing positions. Today *Playboy* has approximately 100 competitors. The year 1969 was a watershed one because the courts then allowed what is known as classic pornographic books to be translated, published, and sold in America, and what a flood was released! The literature that was once underground began to surface. The *"Playboy* era" was translated into the "Eros Era" of the adult bookstore, with more revealing magazines, books, pictures, 8mm films, and other forms of pornography available. This literature includes some of the most filthy language imaginable. Not only does it take God's name in vain, but also every nasty idea possible is discussed. The "dirty-speech movement" of the sixties has become even more profane. Anything that symbolizes God or purity is debased. Stories of ministers or other religious persons are written to humiliate all that is sacred. In the quest for new sensations, every form of violence is depicted, from rape and murder to sexual sadism. Humans are shown engaging in sexual activity with animals. Eroticizing the display of sex in the human body in every form of natural and perverted relationship is shown. A $17 million pornofilm, *Caligula,* depicts the decline and fall of the Roman Empire. The first hard-core film to feature big-name stars such as Peter O'Toole and Malcolm McDowell, *Caligula* contains every violent and unnatural sex act imaginable.

Pornography displays a distorted view of women. Women are shown as a masculine-wish fulfillment, or many times women are depicted as being so lust driven that they will stop at nothing to satisfy themselves. Sex is shown as a physical relationship without love; there is no true love relationship to be found here.

Pornography destroys the privacy of sex. Parents must teach their children that sex is private and beautiful only in the marriage relationship. Dr. Rollo May, a leading contemporary self-theorist, expresses, "The more powerful need is not for sex per se, but for relationship, intimacy, acceptance, and affirmation." Many do not realize the extent of perversion displayed by pornography—people are shown tortured, devoured, and mutilated; women are tortured in the sex act with whips, chains, and racks; people are presented with abnormal sex organs.

Sexual permissiveness has resulted in venereal disease in epidemic proportions, the rise in divorce rates, adultery, the spread of massage parlors, and growing homosexuality. Lust is stimulated by pornography. The Bible says in James 1:14, 15: "But every man is tempted when he is drawn away of his own lust and enticed. Then when lust hath conceived, it bringeth forth sin; and sin, when it is finished, bringeth forth death."

Pornography is a cancer that is changing the character of our republic. It is the responsibility of decent people to wake up and halt its advancement. We must bathe this country in prayer so that in the years ahead we can not only clean up America but also provide an environment and an atmosphere in which our children and our grandchildren can grow up loving God and loving purity. For too long now, moral Americans have been brainwashed and polarized to a position where we are willing to accept what is abnormal as normal. In Philippians 4:8 we find the Apostle Paul saying, "Finally, brethren, whatsoever things are true, whatsoever things are honest, whatsoever things are just, whatsoever things are pure, whatsoever things are lovely, whatsoever things are of good report; if there be any virtue, and if there be any praise, think on these things."

America is a free country. We pride ourselves in freedom of speech and freedom of the press. But freedom ends where someone else's welfare begins. Freedom of the press ends where the welfare of the public and ultimately the welfare of our nation begin. Freedom of speech does not include yelling "Fire!" in a crowded building; it does not include perverting and sickening the moral appetites of men and women.

Liberty cannot be represented by sexual license. Communist theoreticians readily admit that one of the ways that Western societies can be weakened is through sexual laxity.

When the Nazis took Poland in 1939 they flooded the bookshelves with pornography. Their theory was that they would make individuals conscious of only their personal and sensual needs and thus render them more submissive to the oppression that was to come. The Nazis knew what moral decay would do to a people. We Americans are ripe for oppression. Many people brag that they do not attend R-rated movies, but they allow these same movies to be shown on their television sets two years after they are initially shown in the theaters. TV is the greatest vehicle being used to indoctrinate us slowly to accept a pornographic view of life. Pornography is more than a nudey magazine, it is a prevailing atmosphere of sexual license. Readily available, pornography is subconsciously telling our children that this is acceptable.

Our judicial system judges human sexuality by a man-determined code of sexual conduct, not by the Word of God. In 1973 it was decided, by a divided U. S. Supreme Court in the case Miller v. California, that communities must decide what constitutes obscenity. The Court would not even prescribe methods to guide a community in determining what the standards should be. In our nation's capital, a pornographer showed *The Seduction of Amy* at a theater just two blocks from the White House. Two days before that, the theater owner and his two associates had escaped prosecution after a federal jury of seven men and five women could not decide what was obscene. Allan Frank, an award-winning reporter for the Washington *Star*, observes that the experience of the Washington, D.C., jury is typical. He says that on six of twelve counts involving racy adult movies portraying graphic sex acts, the jury acquitted the defendants. On the remaining counts, the jury decided it could not agree on a standard for obscenity.

It is past time that action against pornography is taken. Why is it that when Gallup and Harris polls show that 79 to 80 per cent of Americans oppose pornography, no major strides are being taken to rid our country of this menace? Citizens are ignorant and apathetic. Pornography is not something that is nice to discuss. I was sickened by what I read in the book entitled *How to Stop the Porno Plague* by Neil Gallagher.

Mr. Gallagher points out that *Hustler* magazine has a circulation of 1.5 million. He says, "In the Bicentennial issue of *Hustler*, one finds (July 1976) a vagina wrapped in a small American flag (on the magazine's cover); a full-page color cartoon, 'Chester the Molester,' showing a man seducing a doll-clutching, pig-tailed girl; a centerfold showing caricatures of Jerry Ford, Henry Kissinger, and Nelson Rockefeller involved in sexual acts with an animated Statue of Liberty; and caricatures of George Washington, Paul Revere, and Ben Franklin involved in a variety of sex acts with prostitutes." (p. 13) Mr. Gallagher says, "I cannot tell you the other pictures in *Hustler*. . . . *Hustler* is sold alongside *Reader's Digest, Time,* and coloring books. Children see the covers."

Many of the descriptions in this book describing sections of pornographic magazines are so vile that I cannot even here mention them. The judgment of God is not far from a country that allows Jesus Christ to be depicted in the vilest of sexual scenes. Mr. Gallagher points out that a New York stage drama entitled *Let My People Come* headed for a nationwide tour shows the alleged sexual escapades of the children of Israel while wandering in the wilderness. Mr. Gallagher talks about the movie *Animal Farm,* which shows a feeble-minded woman having intercourse with a giant hog.

Child pornography (pornography that displays adults having sexual relationships with children) is escalating at a frightening rate in the United States of America. I read of one social club that has a slogan on its letterhead that read, "Sex before eight or it's too late." Members of that society swear that they have deflowered a girl before her eighth birthday. There are even such things as child seducers' manuals. There are such things as playing cards that picture naked, spread-eagled children. Children are a heritage of the Lord, and to review the vile and filthy acts committed against them by evil men is enough to prove that there is indeed a devil. Child pornography is indeed one of the vilest forms of child abuse.

The marketable age for sex objects has hit the playground level. A ten-year-old girl poses in a seductive nude ad campaign to promote her career. The sexuality of young girls is exploited commercially in such movies as *Pretty Baby* and *The Exorcist*.

Moral Americans must hold up a standard. Proliferation of pornography into our society is striking evidence of our decadence. The moral fiber of our nation is so deteriorated that we cannot possibly survive unless there is a complete and drastic turnabout soon: A permissive society that tolerates pornography has the same hedonistic attitude that destroyed ancient societies. Pornographers are idolaters. They idolize money and will do anything for materialistic gain. They are men who have reprobate minds and who need divine deliverance. The Bible states that when a man or a woman accepts Jesus Christ as personal Savior he becomes a new creation. When God saves a man or woman He not only forgives of sin but also He imparts a new nature. A saved person is a partaker of the divine nature. God has put His Holy Spirit within that person. God gives that person the ability to live the life he has received. If you are not a Christian and fear becoming a Christian because you think you could not live a good enough life, you must realize that you cannot live the Christian life by yourself. No one but Jesus Christ can help you. He will take up His residence in your body and live through you. I know He will because He did this for me. Only a spiritual revival will rid this nation of pornography and bring her back to a position where God can once again bless her and make her a nation of purity and holiness.

EDUCATION

In his inaugural address on March 4, 1797, John Adams, our second President, stated that one means of preserving our Constitution was to "patronize every rational effort to encourage schools, colleges, universities, academies, and every institution for propagating knowledge, virtue, and religion among all classes of the people." He spoke of the high destiny of this country and of his own duties toward it, having been "found on a knowledge of the moral principles and intellectual improvements of the people deeply engraved on my mind in early life." When John Adams graduated from Harvard, its handbook for "rules and precepts" stated: "Let every student be plainly instructed and earnestly pressed to consider well the main end of his life and studies is to know God, and Jesus Christ, which is eternal life. And therefore to lay Christ in the bottom as the only foundation of all sound knowledge and learning."

Our Founding Fathers knew the importance of education. They considered it a privilege of free men to be educated and to perpetuate their freedom by teaching the religious principles upon which our republic was built. When John Adams was President he said, "So great is my veneration for the Bible that the earlier my children begin to read it, the more confident will be my hope that they will prove useful citizens of their country and respectable members of society."

D. Bruce Lockerbie says in his recently published book *Who*

Educates Your Child?: "Education is a framework like the forms that hold molten lead or liquid concrete, helping to mold character. Education is a mirror to reflect the development of that character. In other words, education is the instrument for carrying out society's philosophical goals." (p. 46)

In the past, parents did not have to worry about the education of their children because the schools—the public schools—were without question the best in the history of the world. I remember when I attended Mountain View Elementary School in Lynchburg, Virginia. I enrolled there in 1940 and spent six years there. Every week we attended chapel. Someone would read the Bible to all of the students and we would have prayer and sing hymns. We were taught to reverence God, the Bible, and prayer. Although, at that time, I was not a Christian and I did not know the Bible or have any religious knowledge, I gained a respect for God, the Bible, the church, and for things that were holy. I learned all those principles in a public school.

Until about thirty years ago, the public schools in America were providing that necessary support for our boys and girls. Christian education and the precepts of the Bible still permeated the curriculum of public schools. The Bible was read and prayer was offered in each and every school across our nation. But our public schools no longer teach Christian ethics, which educate children and young people intellectually, physically, emotionally, and spiritually. The Bible states, "The fear of the LORD is the beginning of knowledge." (Pr. 1:7) I believe that the decay in our public school system suffered an enormous acceleration when prayer and Bible reading were taken out of the classroom by our U. S. Supreme Court. Our public school system is now permeated with humanism. The human mind has been deceived, and the end result is that our schools are in serious trouble.

Since World War II, there has been a continuing infiltration of socialism onto the campus of our major colleges and universities. As the Bible and prayer were removed, they were replaced with courses reflecting the philosophy of humanism. It is no wonder that as we review the 1970s, we find radicals and revolutionaries on our campuses who plundered and defamed their colleges and universities in the name of academic freedom.

Humanism claims a "life adjustment" philosophy. The emphasis is placed on a person's social and psychological growth instead of on factual knowledge. "Socialization" has become the main purpose of education. Students are told that there are no absolutes and that they are to develop their own value systems. The humanist creed is documented in two humanist manifestos, signed in 1933 and 1973. Humanists believe that man is his own god and that moral values are relative, that ethics are situational. Humanists say that the Ten Commandments and other moral and ethical laws are "outmoded" and hindrances to human progress.

Humanism places man at the center of the universe. The philosophy of naturalism projects man as an animal concerned only with fulfilling the desires of the moment. It teaches that man is not a unique and specific creation of God. Man is merely the ultimate product of the evolutionary process who has gained a sense of intelligence that prevents him from acting like an animal.

Naturalism looks on man as a kind of biological machine. In that philosophy of life, sexual immorality is just another bodily function like eating or drinking. Man lives a meaningless existence in which the only important thing is for him to make himself happy in the here and now. It is a philosophy of "do your own thing." Its slogan is "If it feels good, do it." Neither philosophy offers moral absolutes, a right and a wrong. Not only are these philosophies destroying our educational system, but they are destroying the basis and the foundation of the Christian family as well.

Basic values such as morality, individualism, respect for our nation's heritage, and the benefits of the free-enterprise system have, for the most part, been censored from today's public-classroom textbooks. From kindergarten right through the total school system, it almost seems as if classroom textbooks are designed to negate what philosophies previously had been taught. Under the guise of sex education or value clarification, many textbooks are actually perverting the minds of literally millions of students. Let me lay out a brief summary of quotes that I have taken from textbooks I have in hand. These textbooks are actually being used in the classrooms of our American schools. I have found quotes such as these: "To truly induce completely creative thinking we should teach children to question the Ten Commandments, patriotism, the two-party system, monogomy, and laws against incest."

Here is another: "It's tactless if not actually wrong not to lie under certain circumstances."

Another: "To be a better citizen a person needs to learn how to apply for welfare and how to burn the American flag."

"There are exceptions to almost all moral laws depending on the situation."

"Honesty is not something you either have or don't have."

"American society is ugly, trashy, cheap, and commercial, it is dehumanizing, its middle-class values are seen as arbitrary, materialistic, narrow, and hypocritical."

"To be successful in our culture one must learn to dream of failure."

"Only by remaining absurd can one feel free from fear."

A textbook entitled *Human Sexuality: A Course for Young Adults* was approved by the California State Board of Education. Recommended to the board by the State Commission on Curriculum, the book is intended for children aged twelve to fourteen, in the seventh and eighth grades. Sex is described explicitly in words and pictures. The book advises children that because parents are old-fashioned and narrow-minded about moral values, the home is the worst place to learn about sex. It presents the view that perversion is in the eyes of the beholder, saying that unusual sexual behavior should not be considered a perversion simply because it is out of the ordinary. Students are informed that strong disapproval of premarital sexual activity is not shared by the majority of the world's cultures. Infidelity is condoned. The book spoke about subjects such as homosexuality, incest, masochism, masturbation, sadism, and nymphomania.

Many parents would be appalled and shocked if they examined the textbooks from which their children are being taught in America's schools today. Books are very significant factors in society. The textbook business for elementary and secondary schools is an $823-million-a-year business.

When you find an advanced society such as ours, you will find that books have played an important part in the development of that society. The Book of all books has been and always will be the Word of God, the Bible. The foundation for our government, our laws, our statutes, our civilization, the structures of our home, our states, and our churches have come from the Word of God. America's past greatness has come because she has honored the Bible. The attitude America's people take toward the Bible is in direct proportion to the stability of America as a nation.

I believe that the greatness of America can be attributed to the Good Book, and also to the good books of science, literature, history, and biography that have enabled us as a people to assimilate the necessary facts to build a great republic under God.

Textbooks

Mel and Norma Gabler head a group called Educational Research Analysis. The Gablers have become known all across America for their efforts to improve the textbooks of America's schools. It all began one day when their son came home from school in Longview, Texas, with an assignment to write out the Gettysburg Address. They found that the words "under God" had been left out of their son's textbook. Thus began an extensive search of textbooks. The Gablers were absolutely incensed by what they found. They knew that evolution was already taught in textbooks, but they did not know that the very moral values upon which our nation was established were actually attacked in school textbooks. They found this not only in public-school textbooks but also in some private-school textbooks.

A committee in each state determines which textbooks are to

be accepted for use in the school systems of that state. The Gablers took action. They began to appear before the Texas committee every year when new textbooks were presented by the publishers. After doing much homework—obtaining and reading copies of prospective books—they examined and discussed the books openly. One member of a particular committee asked Mrs. Gabler what right she had to take up their time. He questioned her academic expertise. She replied that she was first of all a mother, a parent of three children, a taxpayer, and a registered voter. Because of her efforts, Texas is reported to have the best textbooks of any of the fifty states. Mrs. Gabler says there is still room for improvement but it is far better in Texas than in any other state. Her statement greatly troubles me.

Schools and textbooks are seldom suspected of contributing to the present-day situation in which more than half of our young people favor governmental ownership of industry and believe that most people are not capable of deciding what is best for themselves and, thus, are ready to dispense with freedom of the press. One third of our boys and girls would curb the freedom of speech, and 13 per cent would restrict religious worship by law. Behavior is learned.

Mel Gabler points out in a pamphlet entitled *Have You Read Your Children's School Textbooks?* that the federal government has funded a particular series of studies called "MACOS," which stands for "Man: A Course of Study." Designed for fifth-grade children, this course was hailed by liberals when it came out in 1972 as one of the greatest programs ever developed. Supposedly, MACOS teaches why man is more human than other animals and so on. But as the Gablers have pointed out, the study includes wife-swapping, men practicing cannibalism, the killing of baby girls, and eleven-year-old students role-playing leaving their grandmothers to die. The thirty MACOS booklets are filled with more examples of such cruelty, violence, and death.

MACOS was produced by the National Science Foundation and was the brainchild of Jerome Bruner, a Harvard psychologist specializing in experimental behavior. MACOS was intended to teach the universal bond among all men through a series of discovery lessons on a variety of cultures. The aim was to have children step outside of their own cultures to question values that they may have already learned. The required training for teachers forbids any new questions or clarifications to be inserted. The teacher is helpless. All questions come from manuals that have to be followed exactly, and the students are not allowed to look for answers in extracurricular source material of their own or their parents. All answers must be obtained from the course books, the simulated games, and the films. MACOS is a perfect example of a closed system of government indoctrination for neutralizing the values taught by church and home.

Children who take this course are not to take their booklets home. When parents try to examine these booklets, they find it is very difficult. Parents should be prepared for such pacifying statements as, "The books teach realism; students should learn about other cultures." Students are faced with values that are anti-American, that equate man with the animals, and that display harsh attitudes toward a home and a family. Children are taught that there are no absolute rights or absolute wrongs and that the traditional home is one alternative. Homosexuality is another. Decency is relative.

Inquiries in Sociology notes, "There are exceptions to almost all moral laws depending on the situation." (p. 37) But if God, or the integrity of the Bible, or creationism are included uncritically in a textbook, that book is immediately labeled as biased.

Hitler knew exactly how to indoctrinate people. He went right to the children and in their schoolrooms. Fascism was taught until at one point in time the children became his slaves. Children were ready and willing to turn their parents in to the state for disloyal statements. Prayer and Bible reading were taken out of the schools because they might "offend" some child who did not believe in God. The other 99 per cent of the children had to listen to evolution and secularism, humanism, and vulgarity.

The textbook *Many Peoples, One Nation* (1973), contains

this statement: "No nation on earth is guilty of practices more shocking and bloody than in the United States at this very hour." The National Education Association (NEA) is urging that a film, *The Unknown War*, put together by Soviet filmmakers, be shown to schoolchildren. The film is nothing less than Soviet propaganda.

In the book *Are Textbooks Harming Your Children?* author James Hefley points out that the Gablers were disturbed by a report from an NEA affiliate, the National Council for the Social Studies. The report, "The Study and Teaching of American History," helped to explain the changes in recent history texts. The report said: "Our principle for selecting what is basic in . . . history involves a reference to its predicted outcome. Our 'emphasis' will be determined by what we find going on in the present. . . . Most of us have pledged our allegiance to an organized world community. . . . The teacher who adopts this principle of selection is as intellectually honest as the teacher who relies upon the textbook author—and far more creative. . . ." (p. 31) We find that public education has become materialistic, humanistic, atheistic, and socialistic. This is a far cry from what our Founding Fathers intended education to be. It is a far cry from the motto of the United States of America, "In God We Trust."

The Gablers were incensed when our U. S. Supreme Court declared the official use of voluntary nonsectarian prayer in the public schools unconstitutional, and when a year later the Court outlawed Bible reading and recitation of the Lord's Prayer in classrooms. They saw it as another step closer to the goals of "progressive" education.

The Gablers see only three possible ways for parents to preserve the heritage of family, church, and nation: (1) transfer their children to a Christian school teaching traditional values; (2) teach them at home; (3) fight the self-appointed system of secular humanism.

"Why shouldn't we fight?" Norma commented. "It's our children, our tax money, and our government. And it's our rights that are being violated. If textbooks can't teach Christian principles, then they shouldn't teach against Christianity." (p. 33)

An article in the December 31, 1979, *Time* magazine regarding the Gablers states, "They have become a clearinghouse for critiques written by almost anyone of textbooks, dictionaries, and library books. Texas education officials swear by the Gablers. 'Their ideas about educational materials are the ideas parents want,' says Alton Bowen, deputy commissioner of education."

Fred Reed reports in the December 29, 1979, Washington *Post*: "The decline of education, when sufficiently prolonged, becomes irreversible and alters the structure of society. The point of irreversibility comes when a full generation has been maleducated.

"We seem to be approaching that point. Functional illiteracy is a growth stock, College Board scores continue to decline, professors complain of poorly prepared students, and universities teach remedial English (or try to: finding professors who know grammar is no longer easy).

"There might be hope if teachers were committed to excellence. But the prevailing tone in academic circles is one of apathetic mediocrity and unionism (although many infuriated teachers are exceptions).

"Worse, the people who control the apparatus of education do not want improvement. They see education as an elaborate game of who's-got-a-theory, in which children are regarded as laboratory animals. Their concern is not whether children learn anything, but how they feel about each other.

"If this sounds like an exaggeration, read a few educational journals (every parent should). They contain endless repetition of education's talismanic signature words: interpersonal dynamics, group interaction, cognitive dissonance, and self-image. There is little mention of the substance of scholarship, such as history, long division, and Spanish.

"If the education of what Marxists call 'the masses' deteriorates enough, they must eventually become the masses in a

Marxist sense—unknowing, unreading consumers of television's products. Should quality in education decline far enough, the result must be a sort of peasantrification of the country." (The title of Reed's article is "Half-educated Generation.") An estimated 13 per cent of all high-school graduates are functionally illiterate.

"The amount of cheating that goes on at major colleges and universities is phenomenal. *The Cheating Game*—Bowers's survey of 99 institutions (including such elite ones as Yale, Columbia, Penn, and Stanford)—revealed that at least half the students sampled had engaged in some form of cheating while on campus.

" 'The administration assumes that students coming here have a code of values about cheating, but they don't,' said Fred Hall, the president of Dartmouth 1976 senior class. In many of the lower schools, the rate of cheating ranged as high as a sickening 88 per cent." (pp. 101–2)

"In the no-fault guilt-free new social order, the university's moral authority had languished. 'Character is a word that's dropped out of the university's vocabulary,' said Norman Jacobson, a political-science professor at Berkeley." (p. 102)

"In early 1978 a deeply concerned Harvard president, Derek Vok, admitted, 'We have little reason to believe that Harvard does much to promote moral reasoning, let alone moral conduct.'" (p. 103)

" 'You can't teach it (morality) the way you teach the clarinet. We lack the language to discuss right and wrong,' insisted a University of Chicago professor.

"Between 1974 and 1978 Cornell's mental health center recorded a 44 per cent increase in new student patients. Columbia's counseling service reports a 50 per cent jump in visits over one academic year during the same period." (p. 89)

In the mid-seventies suicide ranked second only to accidents as a cause of death on college campuses.

"At both Berkeley and Stanford the 300-foot bell towers were enclosed at the top to discourage would-be suicides from jumping."

Sexual Anarchy

In his book *Campus Shock*, Lansing Lamont explains that he set out to explore a dozen pre-eminent liberal-arts universities: the eight Ivy League schools of the East (Brown, Columbia, Cornell, Dartmouth, Harvard, Pennsylvania, Princeton, and Yale); the state universities of Michigan at Ann Arbor and California at Berkeley, as well as Stanford and the University of Chicago. His documentary reveals the deeply troubled students on college campuses and universities in the decade of the seventies. The mood of students on many of these major campuses was described as "an epidemic of despair."

Lamont found that sex had become the focal point for much of a young person's educational and social life. Displaced outside of marriage, the sex act fulfilled biological needs apart from accepting emotional and moral responsibilities. "Nor was the plight of Sylvia Webb, a junior at Princeton, by any means an isolated one," he says. "On the first night that her roommate had brought a man up to their dormitory quarters, she had retreated to the bathroom to finish studying for a math examination. When she emerged at 2:00 A.M. the man was still there, and within a week he'd become a regular overnight guest. Thus it is not surprising that there are on what was once a 'distinguished' campus such as Yale, rapes right in campus dormitories."

He found that the "new morality" sowed confusion across many a traditionalist campus, causing hurt and disillusionment. Psychiatrists treated growing numbers of student couples with sexual hangups. At Princeton's sex clinic the traffic in disturbed couples tripled over a two-year period. "It was impossible to just make friends," explained a pretty Cornell sophomore who'd fled to off-campus quarters after her freshman year in a mixed dorm. "The boys had sex uppermost on their minds. They'd wander into your room and ask to sleep with you. The sex came first before you even made an emotional commitment. I didn't know how to handle it and I've done a lot of agonizing since."

"A Harvard woman in her sophomore year become so withdrawn," he said, "partly for fear of sexual pressure 'that I didn't know anyone in the house outside my suite.' The mere sharing of a book could entail sexual expectations."

"At the University of Michigan, the daughter of a Detroit industrialist showed up in tears at the campus psychological clinic. 'She was under tremendous pressure to be deflowered and by God she was,' reported Professor Joseph Adelson, the clinic's director. A young freshwoman at Harvard dropped out after being repeatedly propositioned by a lesbian roommate."

Campus Shock is indeed a disheartening book to say the least. In the pessimism of its pages, I could say "there is hope." And I will continue to try to reach young people with the message that only Jesus Christ is that hope. In the final chapter to his book, Mr. Lamont states: "The shocks came in cumulative bursts of candor from the students—in my dawning realization that so many of them viewed their lives and selves with contempt, that so few of them found their college experience enriching or pleasurable. They recognized the cheating around them, and looked the other way. They sensed the shallowness of their career aims, and plunged blindly ahead. And, though I knew that the old nostalgia for Alma Mater was long gone, I found it still appalling that so many students viewed themselves as mere transients with no loyalties to their college.

"What shocked me most, however, was the numbness, emotional as well as moral, that I encountered everywhere. I remember too well the conclusion of Fred Hall, president of the class of '76 at Dartmouth—that 'more and more students don't react to situations and, more terrifying, don't react to people.'" (p. 128)

"Far too many students in the 1970s have become so obsessed with their entitlements, along with the determination to come out first, that the notion of responsibility seems to have been lost sight of almost entirely.

"On campus after campus, I listened to educators who envisaged a millennium in which the professions were wholly dominated by such attitudes—by businessmen whose preoccupation with the bottom line has obliterated all social concern, by doctors who have lost the ability to diagnose along with any intuitive feel for the patient as a whole person, by lawyers who have lost sight of every goal other than the maximizing of corporate profits. Their vision of the future was, in short, a leadership without a soul presiding over a technological system without a conscience." (p. 131)

Violence in the Schools

Educator Donald R. Howard, in his book *Rebirth of Our Nation*, looks at the 1970s and shows how those years were permeated with the humanistic philosophy that students are not educated until they have been exposed to humanism. But other contents of his book point to the rather inhuman character of many of our schools. I refer to violence. He cites many cases of assault and battery, and actual murder, of teachers in the 1970s.

A UPI story from Washington in the spring of 1976 stated that assault, mugging, vandalism and gang warfare were rampant in America's schools; the writer called for a nationwide crime-control effort. The situation in our schools was described as "a virtual reign of schoolhouse terror."

In January 1978, a massive three-volume report on violence in the public schools was presented to Congress by HEW's National Institute of Education (NIE). Among many shocking findings, this report points out that 2.4 million secondary-school students (11 per cent) have something stolen from them in a typical month. About 282,000 of the students report being attacked in a month; and 130,000 secondary-school teachers report having something stolen from them during a month's time. Some 5,200 teachers are physically attacked, about 1,000 of whom are injured seriously enough to require medical attention.

Is it safe to walk in many of the public schools of our larger cities? Recently I was in a school in New York where the principal and schoolteachers actually stay behind locked doors while school is in progress. Armed security guards keep peace in the school. When school is out, and the young people are gone, the metal doors are locked so that the custodian can clean the building. A large number of the public schools in our nation are hazardous places in which to work and to try to learn.

But the atmosphere of violence is not a problem of the inner-city school alone. The suburbs too are in trouble. The May 21, 1979, *U. S. News & World Report* states, "A wave of violence in many of the nation's schools is again playing havoc with American education. Now it is the communities noted for good schools and quality education that are being scandalized by physical assaults and threats against teachers and students. Handguns, icepicks, explosives, and other weapons are turning up increasingly at schools in wealthy suburbs of Los Angeles, Denver, Washington, D.C., and New York, as well as scores of smaller cities across the nation.

"Violence in our schools reflects violence in our society," says Bennie Kelley, president of the National Association of School Security Directors. "As criminal activity increases in suburbs and smaller cities, it follows that this trend will show up in sub-urban and rural schools. That is exactly what is happening."

The same issue of *U. S. News & World Report* also contains accounts of brutal violence in schools, such as "in Austin, Texas, while thirty of his classmates watched, the thirteen-year-old son of former White House press secretary George Christian shot and killed his English teacher."

There is a frightening problem of vandalism in schools also. The costs of repairing schools and of preventing damage (security measures and additional insurance) amount to more than $600 million a year. This is three times what these expenses totaled in 1971.

Vandalism is not confined to poor urban areas. This is evidenced by an example of vandalism that occurred in December 1978 in a wealthy Virginia neighborhood near Washington, D.C. Three youths were charged with arson in a $4.5 million fire that destroyed a high school. They were sons of prominent community figures, including a two-star Army general. Security authorities say that vandals are usually dropouts, or students on drugs or alcohol. More than 25 per cent of all schools are subject to vandalism in a given month. "The annual cost of school crime is estimated to be around $500 million." Billions of dollars were spent on America's educational system in the 1970s. With these statistics, educators have no reason to look with pride on their innovations in teaching acceptable behavioral patterns. This is what happens when man strays from God and when he makes materialism his god. Our youth are corrupted. We have no leadership. Education has moved from centering on God to focusing on man.

Competency scores in public schools across America are showing that boys and girls are not comprehending the basics such as history, math, and English. Tragically, many graduates of high schools cannot even read their diplomas. The decline in scholastic achievement of the average student coming out of our public educational school system is frightening. Scores by public-school students on the Scholastic Aptitude Tests (SAT) used for college entrance examination have been continually dropping for 14 consecutive years.

On the other hand, during the 1978–79 school year, tests taken by members of the Western Association of Christian Schools (WACS) indicated that first graders scored nine months above the national average and eighth graders scored 12 months above the national average (based on the results of the 1973 Stanford Achievement Test). WACS member schools were compared to 225,000 carefully picked average public-school students. The total test included vocabulary, reading, word-study skills, math, spelling, language, social science, science, and listening.

An Alternative—the Christian School

Is it surprising that Christian parents have found the need to remove their children from the public educational system and to begin educating them in Christian schools? Christian schools are the only hopes of training young men and young women who will be capable of taking the helm of leadership in every level of society. People devoid of character cannot lead a nation. The destiny of any nation is determined by its leaders.

There are 14,000 conservative Christian schools in America and they are increasing at a rate of three per day.

Martin Luther said in the sixteenth century, "I am much afraid that schools will prove to be the great gates of hell unless they diligently labor in explaining the holy Scriptures, engraving them in the hearts of youth. I advise no one to place his child where the Scriptures do not reign paramount. Every institution in which men are not unceasingly occupied with the Word of God must become corrupt." Because of the vacuum in our public schools in the area of character building, Christian educators have found it necessary to begin their own schools. America's school system has always contributed to her greatness and we have a responsibility to teach our children that which is right and that which is good.

In the Christian schools, education begins with God. The objectives are based upon biblical principles, with God as the center of every subject. The philosophies taught stand as witness to society, as the ultimate goal, not as a reflection of man's sinful nature. In science the student learns God's laws for the universe; in history, God's plan for the ages; and in civics, God's requirement of loyalty and support for the government He has ordained.

The principles of honesty, decency, co-operation, and fair play, and the ability to discern what is false and dishonoring to God are presented in a manner that the student can readily comprehend.

This educational process requires more than the school environment. It requires a family that exemplifies these truths and a church with a foundation that reinforces these biblical principles. Edmund Burke said, "Example is the school of mankind, and they will learn at no other." A child's example must first be set in the home before he ever goes to school. Proverbs 22:6 in the Bible states: "Train up a child in the way he should go; and when he is old, he will not depart from it." Many parents who are very hard on schools and educators are actually placing the blame on outsiders when they themselves are at fault. Answering the question "What's wrong with our schools?" Milton Friedman summarizes by saying: "Few institutions in our society are in a more unsatisfactory state than schools. Few generate more discontent or can do more to undermine our liberty." Friedman believes that government intervention has done much to harm schools. He says, "We believe that the growing role government has played in financing and in administering schooling has led not only to enormous waste of taxpayers' money but also to a far poorer educational system than would have developed had voluntary co-operation continued to play a larger role." (*Free to Choose*, pp. 187–88)

Today Christian schools face a myriad of attacks. In some states it is easier to open a massage parlor than to open the doors of a Christian school. Recently the Internal Revenue Service has attacked Christian schools.

The Congress of the United States has refused any funding to the IRS to implement the proposed revenue procedures that would result in the taxation of private schools. U. S. Senator Jesse Helms has stated: "I shed no tears over clipping the wings of the Internal Revenue Service. They have asked for it. By heavy-handedness, by arbitrariness, by harassment of Christian schools, the Internal Revenue Service has asked for precisely what Congress is doing. I am not going to back up one inch, because this kind of tyranny has got to stop. That is my sole interest.

"I have watched these private schools. I know the people who are operating them in my state. I know what kind of citizens they are. I know what kind of character they have. They are not going to engage in any un-American activities. They do not lobby. They simply operate schools conditioned upon precepts that this senator feels made this country great. What we are talking about is the harassment, by the IRS, of good, honest citizens, who are doing the best they can to improve the quality of education for their children. They do not like the drug trafficking going on in public schools; they do not like the violence;

and neither do the teachers who are being assaulted, and sometimes raped and killed in the public schools. They want prayer
in their schools. And I think they are right on all counts. They
have a right to be left alone, and that is what my amendment is
all about."

Additionally, the Ashbrook Amendment to the Treasury Department Appropriations Bill prohibits the IRS from using
funds to investigate private schools.

The amendment was passed in the Senate by a substantial
margin but will be effective only in the 1979–80 fiscal year. Similar amendments must be passed in the future to prohibit these
investigations.

Those two amendments are a victory for Christian schools,
but the guidelines established by them are for fiscal year 1980
only. Approximately two thousand dollars of taxes go each year
to cover the cost of each child enrolled in school. When parents
take their children out of public schools and put them in private schools, they save taxpayers about two thousand dollars per
year. These parents then must pay private tuition in addition to
their taxes.

Economist Milton Friedman states: "Indeed, we believe that
the penalty that is now imposed on parents who do not send
their children to public schools violates the spirit of the First
Amendment, whatever lawyers and judges may decide about the
letter. Public schools teach religion, too—not a formal, theistic
religion, but a set of values and beliefs that constitute a religion
in all but name. The present arrangement abridges the religious
freedom of parents who do not accept the religion taught by the
public schools yet are forced to pay to have their children indoc-
trinated with it, and to pay still more to have their children escape indoctrination." (*Free to Choose*, p. 164)

Christians simply want to educate their children in the way
that they see fit. Recently a Gallup poll was conducted that indicated that 95 per cent of all church people want their children
to have religious instruction, and 74 per cent of all unchurched
people wanted their children to have religious instruction.

On January 23, 1980, a news release went out from the office of Senator Helms announcing the beginning of a nationwide campaign to seek congressional approval of legislation to restore the right of voluntary prayer in public schools. When he spoke at the annual convention of the National Religious Broadcasters Association, Senator Helms described the Supreme Court's decision banning voluntary public-school prayer as a "contradiction of our nation's spiritual heritage and a violation of the First Amendment's guarantee of the free exercise of religion." In 1979 the Senate passed an amendment, S./ 450, which Senator Helms authored, to restore voluntary public-school prayer. This amendment is now pending before the House Judiciary Committee.

Helms commented, "Thus we forfeited by judicial fiat the rights of millions of American schoolchildren to invoke the blessings of God on their work. A handful of determined atheists and agnostics, in collaboration with a handful of pharisees on the Supreme Court, succeeded in their great aim of using the power of the law to eradicate all mention of God and His Word in every public-school classroom in America. And all this was accomplished in the name of civil liberties.

"A greater crime against our children could hardly be conceived. In this case, as in so many others, the Court forced from the Constitution exactly the opposite conclusion from what the Founding Fathers intended. It escaped the Court's notice that this entire country was colonized by individuals seeking free expression of their religious beliefs. The Constitution prohibited the establishment of a religion by the Congress so that the right of freedom of religion would never be threatened.

"It is hardly coincidence that the banishment of the Lord from the public schools has resulted in their being taken over by a totally secularist philosophy. Christianity has been driven out. In its place has been enshrined a permissiveness in which the drug culture has flourished, as have pornography, crime, and fornication—in short, everything but discipline and learning. This is the bitter fruit of the new civil right enacted by our highest court: freedom from religion."

It is fortunate that our Constitution provides, under the system of checks and balances, the authority for a simple majority in both houses of Congress to check the Supreme Court. Senator Helms' bill stresses the word "voluntary." He says that no individual should be forced to participate in a religious exercise that is contrary to his religious convictions. And his bill recognizes this important freedom.

Christians can reverse the decision regarding prayer that our Supreme Court made by exerting forceful pressure upon their representatives in Congress. As we have already pointed out, prayer is allowed in the House and Senate chambers, but it is denied our schoolchildren.

The Senate has already voted favorably, and if the House concurs by a simple majority, only the President's signature would be needed to make it law. Our President has said, "I think that the government ought to stay out of the prayer business," yet he prayed at the signing of the Egypt-Israel peace treaty. Should such distinctions be made by our chief executive officer?

It is the Christian school movement and the restoration of voluntary prayer in public schools that will provide the most important means of educating our children in the concepts of patriotism and morality.

MUSIC

A December 17, 1979, *Time* magazine carried a story entitled, "The Stampede to Tragedy." "It was a tough ticket," the article began. "All 18,348 of them were gone 90 minutes after they went on sale in late September at Cincinnati's Riverfront Coliseum. The Who had not played the area since 1975. It was an event.

"Fans converged from all over. Danny and Connie Burns left their two young children at home, got on a chartered bus in Dayton and headed for the concert.

"Though the music was not billed to begin until 8 P.M., the crowd started building outside the coliseum around 1 o'clock Monday afternoon. By 3, the police had arrived to keep watch. With so long to wait, the kids tried to keep a party mood going. There was some drinking, some grass.

"By early evening there were eight thousand people, most holding general-admission tickets, massed in the coliseum plaza near the west gate. By 7, the doors had still not been opened. The crowd passed impatience, pressed closer together. Danny and Connie Burns were among them.

"Lieut. Dale Menkhaus, detailed to head a squad of twenty-five Cincinnati police on crowd-control assignment, sensed danger. He went looking for someone to open the doors. He found one of the promoters, Cal Levy, who told him this was not possible. The musicians had not completed their rehearsal inside the hall, and not enough ticket takers had arrived.

"The crowd, now clotted tightly together, pressed forward. Around seven-twenty, someone smashed through a closed glass door and crawled through the shards into the hall. Finally the doors of the west gate opened. The crowd surged. Danny Burns was carried with them. He could not see his wife.

"Lieut. Menkhaus heard that 'people were down in the crowd.' There was nothing he could do. The mob was still moving and could not be penetrated. When the initial press slackened, the police started to force their way through. They found the first body at seven-forty-five. In all, there were eight injured and eleven dead—seven men and four women. Three were high-school students, another was a highway worker. One was Connie Burns. According to a coroner's preliminary report, they had died of suffocation.

"Inside the coliseum, Cincinnati Fire Marshal Clifford Drury told Who Manager Bill Curbishley that the show should go on as scheduled. Drury reasoned that the crowd, which did not know what had happened at the west gate, would not sit still for a cancellation. So The Who played a standard two-hour set, and were then instructed to keep the encore short."

What is this group like? *Time*'s cover story tells us: "No other group has ever pushed rock so far, or asked so much from it. No other band has ever matched its sound, a particular combination of sonic onslaught and melodic delicacy that is like chamber music in the middle of a commando raid." *Time* magazine's reporter describes The Who as having "always lived at the outer limits of rock. That is the dangerous borderland where the best rock music is made, the music that lasts and makes a difference. The danger that pervades this territory is not a matter of threat, but a kind of proud, blind, spiritual recklessness, forming a musical brotherhood that could be bound by the words of Russian poet Andrei Voznesensky: 'To live is to burn.'"

For quite a length of time when they first began their group, the four men in The Who received much notoriety for smashing their instruments at the end of each performance. *Time* says, "It was, at first, a flashy, frightening and finally exhilarating thing to see. Drummer Keith Moon blew up his drum kit, and Townshend rammed the neck of his guitar into his amp, while Daltrey slammed his microphone against the stage and Entwistle held tight to his bass, playing stubbornly on like a shipwreck's lone survivor trying to keep dry in a leaking lifeboat. Anyone in the audience could tell those instruments were extensions of, even surrogates for, the four blessed, blitzed maniacs in the band. That was not Pop art onstage; it was a gang war.

"There were no separate peaces. Only nightly shards of instruments lying on the floor of the stage like jigsaw fragments. 'We're always trying to outdo each other onstage,' Daltrey says. 'All of us are a bit mad. We've stayed together for fifteen years because we've never stopped fighting.' Adds Townshend, 'The Who's like an open book. It leads to a kind of unwitting honesty. That's what I think the fans really get fanatic about.'"

The Who's cumulative sales exceed twenty million records. The members of the group are all millionaires several times over. The group's Keith Moon died of drug overdose at age thirty-one. Townshend is devoted to Indian mystic Meher Baba. The *Time* article goes on to give the history of the members of The Who and of their group. They have always been a violent group and fought much with each other. The article states that they are dedicated to rock 'n' roll "excess." "A hotel manager once appeared in Moon's room where he was playing a cassette at top volume and insisted he turn down 'the noise.' In a flash, Moon reduced the room to splinters, announcing 'this is noise. That was The Who.'"

The hearing of the members of the group has been impaired by long exposure to maximum amplification. "When it's noisy," Daltrey says, "I have to lip read." The article quotes one of Townshend's friends saying, "He's perfectly capable of getting off the plane in New York and staying drunk for the entire tour." Townshend says himself, "Rock is going to kill me somehow. Mentally or physically or something, it's going to get me in the end. It gets everybody in the end." The article states, "The members of The Who know what this music means, know its power and its necessary mutability."

In his book *Rock One Hundred,* David Dalton says about the Rolling Stones, "They have participated in and provoked the transformation of the morals and manners of their generation so effectively that to future social historians the Rolling Stones might actually seem to bear out the reactionary ravings that they are the ringleaders of an international conspiracy of rock 'n' roll punks to undermine Western civilization with drugs, music, polymorphous sexuality, and violence."

Satan worship and the occult are often the topics of rock songs. A Rolling Stones record of a few years ago, "Goat's Head Soup," was reported to have been taped live at a voodoo ritual. On one song the screams of those who are allegedly being possessed by demon spirits is heard. The inside of the album jacket has a colored picture of a severed goat's head floating in a boiling caldron. It is a fact that for many years the devil has been worshiped by the symbol of a goat. The Rolling Stones appear as witches on the jacket of their album entitled "Their Satanic Majesty's Request." And on another of their albums, their featured song is "Sympathy for the Devil," which is now the anthem of satanists.

There is a scene entrenched in my memory that will be vivid until the day I die. In 1975 I conducted a tour across the United States. The LBC Chorale, a singing group from Liberty Baptist College, joined me. One evening I preached and the Chorale sang to two hundred people in a banquet room in a coliseum in Seattle, Washington. Our service had been slightly disturbed by a rock concert that was going on in another part of the building. After the conclusion of our meeting I took some of the young people from the Chorale with me to the site of the rock concert. There I witnessed one of the most horrifying scenes I think I will ever see. Thousands of young men and women were lying on the floor engaged in every filthy act imaginable. The discordant sounds in that room were deafening. On the stage a rock-star hero of thousands of American young people stood with outstretched arms in front of a cross with psychedelic fluorescent lights whirling around him. Those young people who were not engaged in some immoral act at the moment bowed down to him. Drug-caused smoke so permeated the atmosphere in that place that policemen on patrol had been instructed to work only thirty-minute shifts inside. As I looked at those young people, our nation's future, my eyes filled with tears. That night I could not sleep.

Few have made so thorough a study of rock music as has Bob Larson. Once deeply involved in the rock scene, Bob Larson performed professionally as a rock entertainer for four years. He was a singer, composer, guitarist, and disc jockey. During his climb to fame a friend introduced him to Jesus Christ. Today he is an evangelist. He is a noted author and lecturer who presents a moral analysis of rock music. In his latest book entitled *Rock*, he makes keen observations, pointing out that rock is more than just an irritating beat. He shows it to be a subtle and pervasive influence on young people. He exposes the rock culture as a dark world of occultism, drugs, and perverted sex. Through an analysis of the musical properties of the rock beat, he shows how it can affect the mind.

When lecturing Mr. Larson says that "The music of rock is what hooks the teen-ager. By its very beat and sound, rock has always implicitly rejected restraints and celebrated moral anarchy. Its repetitious and pulsated rhythms mesmerize the listener and induce a state of moral oblivion. The beat of rock, with amplified intensity, encourages a feeling of complete abandonment to accepted social behavior. The electronic insistence of guitars, accompanied by the neurotic throbbing of drums, compels the shedding of inhibitions. Rock's cacophonous sounds, often performed beyond the auditory threshold of pain, literally assault the listener and immerse him in a physically sensuous experience."

Speaking from experience relates that "Rock is not played to be heard but to be felt. Rock jumps out at you from twenty thousand watts of power to jam you in the skull. You can't objectify its sound. It envelops you with an electronic impact unlike any music ever performed. This attack upon the senses makes the mind easy prey for the lyrics. Unfortunately, most teen-agers don't really understand the powerful effect that rock's message has on their minds. The topical content of rock has molded this generation into an irresponsible and frustrated one."

Bob Larson points out that rock lyrics glorify promiscuous sex and invite immediate physical self-indulgence. "Love means sex to most contemporary rock composers. Meaningful relationships are often described as fruitless and painful. . . . love has a single dimension—desire. Lust is the motivation and conquest is the goal." (*Rock*, p. 14)

"Nothing is left to the imagination. Every intimate detail pertaining to the physical aspects of sex is thoroughly explained to the teenage mind. The mere titles of songs over the last several years would make a sailor blush. Try these recent top ten hits: 'Let's Make a Baby,' 'Do Something Freaky,' 'Afternoon Delight,' 'Sharing the Night Together,' 'Hot Child in the City,' 'You Never Done It Like That,' 'Nobody Does It Better,' 'Lay Down Sally,' 'I'm In You,' 'Torn Between Two Lovers.'" (*Rock*, p. 14)

Not only are the graphics of album jackets often pornographic, but lyrical images are often conveyed in a code language known by teens who listen to rock music. After stating many shocking examples in his book entitled *Rock*, Mr. Larson says, "Parents should know that the examples in this book aren't the worst ones. Some top hits are so lewd that the lyrics can't be printed for fear of having this book classified as pornography." (pp. 15, 16)

Not only does rock music promote promiscuous sex, but it has also done much to advance the drug culture. Mr. Larson knows of literally hundreds of members of rock groups who died horrifying deaths from overdoses of drugs, or who spent time in mental institutions. It is a tragedy that rock stars are the heroes of American young people. Members of rock groups are worshiped as gods. After Jimi Hendrix performed in the Isle of

Wight rock festival before 500,000 fans, he suffocated in a pool of his own vomit as a result of an overdose. He had been paid more than $100,000 for that night. He was a typical hero in the rock world.

"At a recent International Music Conference," writes Mr. Larson, "the spokesman for a major record industry advertising firm stated: 'Record companies and music publishers have earned many millions of dollars from extolling the virtues of forceful rape, armed robbery, or kidnapping? The answer, I think, for many companies is 'yes' as long as there is money in it, and they don't go to jail.'" (*Rock*, p. 27)

Another trend in the musical world is called gay rock. It is performed for and by homosexuals. Bob Larson points out that rock interest in homosexuality is not entirely recent in origin. Bisexual themes in songs were explored as early as the mid-sixties. Today we find such rock stars as David Bowie, whom Mr. Larson describes as "a British singer/composer/guitarist who boasts in interviews and songs that he is bisexual. His wife is an admitted lesbian, and out of their union have come two children. Wearing orange-hued hair and laced high-heeled boots, he moves in female fashion to a rock beat. Bowie often pretends acts of copulation on stage with other males while singing songs about homosexuals such as 'Queen Bitch.' In spite of such perverted extravagance, he has been a major superstar in this era, and his concerts are sellouts wherever he goes. But the wealth and fame his perversion has brought seem to have only resulted in depression. One rock magazine reported that Bowie had expressed the desire to have a tragic death before he hit thirty— that this would have been the perfect ending to his career." (*Rock*, p. 21)

Mr. Larson writes, "All the gay rock groups have to go a long way to beat Alice Cooper. Alice, who claims to be the reincarnation of a seventeenth-century witch, began his rock career by coming out on stage dressed with mascara and in woman's clothing. An Alice Cooper performance is a wedding of perversion and dramatized violence as Alice chops a lifelike doll to pieces, makes love to a writhing snake, and eventually hangs himself on a gallows. In spite of all this, Alice was asked to lecture at the Eastman School of Music in Rochester, New York. His subject was the art of writing popular music.

"The Cooper album, 'Billion Dollar Babies,' had already earned over a million dollars on advance sales before it hit the stands. Included is the song, 'I Love the Dead,' an anthem of necrophilia which Alice sings while simulating sex on stage with a lifelike mannequin. Cooper's album 'Muscle of Love' was planned to include a painting of the group seated at a Thanksgiving dinner in a whorehouse."

The craze today is disco. The Bee Gees, John Travolta, and Saturday Night Fever set disco on fire. Disco is a variant of rock music, but it is more than just a style of music, it is a way of life. The April 2, 1979, issue of *Newsweek* states that the Afro-Cuban background of disco allows it to repeat simple lyric lines like voodoo chants. Drugs and dancing characterize the disco world.

In his pamphlet *Disco and Dancing*, Bob Larson gives this additional information: "The biggest disco group is comprised of five gays and one straight who call themselves the Village People. They come on stage decked out as a hardhat, an Indian, a cowboy, a policeman, a GI, and a homosexual leather freak. Their manager, Jaques Morali (who, himself, is a publicly acknowledged homosexual), admits he formed the group as a 'protest against Anita Bryant.' Morali declares, 'I am sincerely trying to produce songs to make the gay people more acceptable.' Twelve million people have bought their records with tunes like 'YMCA,' a paean of praise to homosexuality that describes the title designation as a place where you can 'hang out with all the boys' and find 'many ways to have a good time.' One album, 'Cruising,' is named after the homosexual practice of driving around to spot other gays who can be propositioned. In spite of such depraved antics, Merv Griffin featured them for ninety minutes on nationwide television, and the U. S. Navy has considered adopting their hit 'In the Navy' for its recruiting program."

Bob Larson points out, "The environment at a disco is designed to induce a druglike state with the mesmerizing influence of the lights, the beat, and the fantasized atmosphere. The neurosensory responses are overloaded until the dancers project their minds to an escapist level of oblivion. In such a stupefied state, the realities of life and the guilt of sin are negated with the same mind-altering intensity associated with hallucinogens or transcendentalism. The impulse for this kind of indulgences was perhaps best expressed by Patti Labelle's disco hit, 'Music Is My Way of Life.'"

The Bible states that the pleasures of sin are but for a season. Young people cannot live in discos. When the discos' lights have been turned off and the effects of the drugs have worn down, young people must face reality. There is no good life outside of Jesus Christ. Until young people find Him as their Savior, they will go on blinded and tortured by Satan, and someday wake up in hell. But this does not have to be the case. It is their choice today whether they will accept Jesus Christ as personal Savior or whether they will reject Him. This is the deciding question of every man and woman who has ever lived or who ever will live.

DRUGS AND ALCOHOL

Drug addiction was once confined to back alleys, to vacant lots, and to the inner city. Today, from the posh offices of prestigious businessmen to the playgrounds of junior high schools, millions of Americans are taking drugs. Studies show that millions of children, some under the age of ten, are habitual users of dangerous drugs like marijuana, barbiturates, and hallucinogens.

"It was a winter night and four teen-age boys were sitting around a fire in the woods, drinking beer.

" 'Here. Take a hit of Moon Acid,' Billy said, offering Steve a small round piece of paper soaked in LSD.

" 'I don't want it,' Steve said. 'It fries your brain.'

"Billy persisted. 'It's great, man. Try it!'

"But Steve shook his head. A tall, good-looking 215-pounder, he was the star of his school's basketball team, and in his own mind he'd been 'in training' since the second grade. His dream was to play professional basketball.

"The dream ended abruptly that night.

"Billy slipped the LSD into Steve's beer 'for kicks,' and he drank it, not knowing.

"Later as he was walking home, Steve began to hallucinate; 'I heard crazy sounds, and I felt like little pieces of my body were dropping off. On the fourth floor of my apartment complex, I saw a bridge a few feet below me and I stepped out onto it.'

"But there was no bridge.

"He woke up in the emergency room of the hospital. The next day doctors told him he was paralyzed from the waist down and would never walk again." (Peggy Mann, "Frightening Facts About Children and Drugs," *Family Weekly* [Nov. 25, 1979], p. 9)

This true story about Steve is tragically not uncommon. Statistics show that many thousands of teen-agers are physically damaged because of their involvement with drugs. Not only are children and teen-agers physically damaged, but also millions are psychologically damaged. Peggy Mann reports that according to the federal government's drug-abuse reporting network, marijuana, which most children mistakenly believe is harmless, accounted for the second largest number of admissions into federally funded drug-treatment facilities in 1979. One third of these children and young people started using pot before they were fourteen years old. The previous year, ten thousand emergency-room visits related to marijuana, either alone or in combination with other drugs; 40 per cent involved ten-to-nineteen-year-olds. Thousands of young people have died from drug overdoses.

Marijuana is smoked openly in dozens of cities. Hallucinogenic plants are cultivated in college dormitories. Many young urban professionals serve cocaine at their fashionable parties. Authorities estimate that in 1978, drugs worth between $35 billion to $45 billion changed hands in the United States. In 1978, drugs with a street value of $2.5 billion were seized in the United States and abroad by government agents.

In New York City today, heroin use is the leading cause of death among teen-agers. Children today are reaping the sins of adults.

Many adults who cannot face life or its pressures or who are immature and irresponsible and live from one "kick" to another are now taking drugs. Of course, there is a proper use of drugs. They have brought much-needed relief to people who suffer. But we Americans look at drug taking as trivial. Advertisements abound advocating this drug for headaches and that drug for stomach aches. Our children are impressionable. They model their behavior after adults. If we are always needing a pill to get us through the day, should we be surprised if they follow our example? Drugs are not cure-alls that should be taken the moment there is the slightest bit of pain.

Francis Schaeffer, in his book *How Should We Then Live?* points out that as the majority of American people accepted personal peace and affluence as their primary values, their children began to question the meaning of life with reference to any values they previously had thought were absolute. He points out that in 1964 at the University of California at Berkeley, students carried the meaninglessness of man into the streets.

Dr. Schaeffer asks the question, "Why should anyone have been surprised?" Many of the teachers taught the ultimate meaninglessness of man and the absence of absolutes. Was it not natural that students turned to drugs? Some approached drug taking as an ideology, and some approached it as a religion. Students were searching for meaning in life. Dr. Schaeffer points out that psychologist Timothy Leary, Gary Schneider, author-philosopher Allan Watts, and poet Allen Ginsberg were all influential in making drugs an ideology. Timothy Leary said that drugs were the sacraments of a new religion.

Timothy Leary once said, "Death to the mind, that is the goal you must have. Nothing else will do."

Young people have sought to solve their problems through taking drugs. Not satisfied with their parents' values of personal peace and materialism, the accumulation of more and more things, they rebelled. Rock festivals took fire around the country and were the scenes of many tragic ends of young people who overdosed on drugs. So it evolved that as the sixties drew to a close and the seventies began, thousands were taking drugs and at an alarmingly young age. Drugs were no longer an ideology, but they began to be in the sixties and continued to be an escape mechanism to the present time. (Schaeffer, pp. 207–8)

Dr. Schaeffer says, "Now drugs remain, but only in parallel to the older generation's alcohol, and an excessive use of alcohol has become a problem among the young people as well. Promiscuous sex and bisexuality remain, but only in parallel to the older generation's adultery. In other words, as the young people revolted against their parents, they came around in a big circle—and often ended an inch lower—with only the same two impoverished values: their own kind of personal peace and their own kind of affluence." (p. 210)

Congressman Lester Wolff, chairman of the House of Representatives' Select Committee on Narcotics Abuse and Control, warns, "Not only is the United States the most pervasive drug-abusing nation in history, but drug abuse among our children has risen, in the past two years, from epidemic to pandemic proportions. It has grown so large that neither this nation—nor any nation in history—has ever before faced a problem that is so insidious and so dangerous. And if we don't recognize the importance of this problem, it will have disastrous effects upon our society."

There are more than 100 federal agencies concerned with drug abuse and prevention in the United States. A 1977 National Institute on Drug Abuse Survey shows that 28 per cent of our nation's teens have used marijuana; 17 per cent, or 4.11 million of our nation's teens, currently smoke pot. The use of marijuana by teen-agers is reaching pandemic proportions in this country. A Defense Department survey indicates that nearly one out of every three soldiers in the Army admits to occasional or frequent use of marijuana; 7 per cent admit to using hard drugs; 40 per cent of enlisted men under the age of 25 in the Navy smoke marijuana.

The National Highway Traffic Administration indicates that 50 per cent of all highway fatalities are caused by drunken drivers. With the lowering of the legal drinking age to 18 came an increase in vandalism and other school disciplinary problems. The lowered age gave younger students opportunities to obtain liquor through friends who became 18 during their senior year. According to the National Clearinghouse for Alcohol Information, Rockville, Maryland, there are 10 million alcoholics in America. Between 1.5 million and 2.5 million of these alcoholics are women, and 3.3 million 14-to-17-year-olds are problem drinkers. "Victims" of alcohol abuse cost our economy more than $42 billion a year.

White House drug-policy adviser Lee Dogoloff says concerning the national scene, "If the present adolescent drug-abuse trends continue, we could soon acquire an unmanageable number of emotionally, intellectually, and socially handicapped young people. We could have a 'diminished generation' unable to function effectively if at all, in an increasingly complex and demanding world. In the area of adolescent drug abuse, therefore, we have neither the luxury of time nor the opportunity for esoteric debate."

In the *Family Weekly* article quoted earlier, Peggy Mann enumerates five grim factors about drug abuse:

1. According to the latest nationwide drug-abuse survey—the 1978 High School Senior Survey—one out of every nine seniors says he smokes pot daily, almost an 80 per cent increase in three-years' time. Of the 50 per cent who smoked pot at all during 1978, 37 per cent said they usually stay high three to six hours, and 6 per cent usually stay high seven hours or more. This, despite the fact that scientific evidence is mounting that shows the sustained use of marijuana has deleterious effects on the lung, brain, sex, and reproductive organs; that it creates cellular damage, psychological damage; and that the younger the user, the greater the damage.

Also, 46 per cent of all pot-smoking high-school seniors said they use one or more additional illegal drugs.

2. According to the most recent national drug-abuse survey covering all ages (1976 through 1977), use of marijuana is twice as high for youngsters as it is for adults, and one in ten pot-smoking youngsters said he also used stronger drugs.

3. The latest state, city, suburban, and rural surveys show that, since the above poll was taken, drug use has

increased at rapid rates in all grade levels; and white, middle-, and upper-income kids are just as deeply involved in drug abuse as minority youngsters in the ghettos. For example, in Maryland—often called "America in miniature," 42.7 per cent of tenth graders and 47 per cent of twelfth graders said they were current users of at least one of the following: marijuana, tranquilizers, quaaludes, amphetamines, heroin, hashish, hallucinogens, barbiturates, inhalants, and methamphetamines.

Throughout the country, junior-high- and high-school kids are getting stoned on the way to school, during school, after school, and at home, where they often "smoke out the window" or burn incense to cover the smell.

4. Drug use is reaching down to even low grade levels. Kevin McEneaney, director of the public-information program of Phoenix House—one of the nation's most successful drug rehabilitation centers—says, "In the many hundreds of drug-education seminars we do in school, we've found that younger and younger children openly admit to various levels of drug taking, ranging from heavy use of inhalants such as amyl or butyl nitrite (often called "poppers") and nitrous oxide (laughing gas), to heavy marijuana use including, in some areas, angel dust and cocaine. Many school officials tell us that kids are now developing drug-abuse patterns at nine or ten, as opposed to several years ago, when it was more like thirteen and fifteen.

One study in California indicated that the children began to experiment with drugs as early as the fifth grade. Drugs are generally given or sold to them by older students. Drug paraphernalia can be purchased by youngsters of any age in "head shops" or through mail order. And butyl nitrite, which produces a sixty-second "rush," can actually be purchased legally.

5. Multidrug use is also rising sharply. In many parts

of the country, "drug games" are in; for example, paper-bag roulette. A bag is passed around on the school bus. Kids put pills in (often collected from the family medicine chest), and take pills out to swallow during the day. Junior-high "fruit-salad parties" are also popular. Admission requirements: Drop pills into the collection plate. Other refreshments may include pot, hashish, psychedelic mushrooms, and cocaine. Older teen parties sometimes feature a grim pamphlet of hors d'oeuvres; LSD, THC (the chief psychoactive ingredient of marijuana), Q's (quaaludes, depressants), and PCP, otherwise known as angel dust (an animal tranquilizer). And always, of course, alcohol, which greatly augments the dangers of any of these drugs. It is a pathetic commentary that many of our public schools have become the main marketplaces for drugs."

Note: *Newsweek*, January 7, 1980, in an article entitled "New Look At Marijuana," confirms "figures compiled for the Health, Education and Welfare Departments NIDA show that in 1978 one in nine high-school seniors smoke pot every day, nearly double to the percentage of daily users in 1975."

Parents must learn as much as possible about the drug problem and drugs to take action against the problem. Their No. 1 priority should be to make their home the place that it should be. Parents must teach their children firm biblical principles so that they will not be tempted when they are exposed to drugs or yield to peer pressure. Many youngsters turn to drugs because they live lonely lives full of anxiety and despair. A home founded on God's Word will provide the love and guidance needed to avoid a life in drugs and despair.

Radiant, happy, well-adjusted young people at Liberty Baptist College have found fulfillment in this life and rest in the promise of one day being united with Jesus Christ. They answer the dilemma of millions of Americans in a simple song entitled, "Jesus Is Still the Answer." (Dimension Music © 1974)

Some men try so hard to prove that God's not really real,
While others say they know for sure His love you cannot feel;
But I know He's real within my soul for one day He cleansed and made me whole,
And Jesus is still the answer for that longing
deep in your soul.

Some men pretend that things of the world have brought them peace of mind,
But with the dawn of each new day new thrills they try to find!
Not until they meet the Prince of Peace can they ever hope to find release,
For Jesus is still the answer for a world that's seeking for peace.

Jesus is still the answer and tho' time and ages roll,
Jesus is still the answer, He's the answer for your soul;
And tho' some may say He doesn't fit with their philosophy,
I know Jesus is still the answer, He's always been and always will be.

Part III

PRIORITY—
REVIVAL IN AMERICA

Listen, America! Our nation is on a perilous path in regard to her political, economic, and military positions. If America continues down the path she is traveling, she will one day find that she is no longer a free nation. Our nation's internal problems are direct results of her spiritual condition. America is desperately in need of a divine healing, which can only come if God's people will humble themselves, pray, seek His face, and turn from their wicked ways. It is now time that moral Americans awake to the fact that our future depends upon how we stand on moral issues. God has no reason to spare us if we continue to reject Him.

America has been great because her people have been good. We are certainly far from being a perfect society, but our heritage is one of genuine concern for all mankind. It is God Almighty who has made and preserved us as a nation, and the day that we forget that is the day that the United States will become a byword among the nations of the world. We will become nothing more than a memory in a history book, like the many great civilizations that have preceded us. America's only hope for survival is a spiritual awakening that begins in the lives of her individual citizens. It is only in the spiritual rebirth of our nation's citizens that we can have a positive hope in the future. The destiny of America awaits that decision.

We are facing many serious issues at this time. Action must

be taken quickly in the areas of politics, economics, and defense. But the most brilliant plans and programs of men will never accomplish enough to save America. The answer to America's continued existence rests with the spiritual condition of her people. When a person allows biblical morality to be the guiding principle of his life, he can have the confidence that "righteousness exalts a nation."

I do not believe that God is finished with America yet. America has more God-fearing citizens per capita than any other nation on earth. There are millions of Americans who love God, decency, and biblical morality. North America is the last logical base for world evangelization. While it is true that God could use any nation or means possible to spread the Gospel to the world, it is also true that we have the churches, the schools, the young people, the media, the money, and the means of spreading the Gospel worldwide in our lifetime. God loves all the world, not just America. However, I am convinced that our freedoms are essential to world evangelism in this latter part of the twentieth century.

I am seeking to rally together the people of this country who still believe in decency, the home, the family, morality, the free-enterprise system, and all the great ideals that are the cornerstone of this nation. Against the growing tide of permissiveness and moral decay that is crushing our society, we must make a sacred commitment to God Almighty to turn this nation around immediately. I know that there are millions of decent, law-abiding, God-fearing Americans who want to do something about the moral decline of our country, but when you ask the average person what can be done about revival in America, he will often reply, "I'm just one person. What can I do, anyhow?" As long as the average moral American believes that, the political and social liberals in this society will be able to pass their socialistic legislation at will. We are late, but I do not believe that we are too late. It is time to put our lives on the line for this great nation of ours.

A BIBLICAL PLAN OF ACTION

In his last epistle, the Apostle Paul gave this plan of action to Christians who were living in the pagan Roman Empire of their day. "I exhort, therefore, that, first of all, supplications, prayers, intercessions, and giving of thanks be made for all men; for kings, and for all that are in authority; that we may lead a quiet and peaceable life in all godliness and honesty. For this is good and acceptable in the sight of God our Savior; who will have all men to be saved and to come to the knowledge of the truth. For there is one God, and one mediator between God and men, the man Christ Jesus; who gave himself a ransom for all, to be testified in due time." (1 Tm. 2:1–6)

In this passage the Apostle Paul emphasized the importance of prayer for those in positions of authority and leadership. He urged that prayers and intercessions be made for all men, including kings and those in authority. Why would a Christian preacher urge other fellow believers to pray for those in authority? The answer to that question is found in Paul's statement in verse 2: "That we may lead a quiet and peaceable life in all godliness and honesty." It is essential that peace prevail in order to mobilize Christians to spread the Gospel of Christ effectively so that all men might have the opportunity to be saved and come to the knowledge of the truth. I am convinced that many Christians have failed to pray genuinely for our President, his Cabinet, the legislature, and those in judicial positions.

These people, representing the highest offices of our country, have a great deal of personal and corporate responsibility placed upon them by the citizens of this free nation. They desperately need our prayerful support. It is easy to become a critic of their failures and shortcomings, while forgetting to hold them up before God in prayer.

The Power of Believing Prayer

Every great revival in the history of the Christian church has been bathed in prayer. God gave Israel a wonderful promise: "If my people, which are called by my name shall humble themselves and pray and seek my face, and turn from their wicked ways, then will I hear from heaven, and will forgive their sin, and will heal their land." (2 Ch. 7:14) Throughout Israel's history, there were times when her kings like Jehoshaphat and Hezekiah went to the Lord in prayer and experienced miraculous intervention of God on their behalf.

The great prayer-warrior, E. M. Bounds, wrote that God's greatest movements in this world have been conditioned upon, continued, and fashioned by prayer. He pointed out that God has always responded just as men have prayed. E. M. Bounds saw prayer as a means of moving God to do what He would not otherwise do if prayer were not offered. He knew prayer to be a wonderful power placed by Almighty God in the hands of His saints, to accomplish great purposes and to achieve unusual results. He knew that the only limits to prayer are the promises of God and His ability to fulfill those promises. Like E. M. Bounds, we too have at our disposal an unbelievable resource in the power of prayer. Recognizing this power, we must return to the priority of believing prayer!

In the middle of the nineteenth century, when our nation was divided over the issue of slavery and people were living in a selfish, materialistic approach to life, God raised up Jeremiah Lanphier to lead a revival of prayer. In 1857 he began a prayer meeting in the upper room of the old Fulton Street Dutch Reform Church in Manhattan. Beginning with only six people, the prayer meeting grew until the church was filled. In time virtually every church in New York City was filled with praying people. By February of 1858, nearly ten thousand people a week were being converted. The impact of these prayer meetings spread from city to city across the United States, Cleveland, Detroit, Chicago, Cincinnati—city after city was conquered by the power of believing prayer.

In 1904 a great revival movement began in Wales; the movement was led by Evan Roberts, a young man who was moved by God to pray for revival while studying for the ministry. In a short time, revival swept over Wales like a tidal wave. The impact on the moral condition of the nation was overwhelming. Judges had almost no cases to try. There were virtually no rapes, robberies, or murders. Drunkenness was cut in half, and many taverns were forced to close for lack of business. The illegitimate birth rate dropped 44 per cent within a year of the beginning of the revival. All of this happened because one man began to pray.

As Christians living at the close of the twentieth century, we must again learn how to pray in faith, believing that God will hear from heaven, that He will forgive our sin, and that He will heal our land! The key to prayer is faith. God is not impressed with the length or the volume of prayer, but with the sincerity of the faith on which it is uttered. Scripture says, "He that cometh to God must believe that he is, and that he is a rewarder of them that diligently seek him." (Heb. 11:6) Even when the condition of our nation seems most desperate, we must believe that God is still on the throne and that He has the power and authority to answer. Our priorities must merge with His priorities. God will give revival when we meet His conditions. If we expect Him to move miraculously on our behalf, we must be moved in faith to believe Him.

The Need for National Repentance

In light of our present moral condition, we as a nation are quickly approaching the point of no return. There can be no doubt that the sin of America is severe. We are literally approaching the brink of national disaster. Many have exclaimed, "If God does not judge America soon, He will have to apologize to Sodom and Gomorrah." In almost every aspect of our society, we have flaunted our sinful behavior in the very face of God Himself. Our movies, television programs, magazines, and entertainment in general are morally bankrupt and spiritually corrupt. We have become one of the most blatantly sinful nations of all time. We dare not continue to excuse ourselves on the basis of God's past blessing in our national heritage. The time for a national repentance of God's people has now come to America.

The great English statesman, Winston Churchill, once said, "The moral climate of a nation will be in direct proportion to the amount of hellfire and damnation that is preached from its pulpits." As a preacher of the Gospel, I could not more heartily agree! Pastors and religious leaders do not enjoy pointing out the sins of people. I entered the ministry nearly thirty years ago because of a genuine love and concern for people. I wanted to see their lives changed, their problems solved, and their families put back together to the glory of God. As much as I labored to help people and to encourage them and to understand their hurts and problems, I soon realized that one of my vital responsibilities was to expose sin even in my own life as well as in theirs. The Bible clearly teaches that it is the preacher's responsibility to "warn every man" against the consequences of sinful living.

Abraham Lincoln once observed, "We have been the recipients of the choicest bounties of heaven. We have been preserved, these many years, in peace and prosperity. We have grown in numbers, wealth, and power, as no other nation has ever grown, but we have forgotten God. We have forgotten the gracious hand which preserved us in peace, and multiplied and enriched and strengthened us; and we have vainly imagined, in the deceitfulness of our hearts, that all these blessings were produced by some superior wisdom and virtue of our own. Intoxicated with unbroken success, we have become too self-sufficient to feel the necessity of redeeming and preserving grace, too proud to pray to the God that made us."

Wallowing in our materialism, self-centeredness, and pride, we decided that we really didn't need God after all. We began to tamper with His absolute standards, making them subject to our own opinions and decisions. We did not immediately discard all of God's laws; rather, we began to tolerate variations in them. That which God says is never right, we determined could sometimes be right, depending on the situation. Our courts, which had once legislated against immorality, began to grant freedom to every man to do that which was right in his own eyes. As people who no longer felt accountable to a holy God, we began to accept and even admire immoral behavior. Where once we were openly shocked at the outwardness of sin, we have now become gradually conditioned to accepting it.

Today we tolerate, laugh at, and even enjoy what twenty years ago would have deeply shocked us.

Having pushed God out of our conscience, we soon discovered that as a nation we could get away with almost anything. All we had to do was change the terminology. What God called a sin, we called a sickness. Man has always tended to find a euphemism to cover the reality of sin. What God called drunkenness, we called alcoholism. What God called perversion, we called an alternate life style. What God called immorality, we called the new morality. What God called pornography, we called adult entertainment. What God called murder, we called abortion.

Is God blind to the sin of our nation? Will He continue to allow us to live in rebellion to His moral standards while He looks upon our idols of silver and gold, on our pride of personal achievement, our monuments to ourselves? Can God bless that which He ought to curse?

The Bible clearly states: "Righteousness exalteth a nation; but sin is a reproach to any people." (Pr. 14:34) God will not be mocked, for whatever an individual or a nation sows, that shall he also reap. America is not big enough to shake her fist in the face of a holy God and get away with it. Sodom and

Gomorrah fell under the judgment of God, so did Israel, Babylon, Greece, Rome, and countless other civilizations as well. Like Israel of old, we are "oppressed, trampled in judgment, intent on pursuing idols." Our crumbling economy, our fractured family structures, and unrestrained immorality, as well as our international reproach are all signs of the fact that we are already headed on a collision course.

Is there no hope? Is our doom inevitable? Can the hand of God's judgment not be stayed? Many of us are convinced that it can. We believe that there is yet an opportunity for a reprieve in God's judgment of this great nation. But that hope rests in the sincerity of national repentance led by the people of God.

First, God's people must be humble. Humility, however, is the very opposite of pride, which so often besets us. Scripture says, "God resists the proud, but gives grace to the humble." (James 4:6) We must acknowledge that we are not deserving of God's favor. We must realize that we are totally inadequate to deal with the sins of our own lives, let alone those of our entire nation. We must acknowledge that we are utterly dependent upon God and His grace to deliver us. Our financial resources will not turn this nation back to God, and our elaborate church structures will not cause Him to change His mind and restrain His judgment. We must allow Him to strip us of all that we put our confidence in, so that we may trust in Him alone.

Second, we must pray. We must not just talk about praying, we must pray! We must lay aside our pious and structured prayers in order to beseech the God of heaven to have mercy on us. Let us echo the prayer of confession offered by Ezra the priest as he fell on his face before God and acknowledged, "O my God, I am ashamed and blush to lift up my face to thee, my God; for our iniquities are increased over our head, and our trespasses are grown up into the heavens."

Third, we must learn to seek the face of God. When King Jehoshaphat called the people of Judah together to seek the face of God, they acknowledged, "We have no might against this great company that cometh against us, neither know we what to do; but our eyes are upon thee." We must turn our eyes from ourselves and seek the face of Almighty God. We must be willing to give up ourselves as the measure of all things, and acknowledge that He alone is the measure of truth.

Fourth, God's people must turn from their wicked ways. It is one thing for us to be concerned about the sins of our nation, but before we are prepared to confess the sins of an unbelieving society, we must repent of our own sins. We have not fulfilled our function as the "salt of the earth." We have failed to speak out for God on serious moral issues. We have often endorsed what we should have opposed. We must repent for judging the wickedness of our nation while ignoring the sin in our own homes. More than ever before America needs fathers who are willing to be godly leaders and moral examples in their own homes. We need mothers who are determined to be models of virtuous living, and we need children who are committed to live in obedience to the moral leadership of their parents. May God forgive us who claim His name for tolerating things in our own lives that are not holy, pure, and undefiled. We need to turn from our sinful ways in our churches as well, for we have all too often substituted playing for praying; feasting for fasting; religion for righteousness; organizing for agonizing; and compatibility for confrontation. We need a return to the kind of churches that lead the vanguard of decency while upholding the moral conscience of our nation.

The Bible is filled with examples of national confession. Both Nehemiah and Ezra poured out their hearts before God in confessing the sins of Israel. The Prophet Daniel, looking back over the seventy-year period of the Babylonian captivity before Christ and, realizing the imminent release of his spiritually unprepared countrymen, announced: "We have sinned, and have committed iniquity, and have done wickedly, and have rebelled, even by departing from thy precepts and from thy judgments . . . yea, all Israel has transgressed thy law, even by departing that they might not obey thy voice." (Dn. 9:5–15)

The time has come for America's Christians to confess the sins of our nation as well. While it is true that we are not a theocracy, as was ancient Israel, we nevertheless are a nation that was founded upon Christian principles, and we have enjoyed a unique relationship toward God because of that foundation. In order to confess sin, we must have a genuine conviction of sin based on an awareness of sin. We need to define and articulate the issues of sin and sinful living, which are destroying our nation today. The secularist will argue: What right do you have to define sin? If our definition rested only upon our personal opinion, he would have every right to reject our message. That is why it is essential that our concept of sin be based clearly upon Scripture itself. One reporter recently asked me if this would not lead to a kind of censorship or a kind of Christian Nazism. My reply was that we cannot allow an immoral minority of our population to intimidate us on moral issues. People who take a weak stand on morality inevitably have weak morals.

We need moral leadership today more than ever before. We need that kind of leadership in the media as well as in our schools and in our churches. Leadership must always be responsible to society. Our freedoms certainly guarantee the right to free speech, but they do not give us the right to use our speech irresponsibly to the harm of others. Just because we have free speech doesn't mean that a person has a right to make obscene phone calls or to yell "Fire!" in a crowded building when there is no fire. I believe that the family is the cornerstone of America, and whatever undermines the family is wrong. If our leaders are to care about this country at all we must care about its people and its families. It is time that we no longer be driven by economic considerations and political favors but instead were determined to stand for right whether it is convenient or not, popular or not.

Facing Our National Sins

While sins of America are certainly many, let us summarize the five major problems that have political consequences, political implications, that moral Americans need to be ready to face.

1. ABORTION—Nine men, by majority vote, said it was okay to kill unborn children. In 1973, two hundred million Americans and four hundred thousand pastors stood by and did little to stop it. Every year millions of babies are murdered in America, and most of us want to forget that it is happening. The Nazis murdered six million Jews, and certainly the Nazis fell under the hand of the judgment of God for these atrocities. So-called Christian America has murdered more unborn innocents than that. How do we think that we shall escape the judgment of God?

2. HOMOSEXUALITY—In spite of the fact that the Bible clearly designates this sin as an act of a "reprobate mind" for which God "gave them up" (Rm. 1:26–28), our government seems determined to legalize homosexuals as a legitimate "minority." The National Civil Rights Act of 1979 (popularly referred to as the Gay Rights Bill) would give homosexuals the same benefits as the 1964 Civil Rights Act, meaning they could not be discriminated against by any employing body because of "sexual preference." Even the ancient Greeks, among whom homosexuality was fairly prevalent, never legally condoned its practice. Plato himself called it "abnormal." If our nation legally recognizes homosexuality, we will put ourselves under the same hand of judgment as Sodom and Gomorrah.

3. PORNOGRAPHY—The four-billion-dollar-per-year pornographic industry is probably the most devastating moral influence of all upon our young people. Sex magazines deliberately increase the problem of immoral lust and thus provoke increased adultery, prostitution, and sexual child abuse. Jesus said that if a man looks upon a woman and lusts after her in his heart, he has committed adultery with her already! Pornography is certainly the No. 1 enemy against marital fidelity and therefore against the family itself. Recent psychological studies are showing without a doubt that divorce caused by adultery is having a devastating affect upon children. Pornography is not a victimless crime—the real victims are wives and children!

4. HUMANISM—The contemporary philosophy that glorifies man as man, apart from God, is the ultimate outgrowth of evolutionary science and secular education. In his new book *The Battle for the Mind*, Dr. Tim LaHaye argues that the full admission of humanism as the religion of secular education came after prayer and Bible reading were excluded from our public schools. Ultimately, humanism rests upon the philosophy of existentialism, which emphasizes that one's present existence is the true meaning and purpose of life. Existentialism has become the religion of the public schools. Applied to psychology, it postulates a kind of moral neutrality that is detrimental to Christian ethics. In popular terminology it explains, "Do your own thing," and "If it feels good, do it!" It is an approach to life that has no room for God and makes man the measure of all things.

5. THE FRACTURED FAMILY—With a skyrocketing divorce rate, the American family may well be on the verge of extinction in the next twenty years. Even the recent White House Conference on Families has called for an emphasis on diverse family forums (common-law, communal, homosexual, and transsexual "marriages"). The Bible pattern of the family has been virtually discarded by modern American society. Our movies and magazines have glorified the physical and emotional experience of sex without love to the point that most Americans do not even consider love to be important at all anymore. Bent on self-gratification, we have reinterpreted our moral values in light of our immoral life styles. Since the family is the basic unit of society, and since the family is desperately in trouble today, we can conclude that our society itself is in danger of total collapse. We are not moving toward an alternate family life style; we are moving closer to the brink of destruction.

Bible-believing Christians and concerned moral Americans are determined to do something about the problems that we are facing as a nation. In our family we were recently sitting in the family room having a time of Bible study and devotions and discussing some of these crucial issues. One of my children asked, "Dad, will I ever grow up to be as old as you are in a free America?" Another one of my children asked, "Will I ever get to go to college?" and "Will I ever get married?" Speaking about the vital issues is not just a question of dealing with our generation but with the generations to come. Our children and our grandchildren must forever be the recipients or the victims of our moral decisions today.

My responsibility as a parent-pastor is more than just concern. The issue of convenience is not even up for discussion. If the moral issues are really matters of conviction that are worth living for, then they are worth fighting for. In discussing these matters further with other pastors and concerned Christian leaders, I have become convinced of the need to have a coalition of God-fearing, moral Americans to represent our convictions to our government. I realize that there would be those pastors who misunderstand our intentions. I know that some object that we are compromising in our involvement with people of different doctrinal and theological beliefs. As a fundamental, independent, separatist Baptist, I am well aware of the crucial is-

sues of personal and ecclesiastical separation that divide funda-
mentalists philosophically from evangelicals and liberals. I do
not believe that it is ever right to compromise the truth in order
to gain an opportunity to do right. In doctrinal and spiritual
matters, there is no real harmony between light and darkness.

I am convinced of two very significant factors. First, our very
moral existence as a nation is at stake. There are many moral
Americans who do not share our theological beliefs but who do
share our moral concerns. Second, we must face the fact that it
will take the greatest possible number of concerned citizens to
reverse the politicization of immorality in our society. Doctrinal
difference is a distinctive feature of a democracy. Our freedoms
have given us the privilege and the luxury of theological disagreement. I would not for a moment encourage anyone to water
down his distinctive beliefs. But we must face realistically the
fact that there are Christians in the world today who have lost
the luxury of disagreement. When the entire issue of Christian
survival is at stake, we must be willing to band together on at
least the major moral issues of the day.

One only needs to travel to Rhodesia, as I was privileged to
do earlier this year, to realize that the Christians there have lost
their opportunity to argue with one another. The recent election of Comrade Mugabe, the new Marxist dictator of that
country, may well have ended any opportunity of genuine
Christian witness there. Petty theological differences do not
mean a whole lot today to Christians living in Russia, China,
Cambodia, Mozambique, or Rhodesia! Undoubtedly, the next
target of communist conquest will be the Republic of South
Africa. The many Christian believers of that great nation need
our prayers that their doors remain open to the Gospel. If we are
not careful the United States will be next. We may not have
the luxury of theological disagreement much longer. The time
may soon come when claiming to be any kind of Christian may
cost you your life!

Our ministry is as committed as it ever has been to the basic
truths of Scripture, to essential and fundamental Christian doc-
trines. But we are not willing to isolate ourselves in seclusion

while we sit back and watch this nation plunge headlong toward hell.

Moral Americans can make the difference in America if we are willing to exert the effort to make our feelings known and if we are willing to make the necessary sacrifices to get the job done. In October 1978, our church entered what seemed at the time to be a losing battle. Pre-election polls in September 1978 in the state of Virginia indicated that there was general apathy regarding pari-mutuel betting. Those in favor of pari-mutuel betting expected it to win approval easily. Convinced that gambling is typical of a nation losing its moral values and that it is a sin based upon a lust for things, we took a strong stand against it. While some of our politicians argue that gambling would increase revenue in the state, I knew that it would ultimately cost taxpayers in increased welfare costs or destroy families and increase police protection in prison costs. Gambling is supported by men who are dominated by greed, and who do not consider the havoc that gambling causes to the home.

Our church took a stand against pari-mutuel betting and rallied other good people in the state of Virginia against it also. On November 7, 1978, pari-mutuel betting was rejected by the voters in the state of Virginia. Virginia newspapers stated, "Both the winners and the losers credited an aggressive campaign by the religious leader as bringing about the betting proposal's demise." Those newspapers went on to quote my comment: "The vote is an indication of what the Christian people in Virginia have been able to do by simply uniting their efforts. This is the first time that six thousand Virginia churches of all denominations have joined hands in a moral campaign, and this should be, as I see it, a forecast of future endeavors together."

To change America we must be involved, and this includes three areas of political action:

1. REGISTRATION

A recent national poll indicated that eight million American evangelicals are not registered to vote. I am convinced that this is one of the major sins of the church today. Until concerned Christian citizens become registered voters there is very little that we can do to change the tide of political influence on the social issues in our nation. Those who object to Christians being involved in the political process are ultimately objecting to Christians being involved in the social process. The political process is really nothing more than a realization of the social process. For us to divorce ourselves from society would be to run into the kind of isolationism and monasticism that characterized the medieval hermits. Many Christians are not even aware of the importance of registering to vote. It is perfectly legal, for example, for a deputy registrar to come right to your local church at a designated time and register the entire congregation. I am convinced that those of us who are pastors have an obligation to urge our people to register to vote. I am more concerned that people exercise their freedom to vote than I am concerned for whom they vote.

2. INFORMATION

Many moral Americans are unaware of the real issues affecting them today. Many people do not know the voting record of their congressman and have no idea how he is representing them on political issues that have moral implications. This is one of the major reasons why we have established the Moral Majority organization. We want to keep the public informed on the vital moral issues. The Moral Majority, Inc., is a nonprofit organization, with headquarters in Washington, D.C. Our goal is to exert a significant influence on the spiritual and moral direction of our nation by: (a) mobilizing the grassroots of moral Americans in one clear and effective voice; (b) informing the moral majority what is going on behind their backs in Washington and in state legislatures across the country; (c) lobbying intensely in Congress to defeat left-wing, social-welfare bills that will further erode our precious freedom; (d) pushing for positive legislation such as that to establish the Family Protection Agency, which will ensure a strong, enduring America; and (e) helping the moral majority in local communities to fight pornography, homosexuality, the advocacy of immorality in school textbooks, and other issues facing each and every one of us.

Christians must keep America great by being willing to go

into the halls of Congress, by getting laws passed that will protect the freedom and liberty of her citizens. The Moral Majority, Inc., was formed to acquaint Americans everywhere with the tragic decline in our nation's morals and to provide leadership in establishing an effective coalition of morally active citizens who are (a) prolife, (b) profamily, (c) promoral, and (d) pro-American. If the vast majority of Americans (84 per cent, according to George Gallup) still believe the Ten Commandments are valid today, why are we permitting a few leading amoral humanists and naturalists to take over the most influential positions in this nation?

Tim LaHaye has formed a code of minimum moral standards dictated by the Bible; his code would be used to evaluate the stand of candidates on moral issues. These minimum standards are:

a. Do you agree that this country was founded on a belief in God and the moral principles of the Bible? Do you concur that this country has been departing from those principles and needs to return to them?

b. Would you favor stricter laws relating to the sale of pornography?

c. Do you favor stronger laws against the use and sale of hard drugs?

d. Are you in favor of legalizing marijuana?

e. Would you favor legalizing prostitution?

f. Do you approve of abortions on demand when the life of the mother is not in danger?

g. Do you favor laws that would increase homosexual rights?

h. Would you vote to prevent known homosexuals to teach in schools?

i. Do you favor capital punishment for capital offenses?

j. Do you favor the right of parents to send their children to private schools?

   k. Do you favor voluntary prayer in the public schools?

   l. Do you favor removal of the tax-exempt status of churches?

   m. Do you favor removal of the tax-exempt status of church-related schools?

   n. Do you believe that government should remove children from their parents' home except in cases of physical abuse?

   o. Do you favor sex education, contraceptives, or abortions for minors without parental consent?

   p. Except in wartime or dire emergency, would you vote for government spending that exceeds revenue?

   q. Do you favor a reduction in taxes to allow families more spendable income?

   r. Do you favor a reduction in government?

   s. Do you favor passage of the Equal Rights Amendment?

   t. Do you favor busing schoolchildren out of their neighborhood to achieve racial integration?

   u. Do you favor more federal involvement in education?

The answers to these questions would be evaluated in the light of scriptural principles.

If you were to ask the average Christian who his congressmen and senators are, there is a good possibility that he could not tell you. Some congressmen have gone so far as to brag that their constituents back home have no idea what their real voting record is. In order to affect our nation's moral future we must become informed about the issue. Dwight Eisenhower once stated: "Our American heritage is threatened as much by our own indifference as it is by the most unscrupulous office seeker or by the most sinister foreign threat. The destiny of this republic is in the hands of its voters."

3. MOBILIZATION

The history of the church includes the history of Christian involvement in social issues. The preaching of John Wesley and George Whitefield led to great revival movements in England and America. The great awakening in colonial America prepared the way for the proper application of freedom stemming from the Revolutionary War. In England, William Wilberforce crusaded against slavery in the British Empire, while Robert Raikes established the Sunday school movement to give children religious training, and elementary training in reading and writing. In the meantime, Lord Shaftesbury lobbied for child-labor laws and protection of the insane. At the same time, John Howard, influenced by the Wesleyan revival, devoted his life and fortune to prison reform in England. William Booth, a Methodist minister, organized the Salvation Army to carry out open-air evangelism and social work. In 1844, George Williams founded the YMCA, to meet the needs of young men in the cities of England and America. Evangelist Dwight L. Moody raised thousands of dollars for the support of the YMCA and other youth movements. During the same period of time the great missionary movement exploded worldwide. William Carey, a Baptist, went to India not only to evangelize but also to organize the people on a self-supporting industrial level. David Livingstone, the great Congregationalist missionary to Africa, not only proclaimed the Gospel but also openly opposed the Arabian slave trade and exploitation of the African natives. Robert Morrison translated the Bible into Chinese and established vocational industrial training schools to help the people. In America, outstanding evangelical preachers such as Charles G. Finney, Albert Barnes, and Lyman Beecher called on Christians to feed the poor, educate the unlearned, reform the prisons, humanize treatment for the mentally ill, establish orphanages, and abolish slavery. Led by the work of Jerry McCalley, there were eventually seventy-six rescue missions opened in New York City alone in the nineteenth century.

The turning point in Christian involvement in social action seems to have been the repeal of prohibition in 1933. A wide variety of Christians and moral Americans were united in the crusade against alcohol for nearly twenty years. Lead by the preaching of evangelist Billy Sunday, prohibition finally became law in 1919. Its eventual repeal caused many Christians to conclude that we have no business trying to legislate Christian morality on a non-Christian society. The Depression and World War II followed shortly thereafter, and Christian concern about social issues hit rock bottom during the fifties and sixties. We have tended to develop the attitude that our only obligation is to preach the Gospel and prepare men for heaven. We have forgotten that we are still our brother's keeper and that the same spiritual truths that prepare us to live in eternity are also essential in preparing us to live on this earth. We dare not advocate our responsibility to the society of which we are so very much a vital part. If we as moral Americans do not speak up on these essential moral issues, who then will? As Christians we need to exert our influence not only in the church but also in our business life, home life, and social and community life as well.

Since government has the power to control various areas and activities of our lives, it is vital that we as concerned Americans understand the importance of our involvement in the political process. Everett Hale, author of *The Man Without a Country*, once said: "I'm only one—but I am one. I cannot do everything —but I can do something. What I can do, I should do, and what I should do, by the grace of God, I will do." In order to make your influence felt, the first thing you must do is to know who to contact in positions of authority. Elected officials depend upon the voice of the people, and elected officials are willing to listen to those groups who will speak out on the issues. It is important for you to know who your elected officials are: your senators, congressmen, governor, state attorney general, state senator, state representative, county officials, etc. One of your important obligations is to write or call your elected officials and express your opinions on moral issues and legislation. In order to support good candidates you need to become familiar with their campaign issues. To do this it would be well to attend your political party's precinct and committee meetings. Don't be afraid to go, and don't be afraid to speak out. At these meetings people are selected as delegates for county and state meetings. In most states the county and state meetings will adopt a party platform. In some states they will elect delegates to the national conventions, which will eventually select the party candidates for President and Vice President.

Another area of involvement is to join with other concerned citizens in your region to promote godly morality. Recently in Virginia, profamily citizens united and showed up in force at the Virginia Conference on Families. Because of this they carried the day, for their view on the family rooted firmly in the tradition of the Bible. They were able to gain a majority representation on the Virginia committee. Not only is it important to vote, but it is important to encourage others to do so as well. Never underestimate the power of your vote in a given election. In 1948 Lyndon Johnson was elected to the U. S. Senate from Texas by less than one hundred votes. Edmund Burke once said: "All that is necessary for the triumph of evil is that good men do nothing."

America was born in her churches, and she must be reborn there as well. The time has come for pastors and church leaders to clearly and boldly proclaim the Gospel of regeneration in Christ Jesus. We need a return to God and to the Bible as never before in the history of America. Undoubtedly we are at the edge of eternity. Some are already referring to us as "post-Christian America." We have stretched the rubber band of morality too far already. A few more stretches and it will undoubtedly snap forever. When that happens we will become like all the other nations preceding us who've fallen under the judgment of God. I love America not because of her pride, her wealth, or her prestige; I love America because she, above all the nations of the world, has honored the principles of the Bible. America has been great because she has been good. We have been the breadbasket of the world, we have fed our enemies and canceled their national debts against us while maintaining an exorbitant debt of our own. We have bound up the wounds of a dying and hurting world. We have rushed to nearly every international disaster in the twentieth century to provide comfort and financial aid. In spite of all of this, we have been cursed and belittled by our friends and foes alike. All too often we have been looked upon as "ugly Americans." Instead of closing our hearts to the needs of the world, we have opened our doors to its peoples. Instead of only exporting the products of our commercial expertise, we have imported the goods of nearly every country in the world. In many ways we have been our brother's keeper. But good deeds alone will not save a nation, nor an individual.

Salvation is of God. Regeneration is the theological term for the new birth. Jesus said to Nicodemus nearly two thousand years ago: "Except a man be born again, he shall not see the kingdom of Heaven." (Jn. 3:5) The Apostle Paul stated: "For whosoever shall call upon the name of the Lord shall be saved." (Rm. 10:13) Regeneration is not based upon moral goodness alone. If our morality could make us acceptable in the sight of God, we could literally work our way to heaven and brag about ourselves. Christians are concerned about moral issues not because they want to brag about themselves but because they have experienced the reality of the life-changing power of God. The Bible clearly states: "For by grace are ye saved through faith; and that not of yourselves; it is the gift of God, not of works, lest any man should boast." (Ep. 2:8-9) Salvation is a gift from God. It is a gift that you need to receive personally by faith. Romans 6:23 says, "For the wages of sin is death, but the gift of God is eternal life through Jesus Christ our Lord." If you have never received Christ as your personal Savior, I would urge you to do so. Acknowledge your sin, accept His forgiveness and the gift of life that He offers.

I am convinced that we need a spiritual and moral revival in America if America is to survive the twentieth century. The time for action is now; we dare not wait for someone else to take up the banner of righteousness in our generation. We have already waited too long. The great American Senator Jesse

Helms said: "Each of us has a part to play in bringing about the great spiritual awakening that must come upon this land before we are brought to our knees by the chastisements of God. Each of us must place our hope and reliance in God, and in that hope and reliance turn our energies to restoring a government and society that serves us as sons of God. . . . Faith and courage are not dispensed by civil governments or revolutions, but by the spirit of God. Americans as a people must once again rise up and reclaim their nation from the slothful, divisive, prodigal, and treacherous individuals who have bartered away our freedoms for a mess of pottage . . . we must return to the author of liberty to enjoy again what once we had so abundantly."

We should thank God every day that we were born in a free land. We must pray that God will help us to assume the obligation to guarantee that freedom to the generations that will follow. In a time when freedom is becoming less and less a privilege to the peoples of the world, we cannot value our American citizenship too highly. No one in the world knows the freedoms that Americans know. Those who so often criticize our country with their anti-American, antimilitary, anticapitalist attitudes must forever realize that the very freedom that allows them to do this is the freedom they are trying to destroy. Let them take anti-Soviet slogans and march up and down the streets of Moscow; they would swiftly disappear.

Right living must be re-established as an American way of life. We as American citizens must recommit ourselves to the faith of our fathers and to the premises and moral foundations upon which this country was established. Now is the time to begin calling America back to God, back to the Bible, back to morality! We must be willing to live by the moral convictions that we claim to believe. There is no way that we will ever be willing to die for something for which we are not willing to live. The authority of Bible morality must once again be recognized as the legitimate guiding principle of our nation. Our love for our fellow man must ever be grounded in the truth and never be allowed to blind us from the truth that is the basis of our love for our fellow man.

As a pastor and as a parent I am calling my fellow American citizens to unite in a moral crusade for righteousness in our generation. It is time to call America back to her moral roots. It is time to call America back to God. We need a revival of righteous living based on a proper confession of sin and repentance of heart if we are to remain the land of the free and the home of the brave! I am convinced that God is calling millions of Americans in the so-often silent majority to join in the moral-majority crusade to turn America around in our lifetime. Won't you begin now to pray with us for revival in America? Let us unite our hearts and lives together for the cause of a new America . . . a moral America in which righteousness will exalt this nation. Only as we do this can we exempt ourselves from one day having to look our children in the eyes and answer this searching question: "Mom and Dad, where were you the day freedom died in America?"

The choice is now ours.

BIBLIOGRAPHY

Barck, Oscar Theodore, Jr., and Lefler, Hugh Talmage. *Colonial America*. New York: The Macmillan Company, 1958.
Boller, Paul F., Jr. *George Washington and Religion*. Dallas, Tex.: Southern Methodist University Press, 1963.
Boorstin, Daniel J. *The Exploring Spirit*. New York: Random House, 1975.
Campbell, Douglas, A. M. *The Puritan in Holland, England, and America*. New York: Harper & Brothers, 1893.
Campbell, Norine Dickson. *Patrick Henry: Patriot and Statesman*. New York: The Devin-Adair Company, 1969.
Commager, Henry Steele (ed.). *Documents of American History*, 5th ed. New York: Appleton-Century-Crofts, 1949.
Crane, Philip M. *The Sum of Good Government*. Ottawa, Ill.: Green Hill Publishers, 1976.
Dooley, Thomas A. *Deliver Us from Evil*. New York: Farrar, Straus and Cudahy, 1956.
Ehrenfeld, David. *The Arrogance of Humanism*. New York: Oxford University Press, 1978.
Ellis, Jane (trans.). *Georgi Vins: Prisoner of Conscience*. Elgin, Ill.: David C. Cook Publishing Company, 1979.
Friedan, Betty. *It Changed My Life*. New York: Random House, 1976.
Friedman, Milton. *Capitalism and Freedom*. Chicago, Ill.: University of Chicago Press, 1962.
Friedman, Milton and Rose. *Free to Choose*. New York: Harcourt Brace Jovanovich, 1980.
Gallagher, Neil. *How to Stop the Porno Plague*. Minneapolis, Minn.: Bethany Fellowship, 1977.
Goldwater, Barry. *The Coming Breakpoint*. New York: Macmillan Publishing Company, 1976.
Green, Harry Clinton, and Green, Mary Wolcott. *The Pioneer Mothers of America*, Vols. 1–3. New York: G. P. Putnam's Sons, 1912.
Hefley, James C. *Are Textbooks Harming Your Children?* Milford, Mich.: Mott Media, 1979.
Helms, Jesse. *When Free Men Shall Stand*. Grand Rapids, Mich.: Zondervan Publishing House, 1976.

Howard, Donald R. *Rebirth of Our Nation.* Lewisville, Tex.: Accelerated Christian Education, 1979.

Jacobs, J. Vernon. *500 Little-known Stories from American History.* Tulsa, Okla.: Christian Crusade Publications, 1964.

Lamont, Lansing. *Campus Shock.* New York: E. P. Dutton, 1979.

Larson, Bob. *The Day the Music Died.* Denver, Colo.: Bob Larson Ministries, 1978.

————. *Rock.* Wheaton, Ill.: Tyndale House Publishers, Inc., 1980.

Linkletter, Art. *Drugs at My Door Step.* Waco, Tex.: Word Books, Publishers, 1973.

Lockerbie, D. Bruce. *Who Educates Your Child?* Garden City, N.Y.: Doubleday & Company, 1980.

Lott, Davis Newton (annot.). *The Inaugural Addresses of the American Presidents.* New York: Holt, Rinehart & Winston, 1961.

Marshall, Peter, and Manuel, David. *The Light and the Glory.* Old Tappan, N.J.: Fleming H. Revell Company, 1977.

McGraw, Onalee. *Secular Humanism and the Schools: The Issue Whose Time Has Come.* Washington, D.C.: The Heritage Foundation, 1976.

Menninger, Karl, M.D. *Whatever Became of Sin?* New York: Bantam Books, 1978.

Minor, Robert S. (ed.). *The Rebirth of a Nation.* Austin, Tex.: Third Century Fund, 1978.

Nathanson, Bernard N., M.D. *Aborting America.* Garden City, N.Y.: Doubleday & Company, 1979.

Owen, Frederick G. *Abraham to the Middle East Crisis.* Grand Rapids, Mich.: Wm. B. Eerdmans Publishing Company, 1939.

Pope, Charles Henry. *The Plymouth Scrap Book.* Boston: C. E. Goodspeed & Company, 1918.

Quebedeaux, Richard. *The Worldly Evangelicals.* New York: Harper & Row, 1978.

Ringer, Robert J. *Restoring the American Dream.* New York: QED/ Harper & Row, 1979.

Schaeffer, Edith. *What Is a Family?* Old Tappan, N.J.: Fleming H. Revell Company, 1975.

Schaeffer, Francis A. *How Should We Then Live?* Old Tappan, N.J.: Fleming H. Revell Company, 1976.

Schaeffer, Francis A., and Koop, C. Everett, M.D. *Whatever Happened to the Human Race?* Old Tappan, N.J.: Fleming H. Revell Company, 1979.

Schauffler, Robert Haven (ed.). *Thanksgiving.* New York: Dodd, Mead & Company, 1926.

Schlafly, Phyllis. *The Power of the Positive Woman.* New York: Jove Publications, 1977.

Simon, William E. *A Time for Truth*. New York: Berkley Publishing Corporation, 1979.

Skinner, B. F. *Beyond Freedom and Dignity*. New York: Alfred A. Knopf, 1971.

Stormer, John A. *The Death of a Nation*. Florissant, Mo.: Liberty Bell Press, 1968.

————. *None Dare Call It Treason*. Florissant, Mo.: Liberty Bell Press, 1964.

Usher, Roland G. *The Pilgrims and Their History*. New York: The Macmillan Company, 1920.

Van Impe, Jack. *Israel's Final Holocaust*. Nashville, Tenn.: Thomas Nelson, 1979.

Walt, General Lewis W., U.S.M.C. (Ret.). *The Eleventh Hour*. New York: Caroline House Publishers, 1979.

Walton, Rus. *One Nation Under God*. Old Tappan, N.J.: Fleming H. Revell Company, 1975.

Whitney, David C. *Founders of Freedom in America*. Chicago: J. G. Ferguson Publishing Company, 1964.